SOLVED EXAMS OF ANATOMY AND PHYSIOLOGY

AS PER PT. B.D SHARMA UNIVERSITY (B.SC NURSING)

RACHNA MAAN SINGH

Dedicated

To

Dear God

My Father and Mother

For leading their children into intellectual pursuits.

Contents

Preface *vii*

Acknowledgements *ix*

1. Question Paper 2022 1
2. Question Paper 2021 28
3. Question Paper 2020 52
4. Question Paper 2019 72
5. Question Paper2018 97

Question Paper 2017 125

Question Paper 2016 127

Question Paper 2015 129

Question Paper 2014 131

Question Paper 2013 133

Preface

Anatomy and physiology are core components of nursing curriculum and every nursing student is expected to have a basic understanding of the structural and functional components of nursing curriculum. This book has sample answers of last 10-year question papers according to pt. B.D Sharma University.

A picture always speaks more than the words. Therefore, all the figures have been redrawn and many illustrations have been added to assist in fast comprehensive and retention of complicated information. I would highly appreciate comments and suggestions from students and teachers for further improvement of this book.

Acknowledgements

I would like to provide my gratitude towards all people who helped me directly or indirectly helped me to complete this project. I want to mention special thanks to Prem Institute of Medical Sciences for providing me time and resources for completing this book.

Rachna Maan Singh
rachnarachna000@gmail.com

CHAPTER I

Question paper 2022

B.Sc Nursing 1st year ,annual exam, 2022
Anatomy and physiology

Note Marks 75

1. attempt all questions and draw suitable diagrams, tables, and graphs where required.
2. attempt part-1 and part-2 in separate answer book.

Part –I anatomy

Q1. Describe in detail: 5+4+4= 13

a. External and internal features of heart
b. Blood supply of long bones
c. Classification of cartilages with examples

Q2.Draw a well labeled diagram to illustrate the following: 4×3=12

a. Relations and ligaments of ovary
b. Relation and blood supply of stomach
c. Relations of the liver.

Q3. Write short note on the following 4×3=12

a. Difference between small intestine and large intestine.
b. Blood supply and function of pituitary gland
c. Venous drainage of heart.

Part-II (physiology)

Q4. Write short note on the following:5+4+4= 13

a. Regulation of Blood Pressure
b. Stages of spermatogenesis
c. Functions of Kidneys

Q5. Write the concept in short with the help of a diagram: 5+4+4= 13

a. Blood groups
b. Structure and function of neurons
c. Conducting system of heart

Q6. write features of the following: 4×3=12

a. Iron deficiency anemia
b. Rickets

c. Placenta

Part –I anatomy

Q1. Describe in detail:5+4+4= 13

a. External and internal features of heart
b. Blood supply of long bones
c. Classification of cartilages with examples.

Answer(a) External and internal features of heart Layers of Heart
The heart wall consists of 3 layers:

- Epicardium: a small outer layer composed of a visceral layer of serous pericardium
- M Myocardium: a dense intermediate layer made up of the heart muscle
- Endocardium: a small inner lining that connects the heart to its valves. It is made up of endothelium and sub-endothelial connective tissue, which is similar to the inner part of the blood vessels.

External Features

- The heart and roots of large vessels are placed in a pericardial sac, approximately in the middle of the thorax. The size of the heart is slightly larger than the folded fist. The heart is surrounded on the sides and back by the lungs, and the front is bound by the sternum and the medial parts of the ribs and the sterno-costal joints.
- It has the shape of a three-dimensional pyramid with apex (front left), base (back), and 4 locations: Sterno-costal / front (formed by right ventricle), diaphragmatic / inferior (formed by the left ventricle and right ventricle segment), left pulmonary (formed by the left ventricle, connected to the left lung), and the right pulmonary (forming the right atrium).
- The heart appears trapezoid in the rear and front view. Thus, it contains 4 boundaries: Right (convex), Lower (horizontal), left (oblique), and above.

The outside of the heart is marked by three large sulci (grooves):

- Coronary (atrioventricular) sulcus: runs around the heart, and separates the atria from the ventricles
- Anterior interventricular sulcus: running near the anterior interventricular septum
- The posterior interventricular sulcus: runs near the interventricular posterior septum

Internal features

- The heart has 4 chambers: right and left atria and right and left ventricles.
- Blood flows normally from right to left: The right atrium to the right ventricle to the left atrium, and finally to the left ventricle.

- Oxygen-rich blood reaches the right atrium through the coronary sinus and the upper and inferior vena cava and drains the right ventricle through the lungs into the lungs.
- Oxygen rich blood then re-enters the left atrium through the 4 pulmonary arteries and drains the left ventricle through the aorta.

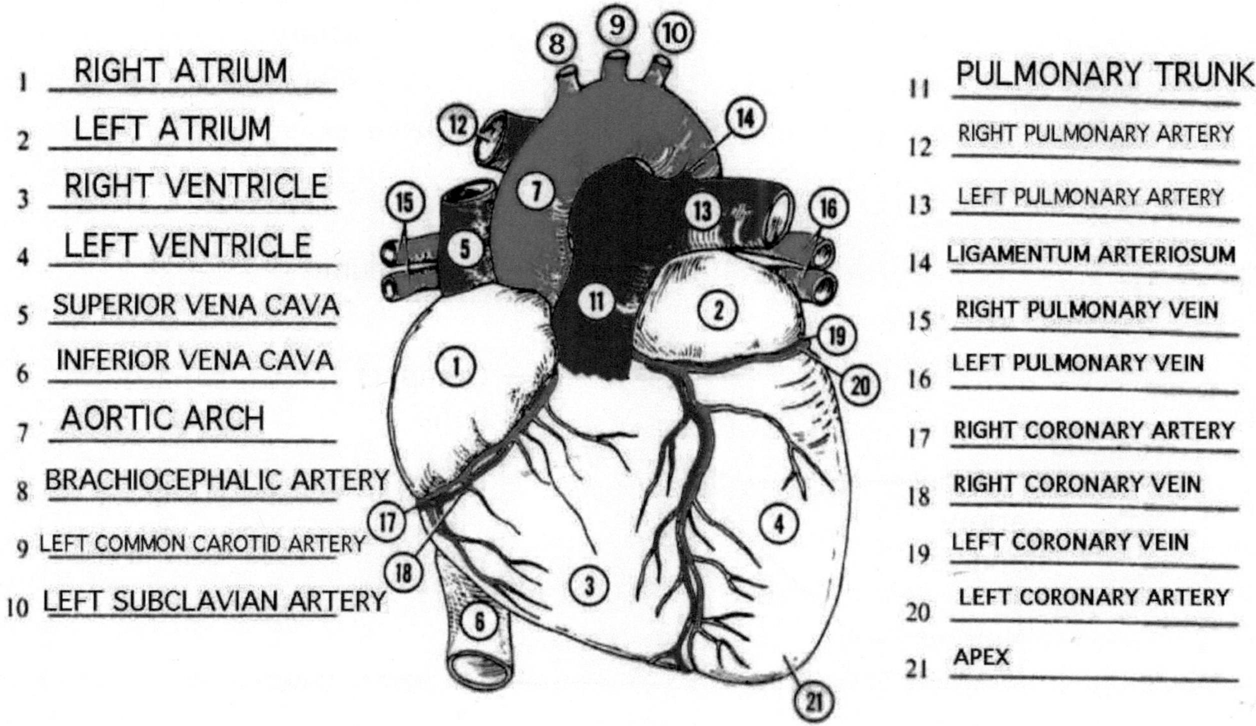

Parts of Heart

Answer(b) Blood supply of long bones

Basic anatomy of long bone:-The central part of the long bone is called the diaphysis. The enlarged bone area is eventually called the epiphysis and the central part of the bone between the two is called metaphysic s. The articular ends of the epiphyseal surface are covered with articular cartilage. One bone is covered with a thick layer of connective tissue called the periosteum. The nutrient forum is an oblique channel usually found in the long bone diaphysis.

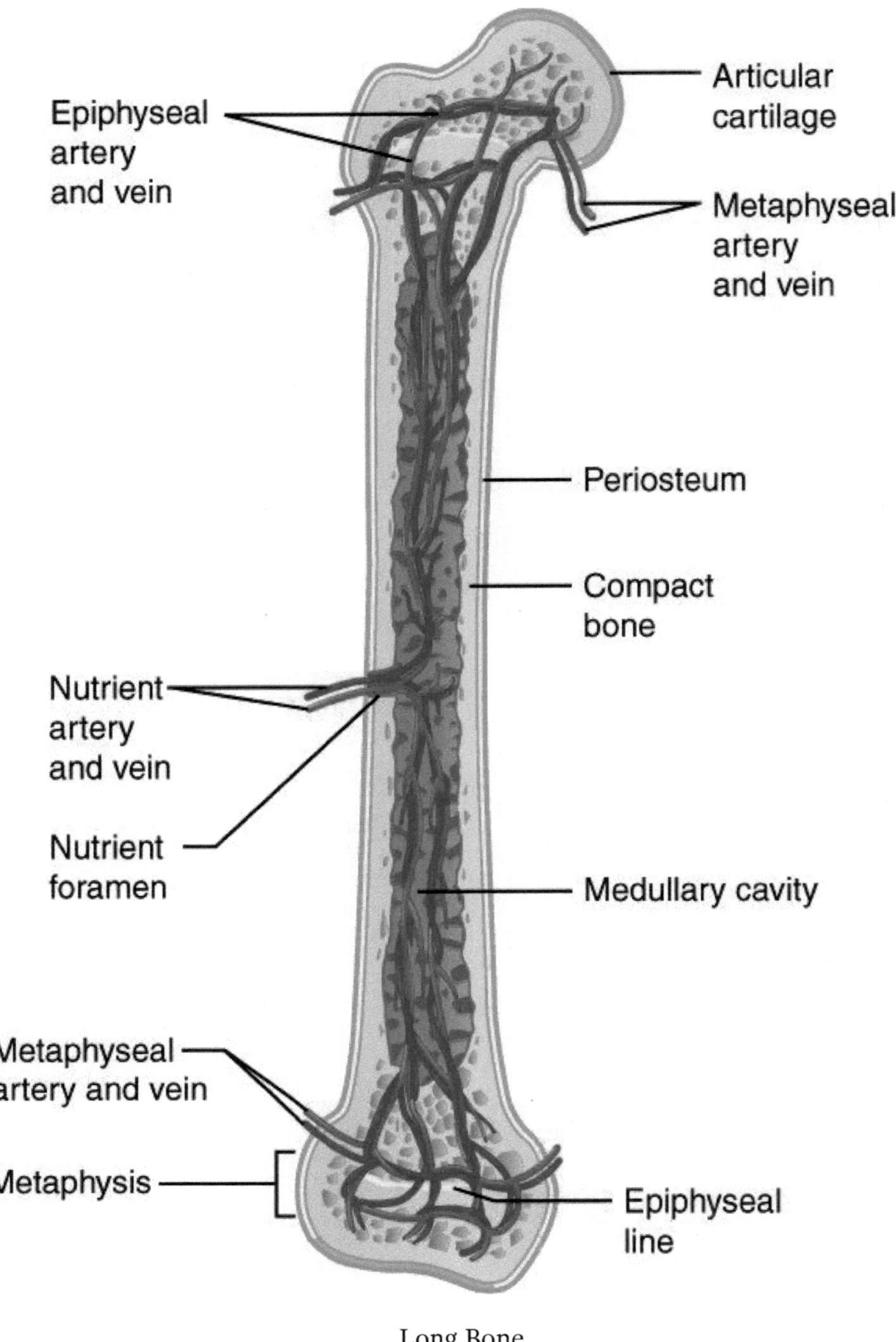

Long Bone

provision of long-term arterial: -

Blood transfusions of long bones account for 5-10% of cardiac output. Normal long bone receives blood from a variety of sources. They are Nutrient arteries, Epiphyseal arteries, Metaphyseal arteries and periosteal arteries.

Food skin: -

Nutrient supply directly to the major systemic arteries. It enters the long bone through the nutrient forum. It then divides into ascending and descending branches. These branches provide small interlocking arteries called radial branches. These branches supply the bone marrow and one-third of the joint bone of the diaphysis. The ascending and descending branches in the metaphysis divide into small twisted branches anastomoses through the metaphyseal and epiphyseal arteries.

Metaphyseal atery: -

Metaphyseal veins from the anastomosis around the joint enter the metaphysis at the edges of the capsule attachment. These are anastomosed with circular veins that make the metaphysic into a large area of long arteries.

Epiphyseal vein: -Epiphyseal arteries are found in periarticular vascular arcades. The epiphysis has holes that allow arteries to enter and exit. In children the epiphyseal arteries are separated from the metaphyseal arteries due to the presence of the epiphyseal plate. In adults the epiphysis and metaphysis are joined together following the binding of the growth plate. Treat epiphyseal veins anastomose freely with metaphyseal and arterial arteries.

As epiphyseal cartilage and articular cartilage progress, the epiphyseal artery pierces epiphyseal cartilage and supplies the epiphysis. If these arteries are reflected in epiphyseal separation, avascular necrosis may occur. In some bones where epiphyseal cartilage does not extend to articular cartilage, epiphyseal vessels enter the bones without piercing the growth plate. This helps prevent avascular necrosis in epiphyseal separation.

Periosteal atery: -

The periosteum has a rich blood supply from the anastomose blood vessels below the periosteum. Periosteal veins act as a low-pressure system and enter the bone at the sides of the face sheath attachment or aponeurosis. They enter the Volksmann canal and supply about one- third of the joint bone of the diaphysis.

Venous drainage: -

The long bones protrude into the medial venous veins, then draw in the arteries, and then into the periosteal veins and emissary veins respectively.

Answer (c) Classification of cartilage by examples.

Cartilage is a semi-rigid but flexible avascular connective tissue located at various points within the body. With a soft structure made up mainly of water, this type of tissue is also extremely strong. Cartilage is found throughout the human body in areas such as the joints, nose, air, intervertebral discs of the spine, and the ear.

Function of Cartilage

The cartilage function is more than a structure, and it has different functions in the life cycle. In the embryo, it provides support and is a precursor to bone. Embryonic cartilage remains similar to the cartilage or provides the lower structure for endochondral ossification, meaning that it also serves as a model for rapid growth and development of the musculoskeletal system.

Cartilage is a soft tissue that allows facial movement and provides a simple supporting structure to the outer ear, as well as the head and nasal septum. In some regions it acts as a shock absorber, gripping areas where the bone meets and prevents scratches and bruises. The joint will also not be able to bend without cartilage flexibility. A combination of roles is seen in the airways, where the cartilage around the trachea prevents fractures and injuries, and the cartilage at the ends of the ribs allows the ribcage to rotate up and down during inspiration. The cartilage also plays a key role in repairing the bone marrow, which, like the fetus, provides an ossification pattern, in this case, in broken bones.

Types of Cartilage

There are three types of cartilage in the human body. Although their components are very similar, the values of each component vary, providing different characteristics for each type. Accordingly, each species has a specific place.

Hyaline Cartilage

The most common type of cartilage is hyaline cartilage. Hyalos is a Greek word meaning glass, which describes the appearance of this type of connective tissue - flexible, blue - white, and glossy. Hyaline cartilage is usually only 2 - 4 mm thick (all cartilage should be thin, as there is no vascularization in this type of tissue, and nutrients and oxygen should be available by distribution). It is an embryonic process of cartilage, and is found in the bones, joints, nose, larynx and trachea.

The fibers of Hyaline cartilage collagen are mainly type II, extremely thin, and are not visible to the microscope due to the same opposing structures as those of the matrix itself.

Fibrocartilage

Found where tendons and ligaments meet, in the pubic symphysis, menisci, sternoclavicular joint, and annulus fibrosus (intervertebral disc center), fibrocartilage is the strongest and most flexible connective tissue. It is reinforced with collagen fiber bundles that run smoothly, allowing for a lower level of elasticity. Due to the abundance of collagen fibers, fibrocartilage is white in appearance. It has no perichondrium and is made up of type II and type collagen.

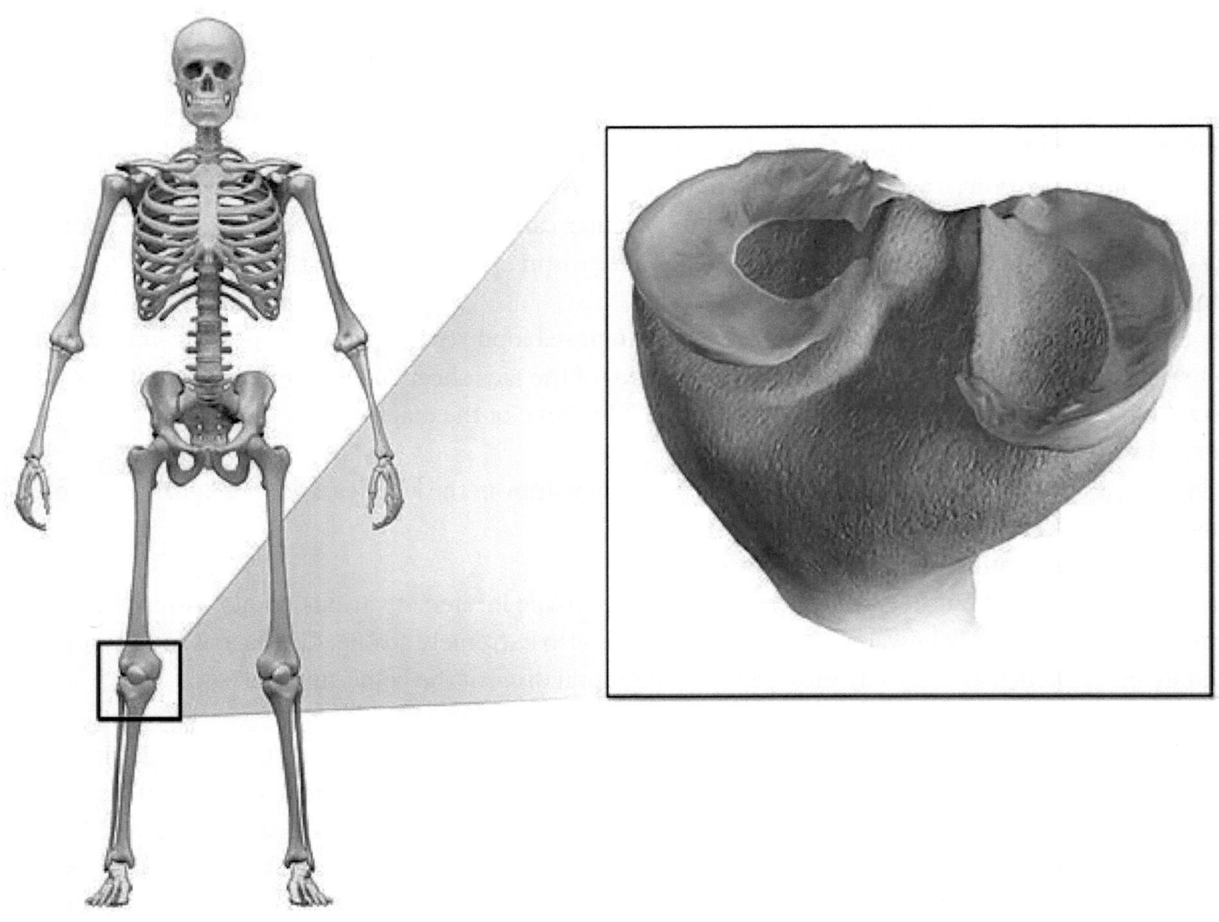

Meniscus of the Knee

Elastic cartilage

Elastic cartilage is found mainly in the outer ear (auricle or pinna), Eustachian tube, and epiglottis. These parts of the anatomy need to be constantly restored. The role of Elastic cartilage is simply structured, providing flexibility and durability due to the combination of elastic fibers and the type of collagen fibers. Yellow in color, and without the formal structure of fibrocartilage when viewed on a slide microscope.

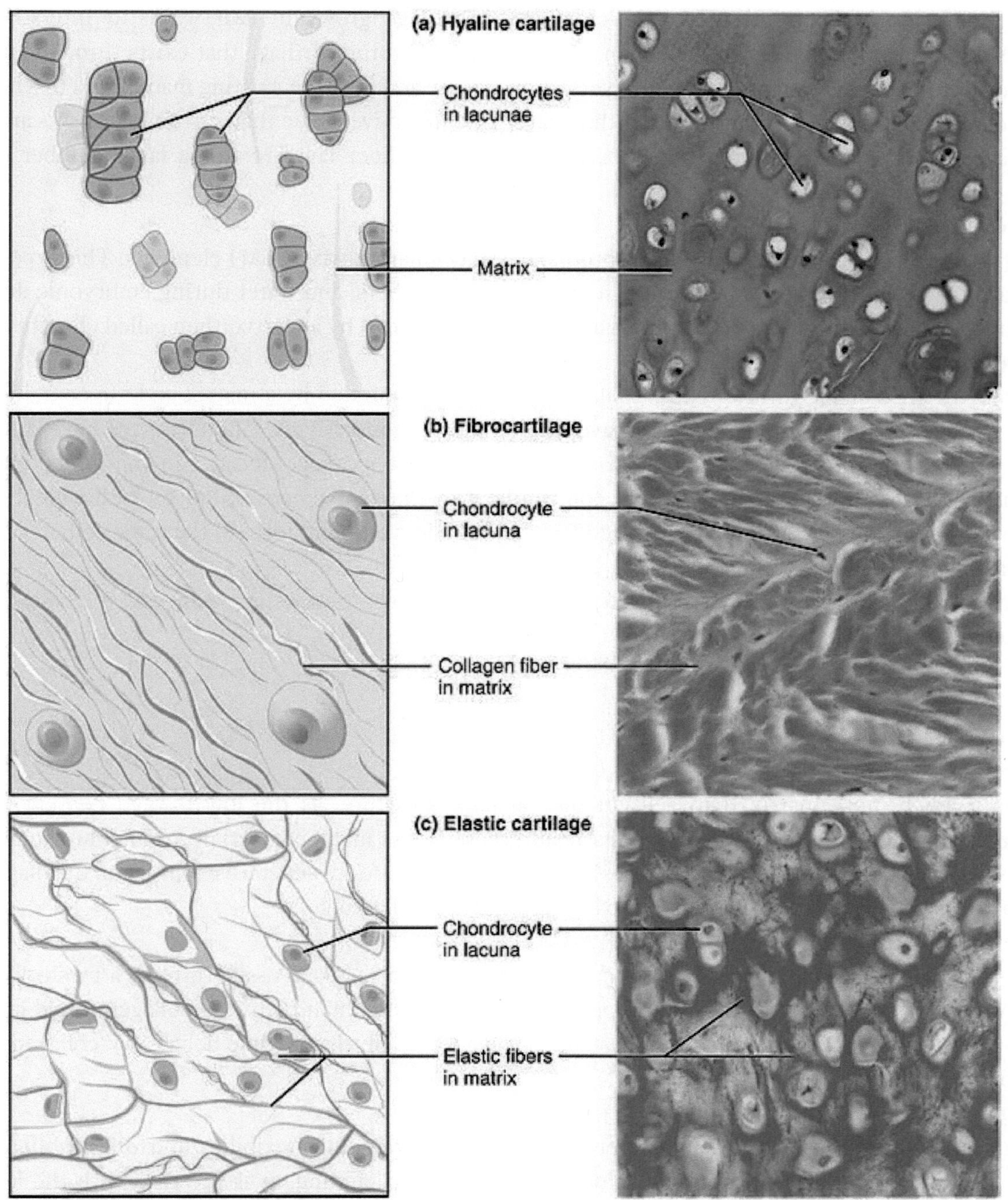

Different cartilages

Main Cartilage Ingredients

Cartilage is made up of specialized cells called chondrocytes and chondroblasts (chondro refers to cartilage), and other extracellular material that forms the cartilage matrix.

All types of connective tissue within the human body are found in the embryonic mesoderm. The bone, the strongest connective tissue, is the last to be formed and can remain in the cartilage after birth. An increase in the amount of cartilage to the bone makes the newborn flexible and safe to

move out of the birth canal. A newborn baby has 300 bones, compared to 206 normal, and all of these are from cartilage.

From the seventh week of embryonic life, the ossification process or osteogenesis gradually replaces the cartilage with bone. This process continues even in childhood. Cartilage grows in two ways. In interstitial growth, chondrocytes multiply and divide, producing an extra matrix within the cartilage that exists throughout childhood and adolescence. In appositional growth, new layers of matrix are added to the existing matrix area by chondroblasts in the perichondrium. The perichondrium is a thick layer of connective tissue that surrounds many cartilage areas. Its outer layer contains collagen-producing fibroblasts, while its inner layer retains a large number of different fibroblasts called chondroblasts.

chondroblasts

As long as it is free to move, chondroblasts produce extracellular matrix (ECM) elements. This type of cell first forms a matrix of hyaluronic acid, chondroitin sulphate, collagen fibers, and water during embryonic development. The chondroblasts eventually become immobile after being surrounded by a matrix, then called chondrocytes.

chondrocytes

Chondrocytes are a stable form of chondroblasts. They are surrounded by a matrix and are contained between fixed spaces called lacunae. One lacuna can have one or more chondrocytes. Chondrocytes have different roles depending on the type of cartilage they are found in. In articular cartilage, located in the joints, chondrocytes increase fusion. In growth plates, chondrocytes control the growth of the epiphyseal plate. Although chondroblasts are ECM producers, chondrocytes retain existing ECM and are a less efficient form of the same cell.

Fibroblasts

Fibroblasts are found in all types of connective tissue. In cartilage, these cells produce I-type collagen. In some cases, fibroblasts transform into chondrocytes.

ECM of cartilage contains three characteristic features:

Extracellular Matrix

There is a much more matrix than cells in the cartilage structure, as the low oxygen content and lack of vasculature do not allow for large numbers. As a result, there is less metabolic activity, and slower new growth of cartilage tissue - one of the most common causes for the elderly to suffer degenerative joint pain. Cartilage continues to grow slowly, however. This can be seen in the big ears and nose of adults.

Collagen

Protein-based collagen matrix provides structure and strength to cartilage tissue through a mesh- like structure of fibrils. Although there are many different types of collagen in the human body, the collagen found in cartilage is mainly type II, with FACIT attached (short collagen associated with fibril and triple helix) XIV collagen determines the range of these fibers.

Proteoglycans

Proteoglycans are large molecules that interact with water, providing flexibility and diminishing properties. Proteoglycan monomers bind to hyaluronic acid by way of protein binding, as is the case with the large protein Aggrecan (chondroitin sulphate proteoglycan 1), shown below

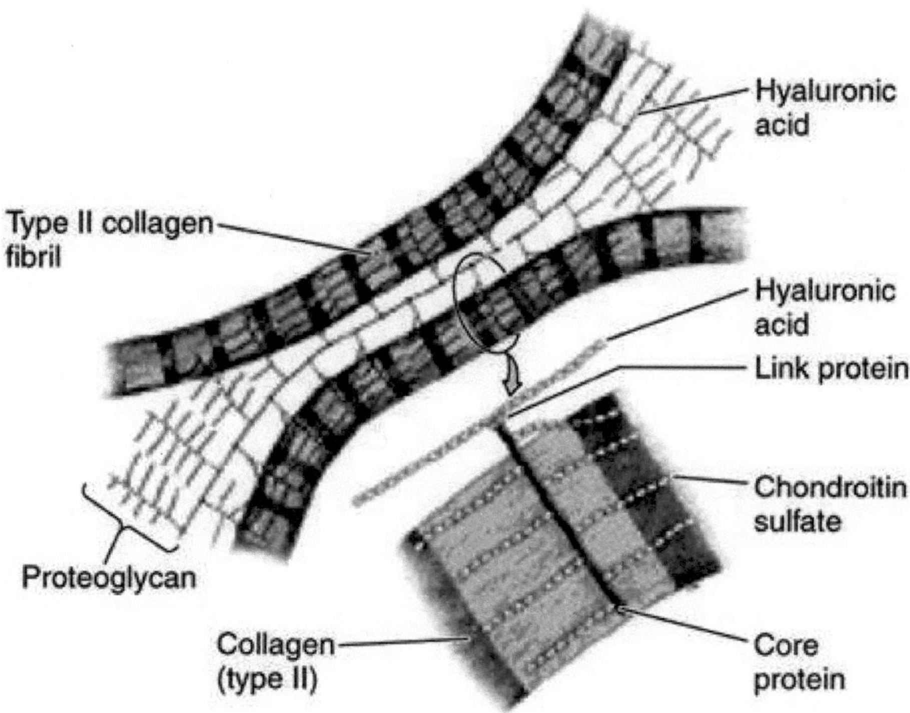

Collagen and aggrecan in hyaline cartilage

The high numbers of negative charges such constructions provide, together with a large surface area, make it possible for proteoglycans to bind to large amounts of water. This creates high osmotic pressure, increases load-bearing, and constitutes the gel-like consistency of the ECM.

Noncollagenous Proteins

Noncollagenous elements of the ECM are small in number and supposed to play a role in maintenance and organization of the cartilage structure on a macromolecular level.

Q2. Draw a well labeled diagram to illustrate the following:-

a. Relations and ligaments of ovary
b. Relation and blood supply of stomach
c. Relations of the liver

Answer (a) Relations and ligaments of ovary

The female gonads are called ovaries. In this article, we will first look at the basic function, location, components, and clinical significance of the ovaries. The last part of the article will cover the lines associated with the ovaries and their vasculature, lymphatic drainage and internal retention.

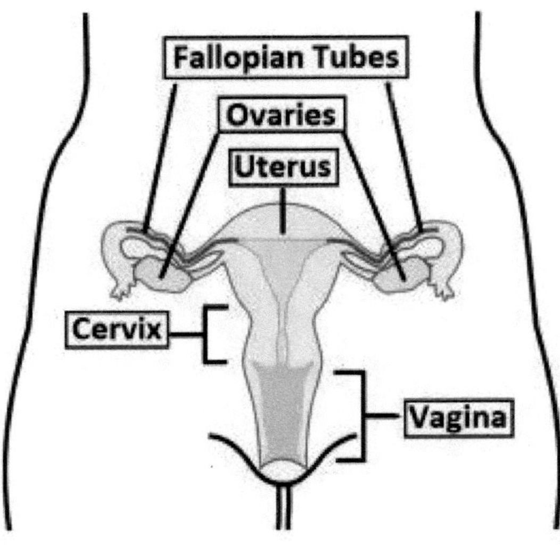

Overview of the female reproductive tract.

- In both men and women, the gonads grow inside the mesonephric ridge and down the abdomen. However, unlike testes, the ovaries stop at the pelvis.
- The ovaries are paired, the oval organs are connected to the back of the wider cervical ligament by the mesovarium (the fold of the peritoneum, which extends beyond the ovaries).
- Neurovascular structures enter the hilum of the ovary through the mesovarium.

The main functions of the ovaries are:

- Producing oocytes (female gamete) in preparation for fertilization.
- Production of the sex hormone hormones estrogen and progesterone, in response to pituitary gonadotrophins (LH and FSH).

Portions of the Ovary

The ovary has three main histological features:

- The surface - composed of a simple cuboidal epithelium (known as the germinal epithelium). Below this layer is a capsule of dense connective tissue.
- Cortex - includes stroma of connective tissue and multiple ovarian follicles. Each follicle contains an oocyte, surrounded by a single layer of follicular cells.
- Medulla - made up of loose connective tissue and a rich neurovascular network, entering the hilum of the ovary.

Muscles

Two peritoneal lines are attached to the ovary;

- Suspensory ligament of the ovary - wrapping the peritoneum from the mesovarium to the pelvic wall. It contains neurovascular structures.

- Ligament of the ovary - from the ovary to the uterus of the uterus. It then extends from the uterus to the connective tissue of the labium majus, like a round uterine muscle.

Neurovascular Supply

The main arterial supply to the ovary travels in paired ovarian arteries. These originate directly in the abdominal aorta (under the renal arteries). There is also a donation from the veins of the uterus.

The venous flow is achieved by paired ovarian veins. The left uterine artery drains to the left renal artery, and the right ovarian artery to the lower vena cava.

The ovaries receive sensitive and parasympathetic innervation from the ovarian and uterine (pelvic) plexuses, respectively. The nerves reach the ovaries through the suspensory ligament of the ovary, to enter the ovary in the hilum.

Lymphatic Supply

Lymph from the ovaries flows to the para-aortic nodes.

The stomach is an organ of the digestive system, specializing in the accumulation and digestion of food. Its structure is complex; it consists of four parts, two curvatures and receives its blood mainly from the celiac trunk. Innervation is provided by the vagus nerves and celiac plexus.

Answer (b) Relation and blood supply of stomach

Abdominal relationships

- **Anteriorly**— abdominal wall, left ventricle, diaphragm and left ventricle.
- **Back** — a small sac, which separates the stomach from the pancreas, the mesocolon intersecting, the left kidney, the left suprarenal, the spleen and the splenic artery.
- **Above** — the left dome of the diaphragm.

The small omentum is attached to the side of the small curvature of the abdomen, the large omentum near the large curvature. These oments contain vascular and lymphatic supply of the abdomen.

Blood Supply of Stomach

- The abdomen is provided by a rich system of arteries found in the celiac trunk, the first large visceral branch of the abdominal aorta.
- A small abdominal curvature is assigned to the left and right abdominal arteries, which are the branches of the celiac trunk and the normal hepatic artery respectively. The major curvature is given to the left and right gastro-omental (gastro-epiploic) arteries, exiting the splenic and gastroduodenal arteries respectively.
- Each of these pairs of arteries develops arterial anastomosis, which means the arteries connect and share the area of supply. This is an important organization, as blood is yet to be brought to a specific location, even if one of its many arteries is blocked, often seen in elderly patients.
- The fundus and the upper part of the abdomen are fed to the short and posterior gastric branches of the splenic artery while the abdominal pylorus is fed to the gastroduodenal artery, a branch of the common hepatic artery.
- Because the stomach is rich in blood, the collapse of the abdominal wall can lead to severe bleeding with some side effects. Under normal circumstances, there is a balance between acid secretion in the stomach, and immune factors (such as gastric mucosal barrier) near the inner lining of the stomach and duodenum. Disruption of this physiologic balance leads to damage to this inner lining, known as the peptic ulcer.
- Abdominal ulcers are the most common cause of upper bowel bleeding. Hemorrhage can occur over a long period of time, leading to blood loss, or it can be rapid, resulting in hemodynamic damage - a condition that requires urgent medical and surgical intervention.

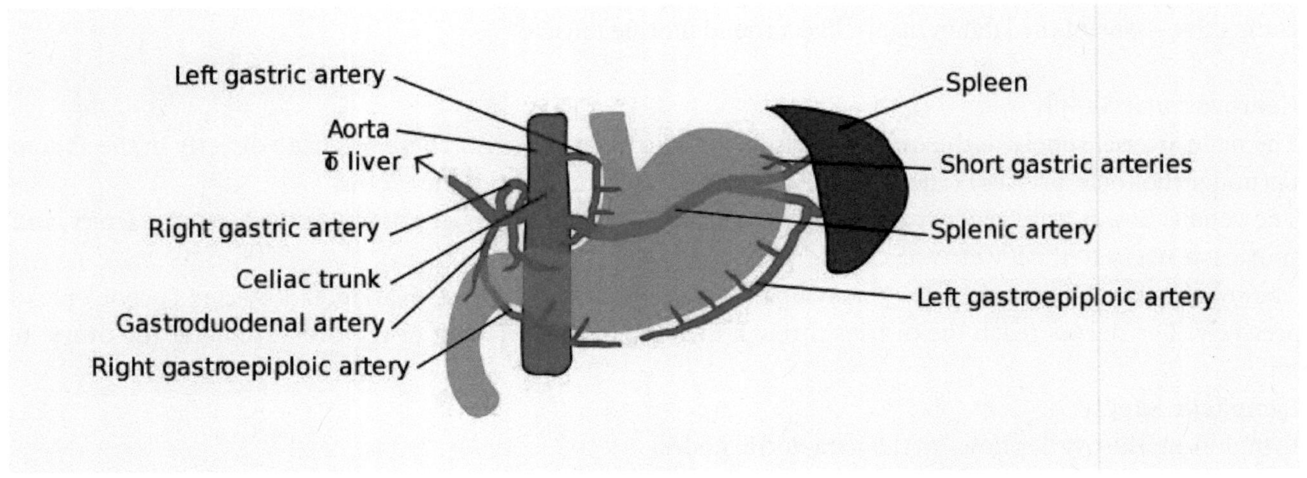

Relation of Stomach

Answer (c) Relations of the liver
RELATIONSHIPS
Overall, the most important and vital relationship of the liver is associated with the diaphragm and the mesentery.
Relations of the liver superior

- Lung
- Right pleura
- Pericardium
- Diaphragm
- Posts
- subphrenic left forearm

Below
The sinus (which opens into the right atrium). The anterior cardiac veins drain directly into the right atrium.

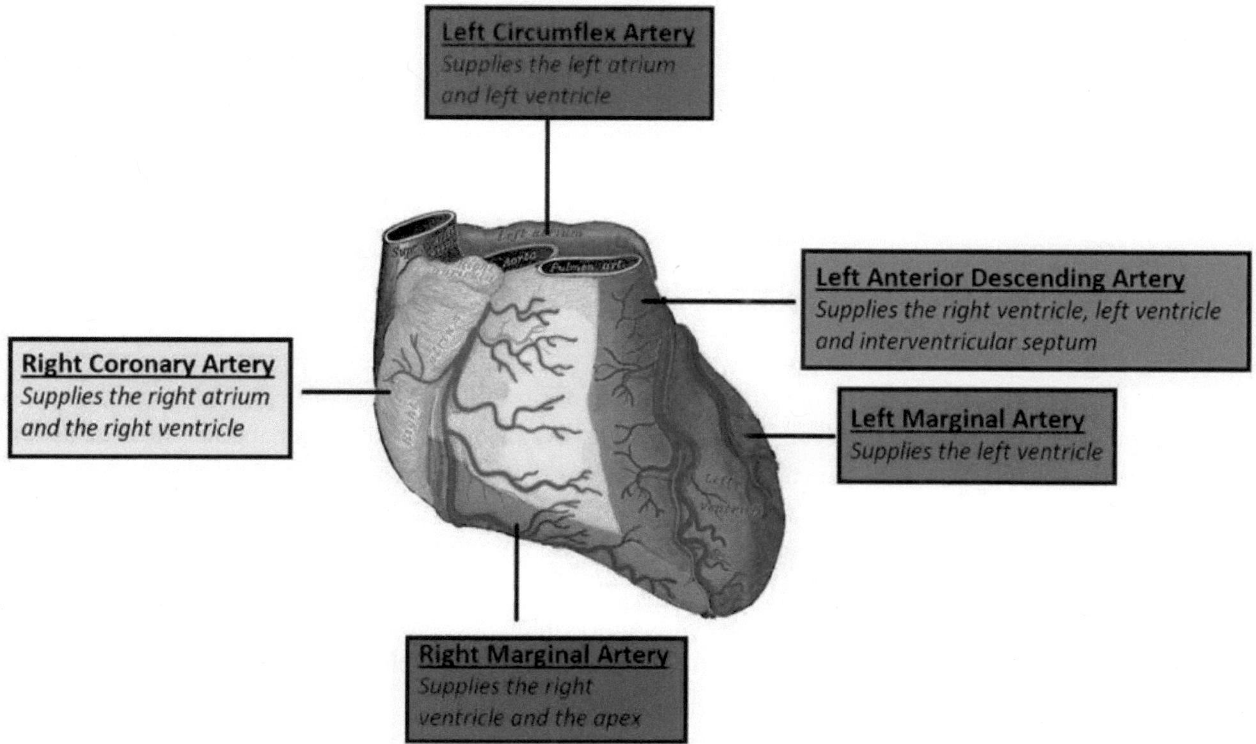

Anterior view of territorial arterial supply to the heart.

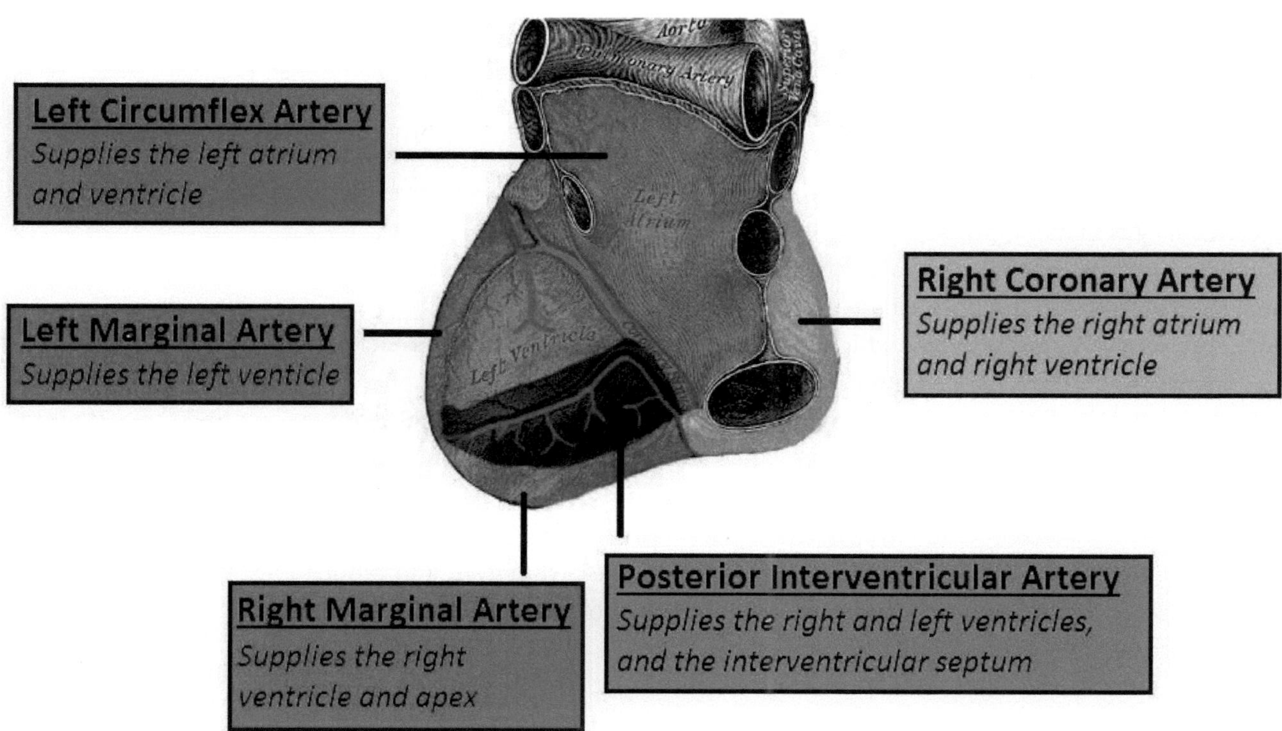

Posterior view of territorial arterial supply to the heart.

Part-II (physiology)

Q4. Write short note on the following

a. Regulation of Blood Pressure
b. Stages of spermatogenesis
c. Functions of Kidneys

Answer(a) Regulation of Blood Pressure

Blood pressure (BP) can provide insight into cardiovascular function. BP is controlled by a variety of complex physiological processes that allow both temporary adaptation and long-term maintenance of BP within a normal range. High or very low blood pressure can lead to a variety of pathologies (e.g., broken blood vessels, reduced perfusion in the limbs) so the mechanisms that maintain BP homeostasis require intensity.

Blood pressure can be measured in many different ways, most commonly systolic and diastolic blood pressure:

- Systolic blood pressure (SBP) represents pressure on the blood vessels when the heart is slow (systole).
- Diastolic blood pressure (DBP) represents pressure on the blood vessels during heartbeat (diastole).

Mean arterial blood pressure (MABP) is another way to check blood pressure:

- What arterial blood pressure means = Heart rate x Resistance to the arteries MABP can be calculated in SBP and DBP using the following formula:
- MABP = DBP + (Pulse pressure / 3)
- Pulse pressure is calculated by releasing DBP from SBP (i.e. SBP - DBP)

Immediate control of blood pressure Baroreceptor reflex

The baroreceptor reflex is a neutral reflex that controls blood pressure in the short term. This reflex is important for maintaining blood pressure throughout the day and in your absence, even a slight change in posture can lead to significant changes in blood pressure.

There are mechanoreceptors known as baroreceptors found in the aortic arch and carotid sinus, which constantly monitor MABP and pulse pressure.1 Increased arterial pressure causes

increased baroreceptor activity, which increases the firing rate of afferent neurons related, possessing this information. at the cardiovascular center in the medulla.

In response to this, the activity of the parasympathetic nervous system (PSNS) increases and the activity of the sympathetic nervous system (SNS) decreases. The result of this decrease in heart rate and systemic vasodilatation jointly reduces MABP.

Conversely, when blood pressure drops, there is less baroreceptor activity which means that the level of afferent fibers pressure decreases, causing the heart center to increase SNS output and reduce PSNS output. an increase in systemic vasoconstriction, resulting in a complete increase in blood pressure.

Baroreceptor reflex

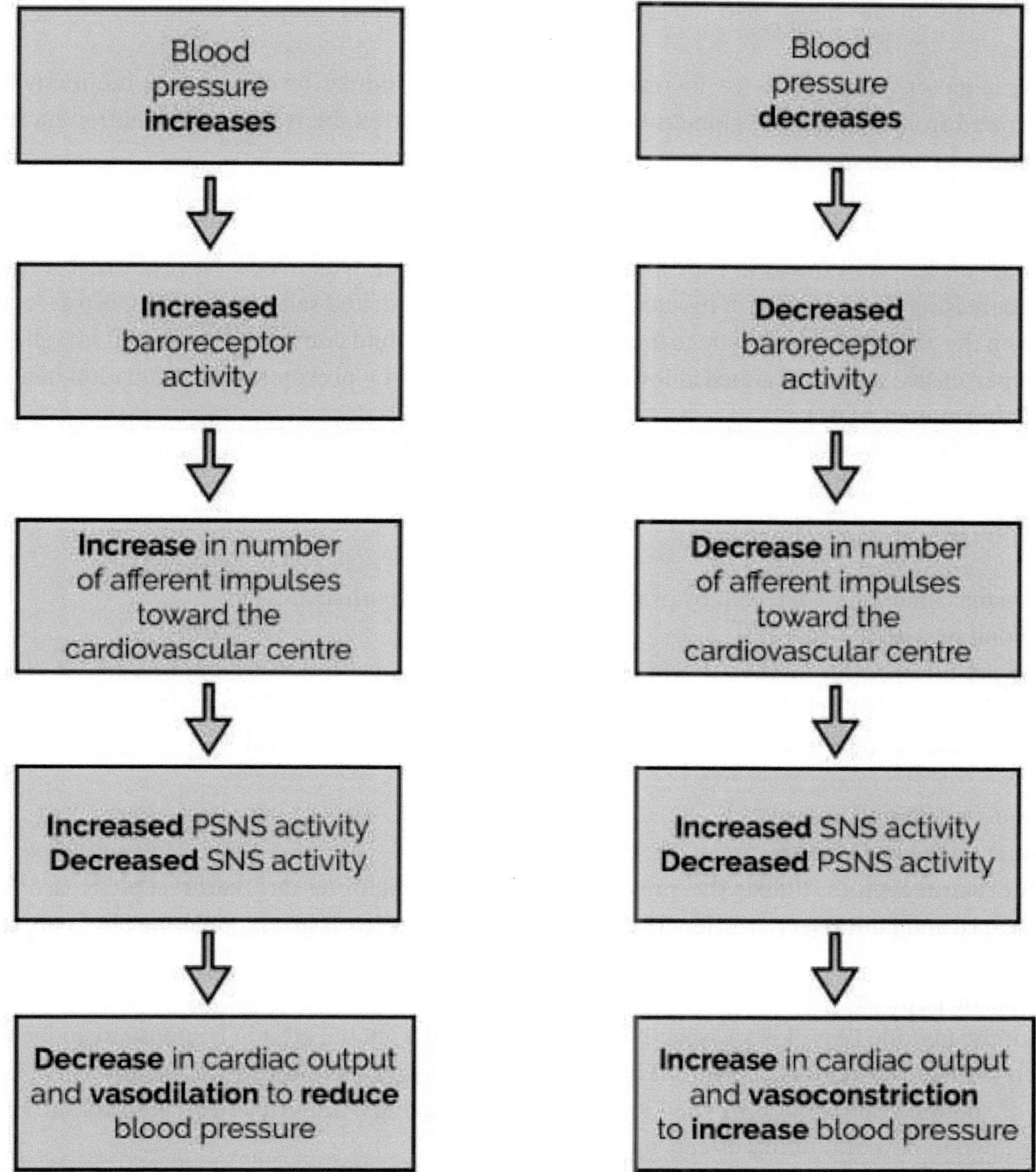

Baroreceptor reflex

Medium and long-term BP control

Renin-angiotensin-aldosterone (RAAS) system

The renin-angiotensin-aldosterone (RAAS) system is an important component of blood pressure control that works to increase blood volume and increase vascular resistance. This process relies on hormonal changes that promote gene expression to produce vasoactive proteins, making it a slower way to control blood pressure compared to the baroreceptor reflex.

The RAAS system begins with renin, a hormone released from granular cells in the juxtaglomerular apparatus, a special structure that includes parts of the distal collecting tubule (DCT) and the adjoining arteriole of glomerulus.

Renin is released as a result of increased salt levels in the blood, decreased renal blood flow, or stimulation from the sympathetic nervous system that activates beta-1 receptors.

Renin converts angiotensinogen, a protein bound to the liver, to angiotensinogen I, later converted to angiotensinogen-converting enzyme (ACE) into angiotensin II. Angiotensin II induces vasoconstriction in the systemic circulation and renal microvasculature, specifically binding to the protruding arteriole.

ACE, found mainly in the lungs, also releases a body of a vasodilator called bradykinin, which causes severe vasoconstriction.

Importantly, angiotensin II works to increase salt reuptake at kidney level and acts indirectly through the aldosterone secreted from them in the glomerulosa of the adrenal cortex. Increased salt retention increases plasma volume and blood pressure.

Angiotensin II is also able to increase plasma levels by stimulating thirst and antidiuretic hormone (ADH), another blood pressure regulator to be discussed soon.

Aldosterone forms key cells found in DCT and accumulates nephron, which increases Na + reabsorption while at the same time increasing K + secretion in tubules.3,7 Aldosterone- mediated salt resorption is also associated with H + secretion. Given the ability of aldosterone to increase the volume of fluid compound in the cell as well as BP, several common antihypertensive drugs are aimed at lowering blood pressure by preventing the formation of aldosterone.

Antidiuretic hormone (ADH)

The antidiuretic hormone, also known as vasopressin, is involved in regulating blood pressure. ADH is made up of cells found in the hypothalamus and released from the nearby posterior pituitary. The following physiological changes lead to the release of ADH:

- increased plasma osmolarity (detected by osmoreceptors in the hypothalamus)
- decreased blood pressure
- Increased levels of angiotensin IIADH works to increase water absorption by binding to V2 receptors, later focusing on the water channels known as aquaporins, named after the AQP-2 channels, are responsible for H2O mutations in the distant part of the nephron, as water cannot pass through them.

Other regulators of blood pressure

Baroreceptors have low pressure

Low-pressure baroreceptors, unlike the previously mentioned high-pressure baroreceptors, are found in the venous system, atria, and pulmonary arteries. They respond to changes in plasma modulating blood pressure through various means.

Atrial natriuretic peptide

Atrial natriuretic peptide (ANP) is a vasoactive peptide released from the atria in response to an increase in atrial pressure, which is linked to venous pressure. The ANP works to lower blood pressure, mainly by vasodilation and the inhibition of sodium reabsorption by the kidneys, the latter having a diuretic effect. aldosterone release.1 ANP has also been shown to have inhibitory effects on vasopressin.

How do vasoactive compounds change SVR and BP?

Vasoactive compounds often alter the resistance to systemic circulation (systemic vascular resistance (SVR) by targeting arterioles, which are very small in the blood vessels. The smooth muscles in these vessels contain a number of receptors that, when bound, trigger any of these reactions, depending on the type of receptor:

- promote smooth muscle contraction, reduce vessel width and increase resistance to systemic arteries
- preventing smooth muscle, later increasing vessel size and reducing systemic resistance of the arteries
- Changes in the width of these small vessels occur throughout the body, increasing the arteriolar tone. As blood pressure decreases, blood pressure rises.

Answer (b) Stages of spermatogenesis

Spermatogenesis and the factors affecting it

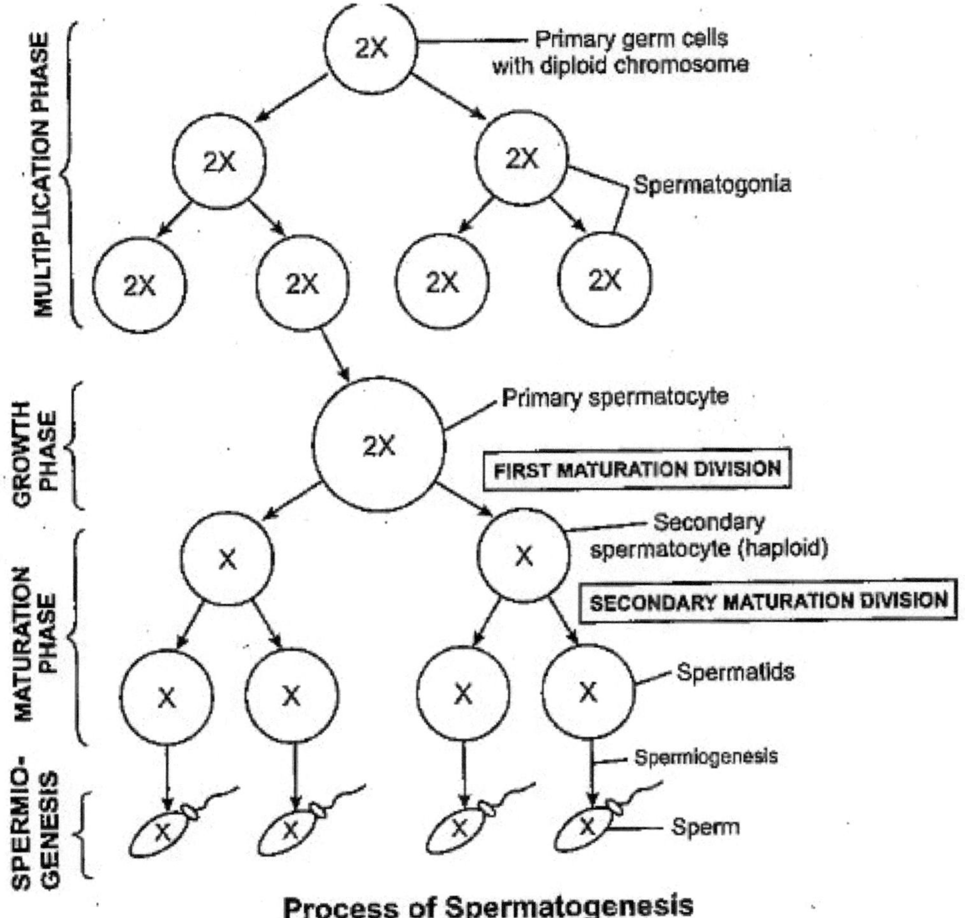

Process of Spermatogenesis

The factors affecting spermatogenesis

- The process of spermatogenesis is very sensitive to environmental changes, especially hormones and temperature.

- Malnutrition (such as vitamins B, E and A), anabolic steroids, iron (cadmium and lead), x-ray exposure, alcohol, and infectious diseases will also adversely affect the rate of spermatogenesis. In addition, the male genital tract is at risk for DNA damage caused by oxidative stress, and it is possible that this damage has a significant impact on pregnancy and pregnancy. Exposure to pesticides also affects spermatogenesis.

Answer (c) Functions of Kidneys

The main function of the kidneys is to make urine and purify the blood. Each kidney produces waste, as well as other chemicals that the body may need. The most important functions of the kidneys are described below.

Waste removal

- Cleansing blood by removing wastes is a very important kidney function.
- The food we eat contains protein. Protein is needed for growth and repair of the body. But as the proteins used by the body produce waste. The collection and storage of these waste products is similar to the storage of toxins within the body. Each kidney filters blood, as well as toxic waste products that end up in the urine.

- Creatinine and urea are two important compounds that can be easily measured in the blood. Their "numbers" in blood tests indicate kidney function. When both kidneys fail, creatinine and urea levels will be higher for blood tests.

Removal of excess fluid

- The second most important function of the kidneys is to control excess fluid by urinating in the urine while retaining the required amount of water in the body, which is essential for life. Too much water in the body leads to inflammation.

Measure minerals and chemicals

- Kidneys play another important role in regulating minerals and chemicals such as sodium, potassium, hydrogen, calcium, phosphorus, magnesium and bicarbonate and maintain normal body fluids.
- Changes in sodium levels can affect a person's mood, while changes in potassium levels can have serious effects on heart rate and muscle function. Maintaining a normal level of calcium and phosphorus is essential for healthy bones and teeth.

Controlling blood pressure

- Kidneys produce various hormones (renin, angiotensin, aldosterone, prostaglandin etc.) that help regulate water and salt in the body, which play an important role in maintaining proper blood pressure control. Disruption in the production of hormones and the regulation of salt and water in a patient with kidney disease can lead to high blood pressure.

Production of red blood cells

- Erythropoietin is another hormone produced by the kidneys; plays an important role in the production of red blood cells (RBCs). During renal failure, the production of erythropoietin decreases, leading to a decrease in RBC production leading to the formation of haemoglobin (anemia). This is why in patients with kidney failure, the amount of haemoglobin does not improve despite the addition of iron and vitamin preparations.

Keeping bones healthy

Kidneys convert vitamin D into an active ingredient in calcium in diet, bone and tooth development, and strong and healthy bones. During kidney failure, a deficiency of active vitamin D leads to weight loss, bone loss, and weakness. Decreased growth may be a sign of kidney failure in children.

Q5. Write the concept in short with the help of a diagram:

a. Blood groups
b. Structure and function of neurons
c. Conducting system of heart

Answer(a) Blood groups

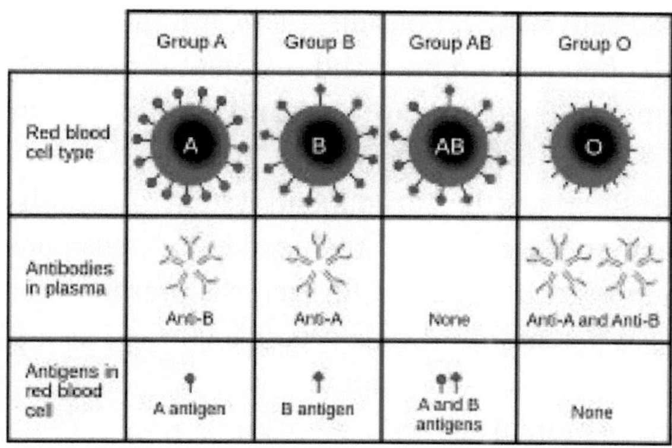

Blood Group

Blood is a fluid that binds to the tissues and is an essential part of the circulatory system. In a healthy person, about 5 liters (12 pints) of blood circulates throughout the body. In this article, blood groups and their types are described in more detail.

Blood Group System

Karl Landsteiner, an Austrian scientist, discovered the ABO blood group system in 1900. In his experiment, he combined various types of blood with plasma and observed that the plasma of certain types of blood produced agglutinates or clusters that formed because of the lack of red molecules. blood cells also cause the immune system to defeat that molecule. He then recorded agglutination and divided the blood types into 4 distinct groups. With the discovery of the ABO blood group, he was awarded the Nobel Prize.

The blood collection system is important for blood transfusions. Our immune system recognizes another type of blood as foreign and attacks it when it is introduced into the body causing a transfusion reaction. Any negative similarity to Rh and ABO blood types, triggers a serious reaction and threatens the life of the transfusion. Therefore, before a blood transfusion is given, it is recommended that a blood group be examined.

ABO and Rh blood groups

During a blood transfusion, the two most important group principles tested were the ABO- system and the Rhesus system.

The ABO blood group system consists of 4 blood groups - A, B, AB, and O and is based primarily on antigen and antibodies in red blood cells and plasma. Both antigens and antibodies are protein molecules where antigens are present in the face of Red Blood Cells and antibodies present in plasma are involved in protecting the immune system.

On the other hand, the Rh blood system contains 50 blood group antigens. In the Rh system, the most important antigens are D, C, c, E, and e. ABO and Rh blood systems are discussed in detail below.

1. **ABO blood Group program**

The basis of ABO collection consists of two antigens - Antigen A and Antigen B. The ABO collection system is divided into four types based on the presence or absence of antigens in the area of red blood cells and plasma antibodies.

- **Group A** - contains antigen A and antibody B.
- **Group B** - contains antigen B and antibody A.
- **Group AB** - contains both A and B antigens and no antibodies (at least A or B).
- **Group O** - does not have A or B antigens and both A and B antibodies.

The ABO group system is important during blood donation or blood transfusions as diversity of blood groups can lead to the accumulation of red blood cells with various disorders. It is important that the blood cells are the same at the time of transfusion, that is, the coherence of donor and recipient is required. For example, a person with blood type A can receive blood from group A or O as there are no A and O antibodies in blood group A.

2. Rh Blood Group System

In addition to the ABO blood system, another prominent system is the Rh blood group. About two-thirds of human beings contain a third antigen on the surface of their red blood cells known as Rh factor or Rh antigen; this determines whether the blood group is good or bad. If Rh factor is present, each person has a rhesus positive (Rh + ve); if Rh factor is not present each person has rhesus negative (Rh-ve) as it produces Rh antibodies. Therefore, coherence between provider and person is also important in this case.

Answer (b) Structure and function of neurons

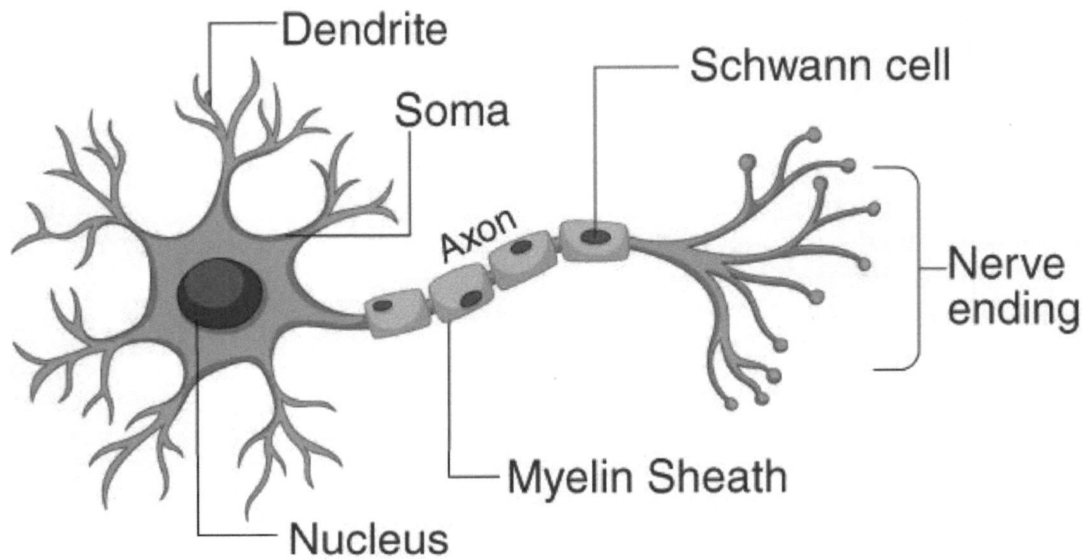

Structure of Neuron

Neurons are the building blocks of the nervous system. They receive and transmit signals from various parts of the body. This is done by physical and electronic means. There are several different types of neurons that aid in the transmission of information.

Sensory neurons carry information from sensory receptor cells present throughout the body to the brain. In turn, motor neurons transmit information from the brain to the muscles. Interneurons transmit information between different neurons in the body.

Components of Neuron

Here are the different parts of a neuron:

Dendrites

These are branch-like structures that receive messages from other neurons and allow the transmission of messages to the cell body.

Cell Body

Each neuron has a cell body with a nucleus, Golgi body, endoplasmic reticulum, mitochondria and other elements.

Axon

Axon is a tube-like structure that carries electrical energy from a cell body to axon terminals that transmit energy to another neuron.

Synapse

It is the site of chemical interactions between one terminal neuron and dendrites of another neuron.

Neuron functions

The key functions of a neuron are:

Chemical Synapse

In chemical synapses, the force of action affects other neurons through a gap that exists between two neurons known as synapses. The force of action is carried by an axon to a postsynaptic term that initiates the release of chemical messengers known as neurotransmitters. These neurotransmitters stimulate postsynaptic neurons that produce unique action power.

Electrical Synapse

When two neurons are connected to a gap junction, it results in an electrical synapse. These gaps include ion channels that aid in the direct transmission of a direct electric signal. These are much faster than chemical synapses.

Answer (c) Conducting system of heart

5 Elements of the Conduction Pathway

The conduction system of the heart controls its pumping action, which results in the delivery of blood to the different organs and tissues of the body. This conduction system is composed of a group of special cells found in the walls of the heart muscle, which send the electrical impulses and cause the heart muscle to contract.

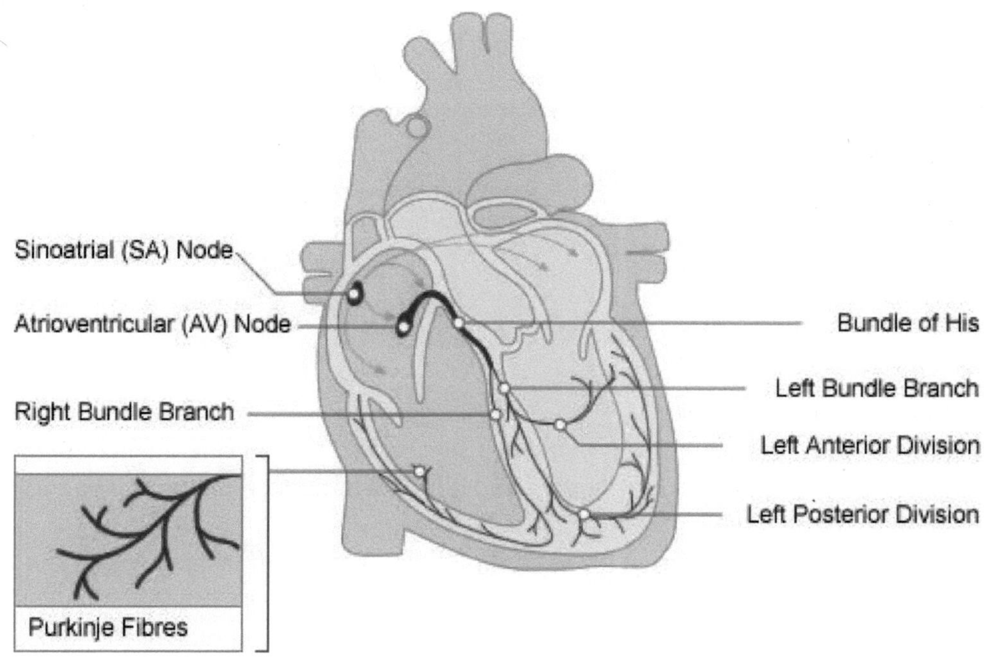

conduction pathway

It is made up of the following components:

<u>**SA (Sinoatrial) Location.**</u>

- The SA node is located in the upper right room (atrium) of the heart.

- It initiates stress which causes nervous breakdown and produces action, electrical activity, which extends into the upper two chambers (atria) and the AV node.
- Sets the heart rate.

AV (Atrioventricular) node

- This group of cells is located between the atria and the ventricles.
- Transmits electrical impulses from the atria, where the action force is temporarily delayed as it decreases, to the AV mass.

AV bundle (His Bundle)

- The electrical connection between the atria and the lower chambers of the heart (ventricles) is the bulk of the AV.
- Allows movement of action from the septum in the atria to the septum that separates the ventricles, and connects the AV node to the ventricular Bundle branches.

Lots of branches

- These transfer the action force to the interventricular septum of the heart.

Purkinje fibers

- These fibers start at the interventricular septum down to the top of your heart, and continue to the ventricular muscles (myocardium).
- They transfer electrical energy to the ventricular muscle cells.

- From an electrical event (force of action), a mechanical event (muscle contraction) occurs when the contraction cells act in an orderly fashion, leading to a heartbeat.

The conduction system of the heart works as follows:

Step 1: Pacemaker Impulse Generation

The SA node is known as a natural pacemaker because it sets the heart rate. This is where the contraction of the heart muscle begins, from the pressure causing the right and left atria to narrow and push blood into the ventricles.

Step 2: AV Node Impulse Conduction

From atria, an electrical signal is transmitted to the AV node, a group of cells located within the atria.

Step 3: AV Bundle Impulse Conduction

The electric current then travels through the bulk of His AV, splitting into a branch of the right and left bulk.

Step 4: Purkinje Fibers Impulse Conduction

Then the force of action spreads through Purkinje fibers, causing the left and right ventricles to contract. The tight contraction of the ventricles causes blood to flow from the right ventricle to the lungs, and from the left ventricle to the rest of the body. After the ventricles reach, they are relaxed and filled with more blood from the atria as the electrical impulses from the SA node begin the heart cycle again.

Q6. write features of the following:

a. Iron deficiency anemia

b. Rickets
c. Placenta

Answer(a) Iron deficiency anemia

Iron deficiency anaemia is a common type of anaemia - a condition in which the blood does not have healthy red blood cells. Red blood cells carry oxygen to the body's tissues.

As the name implies, the lack of iron anemia is due to insufficient iron. Without enough iron, your body cannot produce enough of the red blood cells that make it able to carry oxygen (hemoglobin). As a result, a lack of iron anemia can leave you exhausted and short of breath.

You can correct iron deficiency anemia by adding iron supplementation. Sometimes additional testing or treatment for iron deficiency anemia is needed, especially if your doctor suspects that you are bleeding internally.

Symptoms

Initially, iron deficiency anemia can be so mild that it is undetectable. But as the body becomes more deficient in iron and anemia worsens, the signs and symptoms become worse.

Signs and symptoms of iron deficiency anemia may include:

- Excessive fatigue
- Weaknesses
- Pale skin
- Chest pain, rapid heartbeat or shortness of breath
- Headache, dizziness or light headedness
- Cold hands and feet
- Swelling or pain in your tongue
- Wrinkled nails
- Unusual cravings for unhealthy substances, such as ice, dirt or starch
- Anorexia nervosa, especially in infants and children with iron deficiency anemia

Causes

Iron deficiency anemia occurs when your body does not have enough iron to produce hemoglobin. Hemoglobin is a component of red blood cells that give blood its red color and enable red blood cells to carry oxygen throughout your body.

If you do not eat enough iron, or if you lose a lot of iron, your body will not be able to produce enough hemoglobin, and iron deficiency anemia will eventually develop.

Causes of iron deficiency anemia include:

- **Loss of blood.** The blood contains iron inside the red blood cells. So when you lose blood, you lose some iron. Women who are having a hard time are at risk of getting iron deficiency anemia because they lose blood during menstruation. Slow, chronic blood loss in the body - such as peptic ulcer, hiatal hernia, colon polyp or colorectal cancer - can cause iron deficiency anemia. Gastrointestinal bleeding may be the result of frequent use of painkillers, especially aspirin.
- **Lack of iron in your diet**. Your body regularly receives iron from your diet. If you eat too little iron, over time your body may become deficient in iron. Examples of foods rich in iron include meat, eggs, leafy green vegetables and iron foods. In order to grow and develop well, infants and children need iron in their diet, too.
- **Inability to absorb iron.** Iron from food enters your bloodstream through your small intestine. Intestinal disorders, such as celiac disease, which affects the ability of your intestines to absorb nutrients from digested foods, can lead to iron deficiency anemia. If part of your small intestine has been removed or surgically

removed, this may affect your ability to absorb iron and other nutrients.

- **Pregnancy.** In addition to iron supplementation, iron deficiency anemia occurs in many pregnant women because their iron stores need to supply their growing blood and become a source of hemoglobin in the developing fetus.

Risk factors
These groups of people may be at increased risk for iron deficiency anemia:

- Women. Because women lose blood during menstruation, women are often at greater risk for iron deficiency anemia.
- **Infants and children.** Infants, especially those born prematurely or born prematurely, who do not get enough iron from breast milk or bottle-fed milk may be at risk of iron deficiency. Babies need extra iron during puberty. If your child does not eat a healthy, varied diet, he or she may be at risk of anemia.
- **Vegetarians.** People who do not eat meat may be at greater risk for iron deficiency if they do not eat other foods rich in iron.

- **Regular blood donors.** People who regularly donate blood may have an increased risk of developing iron anemia as blood donations can deplete metal stores. Low hemoglobin related to blood donation may be a temporary problem that can be corrected by eating a diet rich in iron. If you are told that you cannot donate blood because of low hemoglobin, ask your doctor if you should be concerned.

Problems
Medium iron deficiency anemia usually does not cause problems. However, if left untreated, iron deficiency anemia can be severe and lead to health problems, which include the following:

- **Heart problems.** Iron deficiency anemia can lead to rapid or irregular heartbeat. Your heart should pump a lot of blood to compensate for the lack of oxygen in your blood if you have anemia. This can lead to increased heart rate or heart failure.
- **Complications during pregnancy.** In pregnant women, severe iron deficiency anemia has been linked to premature births and low birth weight babies. But this condition is avoided for pregnant women who receive iron supplements as part of their prenatal care.
- **Growth problems.** In infants and toddlers, severe iron deficiency can lead to anemia and delayed growth and development. In addition, iron deficiency anemia is associated with an increased risk of infection.

Prevention
You can reduce your risk of iron deficiency anemia by choosing foods rich in iron. Choose foods rich in iron
Iron-rich foods include:

- Red meat, pork and poultry
- Seafood
- Beans
- Dark green leafy vegetables, such as spinach
- Dried fruits, such as dried rice and apricots
- Iron-fortified cereals, breads and pastas
- Peas

Your body absorbs more nutrients from the body than from other sources. If you choose not to eat meat, you may need to increase your intake of iron-based foods, which are based on plants to absorb the amount of iron that a person eats.

Choose foods that contain vitamin C to improve iron absorption.

Answer (b) Rickets

Rickets are a child's rheumatoid arthritis in which the bones are soft and fragile. Bones tend to be weakened by a lack of nutrients, especially Vitamin D3. It is also caused by a lack of calcium and phosphate in the body. Weak bones can cause bone loss. Vitamin D is best found in sun exposure to the skin. Other good sources of Vitamin D are oily fish (such as tuna and salmon) and egg yolks.

It is a disorder that is common in infants, especially those with dark skin due to the lack of sunlight, and is also seen in premature infants. This condition of rickets in adults is called osteomalacia which is usually seen with soft bones. Diagnosis of rickets is usually done by blood tests and X-rays. Blood tests show the condition in terms of low levels of calcium and phosphorus as well as high levels of naturally alkaline phosphatase. With X-ray, it is shown to change the shape of the bones. Bone biopsies also help in their diagnosis.

Types of rickets

Rickets are of the following types:

1. Nutritional Rickets-This is due to foods that do not contain calcium, phosphorus and vitamin D.
2. Hypophosphatemic Rickets- Caused by low phosphate levels. It is a genetic problem linked to X where the kidneys cannot control the amount of phosphate released in the urine.
3. Renal Rickets - People with kidney problems have renal rickets. They cannot control the amount of calcium and phosphate released in the urine.

Symptoms of rickets

Symptoms of rickets include:

- Reduced growth and short stature
- Bone fractures
- Osteoporosis
- Pain in the bones of the arms, legs, waist and spine
- Dental impairment
- Bone deformities such as bowlegs, and extruded chest bone.

Problems with rickets

Vitamin D is needed to absorb calcium from food. Lack of calcium and vitamin D or the same inability to absorb the same cause rickets.

Vitamin D is found in sunlight and food. Vitamin D is produced when the skin is exposed to the sun. The use of sunscreen prevents radiation and as a result the production of Vitamin D on the skin decreases.

Fish oil and olive oil and egg yolk are rich in Vitamin D. In addition, some grains, milk and fruit juices also contain Vitamin D.

In some cases, rickets can be inherited as a genetic disorder. It usually occurs in children as the bones grow faster in them, especially in children with the following traits:

- **Dark color** - excess melanin pigment
- **Absence of calcium**-rich, phosphorus-rich foods
- Lack of sunlight
- When infants are breastfed without Vitamin D supplements
- Having diseases that prevent the absorption of Vitamin D.

Treatment of rickets

This condition can be treated under proper supervision if the cause is found early. It can also be treated without severe orthopaedic impairment; However, certain conditions may require surgical intervention.

- Riches can be treated by eating foods rich in vitamins and minerals, especially vitamin D, calcium-rich and phosphorus-rich foods.
- Vitamin D supplements need to be given to infants of breastfeeding age. Adequate skin exposure to sunlight improves the condition.
- If rickets are caused by a genetic disorder, the patient is given vitamin D hormones and phosphorus medications.
- Foundations may be needed in the event of a bone defect in order to position the bones properly as the child grows.

Risks Involved

The main risk factors for rickets are given below:

- Babies between the ages of 3 and 36 months are more likely to be infected. This is the time when more calcium and phosphate are needed for bones to develop.
- Children who are lactose intolerant are at risk of developing rickets. Also, infants who rely on breast milk become infected because breast milk lacks vitamin D.
- Black children are more likely to get the disease. Dark skin does not react strongly to sunlight and therefore does not produce vitamin D.
- Children who live in areas with little sunlight or who spend a lot of time indoors may be victims of the disease.
- It can be passed on from one generation to the next.

Answer(c) Placenta

Placenta refers to a temporary vascular organ found in mammals, which attaches to the fetus in the mother's womb during pregnancy.

- The placenta is the passage that connects the fetus to the mother. The placenta facilitates the exchange of nutrients and oxygen in the fetus.
- It is also responsible for collecting carbon dioxide and waste products from the fetus. In appearance, the placenta is disk-shaped and reaches a height of 22 cm. The placenta is also rich in blood vessels.
- The placenta is found only in mammals. The umbilical cord connects the baby to the placenta, facilitating the transfer of material.
- The placenta usually attaches to the top, bottom, side, front or back of the uterus. In severe cases, the placenta attaches to the lower part of the uterus leading to a condition known as placenta previa.

Factors affect the health of the placenta

Various factors can affect the health of the placenta during pregnancy, and some are under your control and some are not. For example:

- **Mother's age.** Other placental problems are more common in older women, especially after the age of 40.
- **Rest in water before cutting.** During pregnancy, your baby is surrounded by a fluid- filled fluid called the amniotic sac. If the sac leaks or breaks before the cut, also called your fluid rupture, the risk of certain placenta problems increases.
- **High blood pressure**. High blood pressure can affect your placenta.

- Twins or other mass pregnancies. If you are pregnant with more than one child, you may be at increased risk for certain placental problems.
- **Dehydration disorders.** Any condition that impairs your blood's ability to clot or increases its chances of clotting increases the risk of certain placental problems.
- **Pre-uterine surgery**. If patient have had previous surgery on your uterus, such as C- section or surgery to remove fibroids, you are at greater risk for certain placental problems.
- **Previous placental abruption**. If patient have had a placenta problem during a previous pregnancy, you may have a higher risk of relapsing.
- **Drug use.** Certain placental problems are more common in women who smoke or use cocaine during pregnancy.
- **Abdominal pain.** Abdominal trauma - such as a fall, car accident or other type of stroke - increases the risk of premature placental abruption.

CHAPTER II

Question Paper 2021

B.Sc Nursing 1st year ,annual exam, 2021
Anatomy and physiology

Note Marks 75

1. attempt all questions and draw suitable diagrams, tables, and graphs where required.

2.attempt part-1 and part-2 in separate answer book.

Part –I anatomy

Q1. Describe in detail:

a. External and internal features of liver
b. Blood supply of heart
c. Urinary bladder and its blood supply

Q2. Draw a well labeled diagram to illustrate the following:

a. Blood supply of bones
b. Mediastinal surface of right lung
c. Blood supply of inferior surface of cerebrum

Q3. Write short note on the following:

a. Deep fascia and its modifications
b. Red nucleus
c. Buccinator muscle and its nerve supply

Part-II (physiology)

Q4. Write short note on the following:

a. regulation of body temperature
b. factor influencing blood pressure
c. functions of skin

Q5. Write the concept in short with the help of a diagram:

a. Contraceptive methods in humans
b. Formation of T-cells and B- cells.
c. Urinary bladder

Q6. write features of the following:

a. Pituitary and thyroid dwarfism
b. Color blindness
c. Male fertility system

Part-I Anatomy

Q1. Describe in detail

a. External and internal features of liver
b. Blood supply of heart
c. Urinary bladder and its blood supply

Answer (a) Anatomy of the Liver

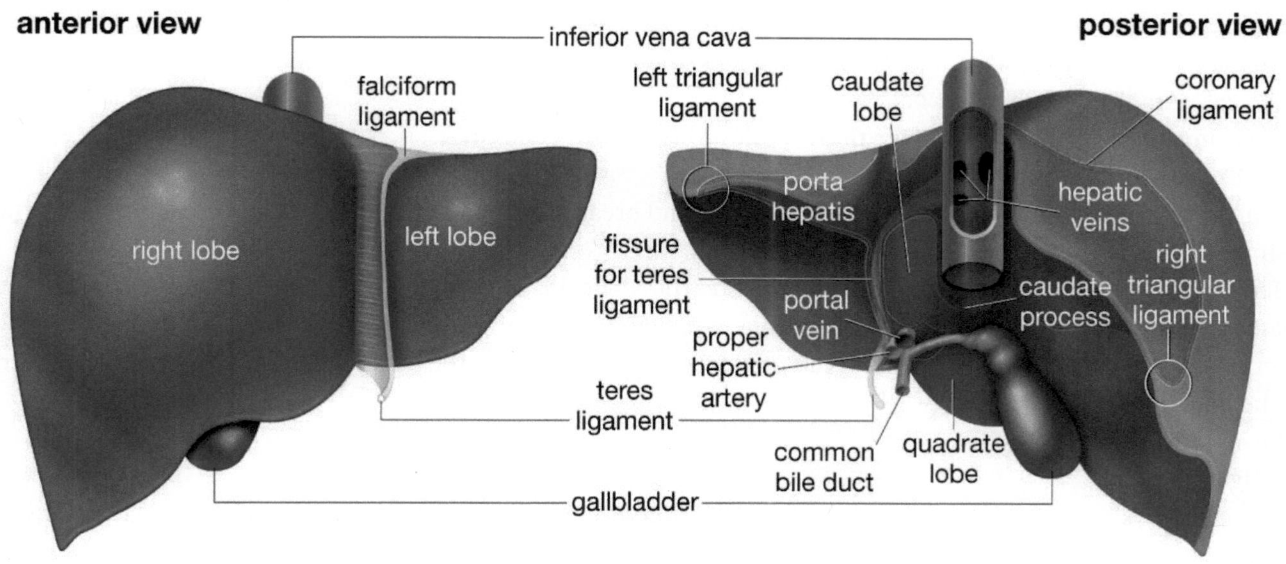

Normal Liver

The liver is a roughly triangular organ that extends across the entire abdominal cavity just inferior to the diaphragm. Most of the liver's mass is located on the right side of the body where it descends inferiorly toward the right kidney

The liver consists of 4 distinct lobes — the left, right, caudate, and quadrate lobes.

The left and right lobes are the largest lobes and are separated by the falciform ligament. The right lobe is about 5 to 6 times larger than the tapered left lobe.

The small caudate lobe extends from the posterior side of the right lobe and wraps around the inferior vena cava.

The small quadrate lobe is inferior to the caudate lobe and extends from the posterior side of the right lobe and wraps around the gallbladder.

1. Bile Ducts

The tubes that carry bile through the liver and gallbladder are known as bile ducts and form a branched structure known as the biliary tree. Bile produced by liver cells drains into microscopic canals known as bile canaliculi. The countless bile canaliculi join together into many larger bile ducts found throughout the liver.

These bile ducts next join to form the larger left and right hepatic ducts, which carry bile from the left and right lobes of the liver. Those two hepatic ducts join to form the common hepatic duct that drains all bile away from the liver. The common hepatic duct finally joins with the cystic duct from the gallbladder to form the common bile duct, carrying bile to the duodenum of the small intestine. Most of the bile produced by the liver is pushed back up the cystic duct by peristalsis to arrive in the gallbladder for storage, until it is needed for digestion.

2. Blood Vessels

The blood supply of the liver is unique among all organs of the body due to the hepatic portal vein system. Blood traveling to the spleen, stomach, pancreas, gallbladder, and intestines passes through capillaries in these organs and is collected into the hepatic portal vein. The hepatic portal vein then delivers this blood to the tissues of the liver where the contents of the blood are divided up into smaller vessels and processed before being passed on to the rest of the body. Blood leaving the tissues of the liver collects into the hepatic veins that lead to the vena cava and return to the heart. The liver also has its own system of arteries and arterioles that provide oxygenated blood to its tissues just like any other organ.

3.Lobules

The internal structure of the liver is made of around 100,000 small hexagonal functional units known as lobules. Each lobule consists of a central vein surrounded by 6 hepatic portal veins and 6 hepatic arteries. These blood vessels are connected by many capillary-like tubes called sinusoids, which extend from the portal veins and arteries to meet the central vein like spokes on a wheel.

Each sinusoid passes through liver tissue containing 2 main cell types:

Kupffer cells and hepatocytes.

Kupffer cells are a type of macrophage that capture and break down old, worn-out red blood cells passing through the sinusoids.

Hepatocytes are cuboidal epithelial cells that line the sinusoids and make up the majority of cells in the liver. Hepatocytes perform most of the liver's functions — metabolism, storage, digestion, and bile production. Tiny bile collection vessels known as bile canaliculi run parallel to the sinusoids on the other side of the hepatocytes and drain into the bile ducts of the liver.

Physiology of the Liver

1.Digestion

The liver plays an active role in the process of digestion through the production of bile. Bile is a mixture of water, bile salts, cholesterol, and the pigment bilirubin. Hepatocytes in the liver produce bile, which then passes through the bile ducts to be stored in the gallbladder. When food containing fats reaches the duodenum, the cells of the duodenum release the hormone cholecystokinin to stimulate the gallbladder to release bile. Bile travels through the bile ducts and is released into the duodenum where it emulsifies large masses of fat. The emulsification of fats by bile turns the large clumps of fat into smaller pieces that have more surface area and are therefore easier for the body to digest.

Bilirubin present in bile is a product of the liver's digestion of worn-out red blood cells. Kupffer cells in the liver catch and destroy old, worn-out red blood cells and pass their components on to hepatocytes. Hepatocytes metabolize hemoglobin, the red oxygen-carrying pigment of red blood cells, into the component's heme and globin. Globin protein is further broken down and used as an energy source for the body. The iron-containing heme group cannot be recycled by the body and is converted into the pigment bilirubin and added to bile to be excreted from the body. Bilirubin gives bile its distinctive greenish color. Intestinal bacteria further convert bilirubin into the brown pigment stercobilin, which gives feces their brown color.

2. Metabolism

The hepatocytes of the liver are tasked with many of the important metabolic jobs that support the cells of the body. Because all of the blood leaving the digestive system passes through the hepatic portal vein, the liver is responsible for metabolizing carbohydrate, lipids, and proteins into biologically useful materials.

Our digestive system breaks down carbohydrates into the monosaccharide glucose, which cells use as a primary energy source. Blood entering the liver through the hepatic portal vein is extremely rich in glucose from digested food. Hepatocytes absorb much of this glucose and store it as the macromolecule glycogen, a branched polysaccharide that allows the hepatocytes to pack away large amounts of glucose and quickly release glucose between meals. The absorption and release of glucose by the hepatocytes helps to maintain homeostasis and protects the rest of the body from dangerous spikes and drops in the blood glucose level. (See more about glucose in the body.)

Fatty acids in the blood passing through the liver are absorbed by hepatocytes and metabolized to produce energy in the form of ATP. Glycerol, another lipid component, is converted into glucose by hepatocytes through the process of gluconeogenesis. Hepatocytes can also produce lipids like cholesterol, phospholipids, and lipoproteins that are used by other cells throughout the body. Much of the cholesterol produced by hepatocytes gets excreted from the body as a component of bile.

Dietary proteins are broken down into their component amino acids by the digestive system before being passed on to the hepatic portal vein. Amino acids entering the liver require metabolic processing before they can be used as an energy source. Hepatocytes first remove the amine groups of the amino acids and convert them into ammonia and eventually urea. Urea is less toxic than ammonia and can be excreted in urine as a waste product of digestion. The remaining parts of the amino acids can be broken down into ATP or converted into new glucose molecules through the process of gluconeogenesis.

3. Detoxification

As blood from the digestive organs passes through the hepatic portal circulation, the hepatocytes of the liver monitor the contents of the blood and remove many potentially toxic substances

before they can reach the rest of the body. Enzymes in hepatocytes metabolize many of these toxins such as alcohol and drugs into their inactive metabolites. And in order to keep hormone levels within homeostatic limits, the liver also metabolizes and removes from circulation hormones produced by the body's own glands.

4. Storage

The liver provides storage of many essential nutrients, vitamins, and minerals obtained from blood passing through the hepatic portal system. Glucose is transported into hepatocytes under the influence of the hormone insulin and stored as the polysaccharide glycogen. Hepatocytes also absorb and store fatty acids from digested triglycerides. The storage of these nutrients allows the liver to maintain the homeostasis of blood glucose. Our liver also stores vitamins and minerals - such as vitamins A, D, E, K, and B12, and the minerals iron and copper - in order to provide a constant supply of these essential substances to the tissues of the body.

Unfortunately, one common hereditary disorder called hemochromatosis causes the liver to store too much iron, potentially leading to liver disease. Modern DNA health testing can help you find out if you are genetically at higher risk of acquiring this condition or others like Gaucher disease ad alpha-1 antitrypsin deficiency, all of which increase your risk of developing liver disease.

5. Production

The liver is responsible for the production of several vital protein components of blood plasma: prothrombin, fibrinogen, and albumins. Prothrombin and fibrinogen proteins are coagulation factors involved in the formation of blood clots. Albumins are proteins that maintain the isotonic environment of the blood so that cells of the body do not gain or lose water in the presence of body fluids.

6. Immunity

The liver functions as an organ of the immune system through the function of the Kupffer cells that line the sinusoids. Kupffer cells are a type of fixed macrophage that form part of the mononuclear phagocyte system along with macrophages in the spleen and lymph nodes. Kupffer cells play an important role by capturing and digesting bacteria, fungi, parasites, worn-out blood cells, and cellular debris. The large volume of blood passing through the hepatic portal system and the liver allows Kupffer cells to clean large volumes of blood very quickly.

Answer (b) Blood supply of heart

- The heart is made of muscle. The strong muscular walls contract (squeeze), pumping blood to the arteries. The major blood vessels connected to your heart are the aorta, the superior vena cava, the inferior vena cava, the pulmonary artery (which takes oxygen-poor blood from the heart to the lungs where it is oxygenated), the pulmonary veins (which bring oxygen-rich blood from the lungs to the heart), and the coronary arteries (which supply blood to the heart muscle).

- On the inside, the heart is a four-chambered, hollow organ. It is divided into the left and right side by a wall called the septum. The right and left sides of the heart are further divided into

two top chambers called the atria, which receive blood from the veins, and two bottom chambers called ventricles, which pump blood into the arteries.

- The atria and ventricles work together, contracting and relaxing to pump blood out of the heart. As blood leaves each chamber of the heart, it passes through a valve. There are four heart valves within the heart:
- Mitral valve
- Tricuspid valve
- Aortic valve
- Pulmonic valve (also called pulmonary valve)

- The tricuspid and mitral valves lie between the atria and ventricles. The aortic and pulmonic valves lie between the ventricles and the major blood vessels leaving the heart.
- The heart valves work the same way as one-way valves in the plumbing of your home. They prevent blood from flowing in the wrong direction.
- Each valve has a set of flaps, called leaflets or cusps. The mitral valve has two leaflets; the others have three. The leaflets are attached to and supported by a ring of tough, fibrous tissue called the annulus. The annulus helps to maintain the proper shape of the valve.
- The leaflets of the mitral and tricuspid valves are also supported by tough, fibrous strings called chordae tendineae. These are similar to the strings supporting a parachute. They extend from the valve leaflets to small muscles, called papillary muscles, which are part of the inside walls of the ventricles.

How Does Blood Flow Through the Heart?

The right and left sides of the heart work together. The pattern described below is repeated over and over, causing blood to flow continuously to the heart, lungs, and body.

Right side

- Blood enters the heart through two large veins, the inferior and superior vena cava, emptying oxygen-poor blood from the body into the right atrium.
- As the atrium contracts, blood flows from your right atrium into your right ventricle through the open tricuspid valve.
- When the ventricle is full, the tricuspid valve shuts. This prevents blood from flowing backward into the atria while the ventricle contracts.
- As the ventricle contracts, blood leaves the heart through the pulmonic valve, into the pulmonary artery and to the lungs where it is oxygenated.

Left side

- The pulmonary vein empties oxygen-rich blood from the lungs into the left atrium.
- As the atrium contracts, blood flows from your left atrium into your left ventricle through the open mitral valve.
- When the ventricle is full, the mitral valve shuts. This prevents blood from flowing backward into the atrium while the ventricle contracts.
- As the ventricle contracts, blood leaves the heart through the aortic valve, into the aorta and to the body.

How Does Blood Flow Through Your Lungs?

Once blood travels through the pulmonic valve, it enters your lungs. This is called the pulmonary circulation. From your pulmonic valve, blood travels to the pulmonary artery to tiny capillary vessels in the lungs.

Here, oxygen travels from the tiny air sacs in the lungs, through the walls of the capillaries, into the blood. At the same time, carbon dioxide, a waste product of metabolism, passes from the blood into the air sacs. Carbon dioxide leaves the body when you exhale. Once the blood is purified and oxygenated, it travels back to the left atrium through the pulmonary veins.

What Are the Coronary Arteries?

Like all organs, your heart is made of tissue that requires a supply of oxygen and nutrients. Although its chambers are full of blood, the heart receives no nourishment from this blood. The heart receives its own supply of blood from a network of arteries, called the coronary arteries.

- At rest, a normal heart beats around 50 to 99 times a minute. Exercise, emotions, fever, and some medications can cause your heart to beat faster, sometimes to well over 100 beats per minute.

Answer (c)

Urinary bladder and its blood supply

The **bladder** is an organ of the urinary system. It plays two main roles:

- **Temporary storage of urine** – the bladder is a hollow organ with distensible walls. It has a folded internal lining (known as rugae), which allows it to accommodate up to 400- 600ml of urine in healthy adults.
- musculature of the bladder contracts during micturition, with concomitant relaxation the sphincters.

Shape of the Bladder

The appearance of the bladder varies depending on the amount of urine stored. When full, it exhibits an **oval** shape, and when empty it is flattened by the overlying bowel.

The external features of the bladder are:

Apex – located superiorly, pointing towards the pubic symphysis. It is connected to the umbilicus by the median umbilical ligament (a remnant of the urachus).

Body – main part of the bladder, located between the apex and the fundus

Fundus (or base) – located posteriorly. It is triangular-shaped, with the tip of the triangle pointing backwards.

Neck – formed by the convergence of the fundus and the two inferolateral surfaces. It is continuous with the urethra.

Urine enters the bladder through the left and right ureters, and exits via the urethra. Internally, these orifices are marked by the **trigone** – a triangular area located within the fundus.

In contrast to the rest of the internal bladder, the trigone has smooth walls (this is explained by the different embryological origin: the trigone is developed by the integration of two **mesonephric ducts** at the base of the bladder).

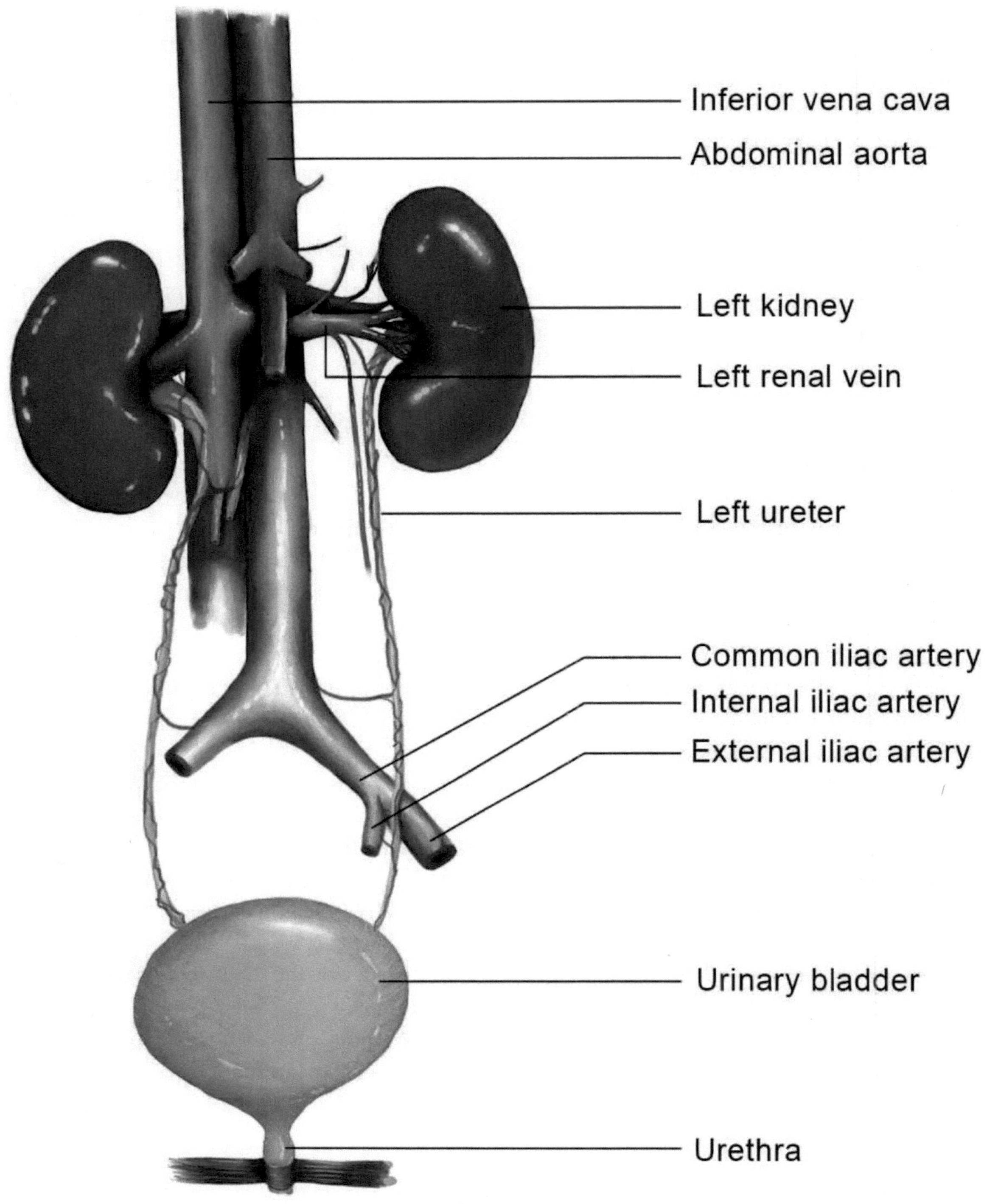

Urinary system anatomy

Blood supply of bladder

- Arterial supply is via the **superior vesical** branch of the internal iliac artery. In males, this is supplemented by the inferior vesical artery, and in females by the vaginal arteries. In both sexes, the obturator and inferior gluteal arteries may also contribute small branches.

- Venous drainage is achieved by the vesical venous plexus, which empties into the internal iliac veins. The vesical plexus in males is in continuity at the retropubic space with the **prostate venous plexus** (plexus of Santorini), which also receives blood from the dorsal vein of the penis

Lymphatics

The superolateral aspect of the bladder drains into the **external iliac** lymph nodes. The neck and fundus drain into the internal iliac, sacral and common iliac nodes.

Q2. Draw a well labeled diagram to illustrate the following:

a. Blood supply of bones
b. Mediastinal surface of right lung
c. Blood supply of inferior surface of cerebrum

Answer (a) Blood supply of bones:

Blood supply to the long bones comes from these three main sources:

- Nutrient artery system
- Metaphyseal-epiphyseal system
- Periosteal system

  - The nutrient artery system is a high-pressure system that branches from major systemic arteries. It enters through the cortex via the nutrient foramen and then migrates into the medullary canal. There it branches into ascending and descending branches that then further branch out into arterioles and supply the inner 2/3 of bone within the Haversian system.
  - The metaphyseal-epiphyseal arteries arise from the periarticular plexus, that is found around the joint area of a long bone.
  - The periosteal artery system is a low-pressure system that supplies the outer 1/3 of bone and is connected through Haversian and Volkmann canals. These canals are part of the osteon structure of the cortex.

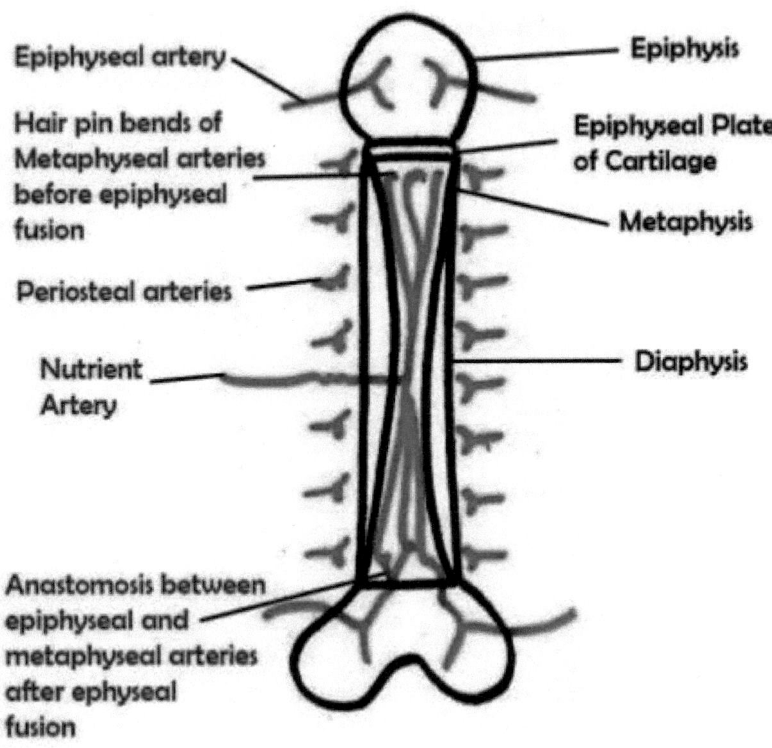

Blood supply of bone

ANSWER (b) <u>Mediastinal surface of right lung:</u>

- Cardiac area is related with Anterior surface of Right auricle, Anterior and right surface of right atrium, Part of anterior surface of right ventricle .
- In front of hilum upper part : Groove for SVC.
- In front of hilum lower part groove for IVC are present.
- Above the hilum : groove for azygous vein.
- Behind the hilum : osophagus except upper and lower part.
- From apex to groove for azygous vein:Anterioposteirly.
- Right brachiocephalic vein,Trachea,Osophagus.
- Three neural structures:right phrenic nerve, Right vagus nerve, Right sympathetic chain.

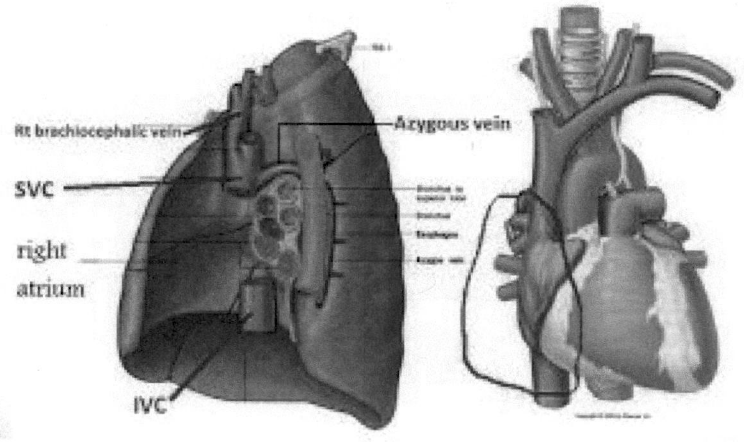

Right Lung

ANSWER (c) Blood supply of inferior surface of cerebrum

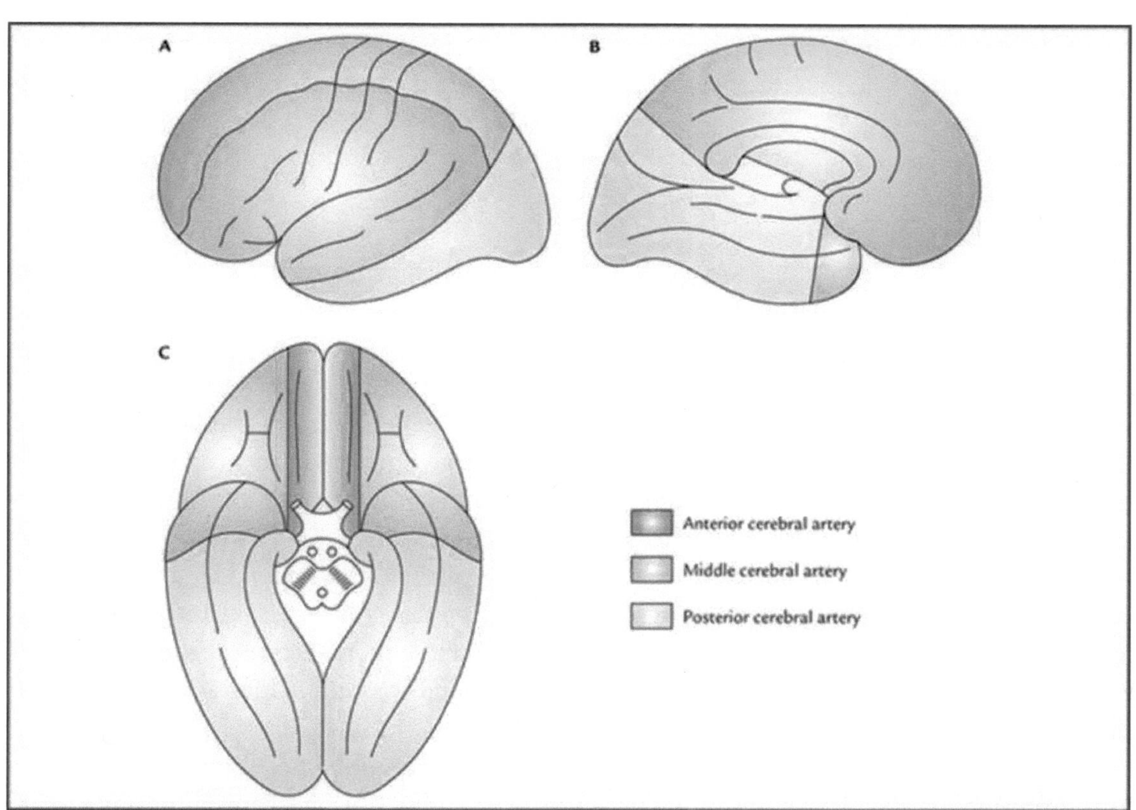

Blood supply of brain

Arterial supply of the superolateral (**A**), medial (**B**), and inferior (**C**) surfaces of the cerebral hemisphere.

- Most of the superolateral surface (about two-third) is supplied by the **middle cerebral artery**. The region of cerebral cortex supplied includes the greater parts of primary motor and sensory areas, and frontal eyefield. In the left (dominant) hemisphere it includes the Broca's and Wernicke's speech areas.
- A narrow strip of cerebral cortex (about 2.5 cm in width) adjoining superomedial border up to the parieto-occipital sulcus is supplied by **anterior cerebral artery**. The upper parts of primary motor and sensory areas lie in this region.
- A narrow strip along the lower border of temporal lobe (excluding temporal pole) and occipital lobe are supplied by **posterior cerebral artery**. The posterior parts of visual area fall in this area.

Q3. Write short note on the following:

a. Deep fascia and its modifications
b. Red nucleus
c. Buccinator muscle and its nerve supply

ANSWER (a) Deep fascia and its modification

Deep fascia is a fascia, a layer of dense irregular connective tissue that wraps the neck, the limbs and body wall like a bandage or stocking

It covers muscles, nerves, bone and blood vessel.

Important features of deep fascia:

- It is devoid of fat
- It is inelastic and tough
- It has nerve supply and very sensitive structure.
- It is a golden rule that when fascia approaches bone it becomes attached to it , blending with the covering periosteum

Modification of deep fascia:

1. Each muscle is covered by deep fascia known as epimysium which sends in the septa to enclose each muscle fasciculus known as perimysium. From the perimysium septa pass to enclose each Muscle fiber. These fine septa are the endomysium. This connective tissue layer supports the muscle and convey nerve, blood vessels and lymphatics.
2. Deep fascia covers each nerve as epineurium, each nerve fascicle as perineurium and individual nerve fibered as endoneurium. These connective tissue coverings support the nerve fibers and carry capillaries and lymphatics.
3. From deep fascia, the intermuscular septa is arises which separating functionally different group of muscles into separate compartments.
4. It also forms septa between various muscles. These septa are specially well developed in the calf muscles of lower limb. The contraction of calf muscles in the tight sleeve of deep fascia helps in pushing the venous blood and lymph towards the 'heart. Thus, the deep fascia helps in venous and lymphatic return from the lower limb.
5. The deep fascia is dense around the artery and rather loose around the vein to give an allowance for the vein to distend.deep fascia forms sheaths around large arteries, e.g., carotid sheath, axillary sheath.
6. Deep fascia is modified to form the capsule, synovial membrane and bursae in relation to the joints.
7. Deep fascia forms tendon sheaths wherever tendons cross over a joint. This mechanism prevents wear and tear of the tendon.
8. In the region of palm and sole it is modified to form aponeuroses. in the forearm and leg, the deep fascia is modified to form the interosseous membrane, which keeps:

- The two bones at optimum distance
- Increases surface area for attachment of muscles.
- Transmits weight from one bone to other

ANSWER (b) Red nucleus

The **red nucleus** is a paired oval-shaped, midline structure that appears bright red in the freshly dissected specimen. This unique appearance has been attributed to the high vascularity of the structure in addition to the high level of iron pigments within the cytoplasm of its constituent neurons. The nuclei blend rostrally with the nearby reticular formation and interstitial nucleus.

- At about 5mm in diameter, it spans the region from the inferior extent of the superior colliculus to the subthalamic part of the diencephalon in the midbrain. Each consists of caudal magnocellular and rostral parvocellular parts that give rise to specific efferent tracts. Each red nucleus is pierced by (but does not communicate with) the oculomotor nerve (CN III) before the nerve leaves the midbrain and passes through the interpeduncular fossa. Fibers of the superior cerebellar peduncle and the retroflex fasciculus also cross this structure. This gives the red nucleus a perforated appearance when stained with Weigert stains.
- Anterior to the red nucleus is the anterior tegmental decussation, interpeduncular nuclei and the medial third of the pars reticulata of the substantia nigra. Laterally, the cerebellothalamic fibers and the medial lemniscus tract can be seen. The central tegmental tract (which is a paired structure) is located posterior to each red nucleus. Other posteriorly related structures include the medial longitudinal fasciculi, oculomotor nuclei, mesencephalic nuclei and tracts, trigeminothalamic (anterior and posterior tracts) and the periaqueductal grey region.

LOCATION

As previously stated, the nuclei are midline structures found within the tegmentum of the midbrain at the level of the superior colliculi. The tegmentum is the region of the midbrain anterior to the cerebral aqueduct and posterior to the crus cerebri. The transition point from the tegmentum to the crus cerebri is demarcated by a hyper-pigmented band known as the substantia nigra. The medial third of the pars reticulata of the substantia nigra is proximal to the red nucleus (while the pars compacta is distal to the same).

ANSWER (c) Buccinator muscle and its nerve supply

The buccinator muscle is a thin quadrilateral facial muscle that is the main component of the cheek. Buccinator has a number of origin points which is the basis for subdividing the muscle fibers into superior, inferior and posterior parts.

- This muscle is the main muscle of the cheek, that provides it with structure and tightness. It compresses the cheek against the molar teeth, which is important to keep the food bolus central in the oral cavity, and to prevent the cheeks from being bitten during mastication. In addition, the buccinator is the main muscle involved in playing wind instruments, as it expels air from the distended cheeks.

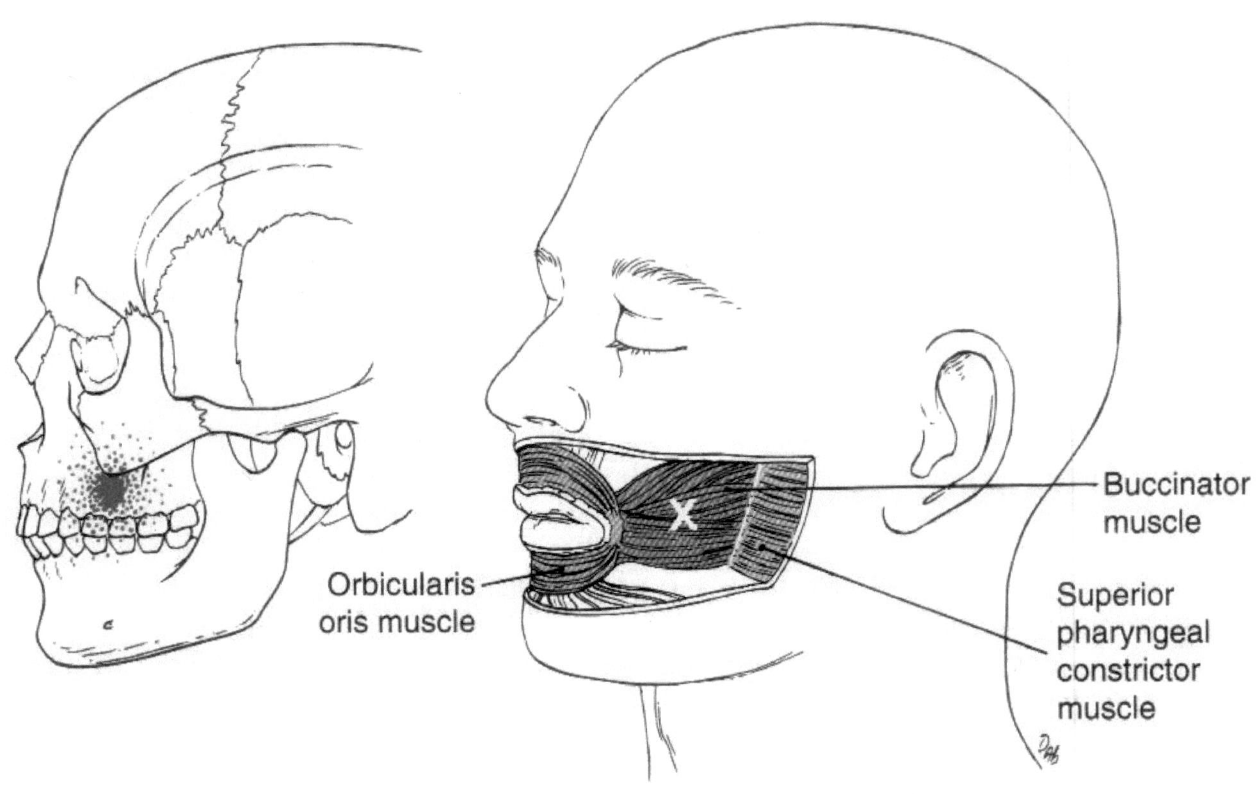

Buccinator muscle

BLOOD SUPPLY AND LYMPHATICS :

- The main blood supply to the buccinator comes from three arteries which form extensive anastomotic vascular plexus on the muscle's lateral surface and within its fibers.
- The posterior part of the muscle is supplied by the buccal artery, which is a branch of the internal maxillary artery.
- The artery runs in an anteroinferior direction under the external pterygoid muscle to reach the posterior part of the muscle.
- The facial artery, via its numerous branches, supplies the posterior, inferior, and anterior part of the muscle.
- The posterior buccal branch, which is the largest branch of the facial artery supplies the posterior half of the muscle. Inferior buccal branches of the facial artery supply the inferior half of the muscle.
- It then runs anterosuperiorly to give off anterior buccal branches which supply the anterior half of the muscle.
- Two small branches form the posterosuperior alveolar artery, which is a branch of internal maxillary artery enter the buccinator muscle posterosuperiorly and supply the surrounding area.
- Venous drainage of the muscle occurs through the pterygoid plexus and internal maxillary vein.

PART -II PHYSIOLOGY

Q4. Write short note on the following

a. regulation of body temperature
b. factor influencing blood pressure
c. functions of skin

Regulation of body temperature

- Thermoregulation is a mechanism by which mammals maintain body temperature with tightly controlled self-regulation independent of external temperatures. Temperature regulation is a type of homeostasis and a means of preserving a stable internal temperature in order to survive. Ectotherms are animals that depend on their external environment for body heat, while endotherms are animals that use thermoregulation to maintain a somewhat consistent internal body temperature even when their external environment changes.

- Humans and other mammals and birds are endotherms. Human beings have a normal core internal temperature of around 37 degrees Celsius (98.6 degrees Fahrenheit) measured most accurately via a rectal probe thermometer.
- This is the optimal temperature at which the human body's systems function. Thermoregulation is crucial to human life; without thermoregulation, the human body would cease to function. Thermoregulation also plays an adaptive role in the body's response to infectious pathogens.

DEVELOPMENT

- The brain, more specifically the hypothalamus, controls thermoregulation. If the hypothalamus senses internal temperatures growing too hot or too cold, it will automatically send signals to the skin, glands, muscles, and organs.
- For example, if the body is generating heat during high-level exercise or if the external ambient temperature is elevated enough to cause a rise in the core temperature, afferent signals to the hypothalamus result in efferent signals to the cells of the skin to produce sweat. Sweating is one mechanism the body can use to cool itself as heat is lost through the process of sweat evaporation.
- In contrast, when the body experiences a cold environment, a shivering reflex results in skeletal muscles contracting and generating heat; additionally, the arrector pili muscles (a type of smooth muscle) raise the bodily hair follicles to trap the heat generated.

MECHANISM

- Thermoregulation has three mechanisms: afferent sensing, central control, and efferent responses. There are receptors for both heat and cold throughout the human body. Afferent sensing works through these receptors to determine if the body core temperature is too hold or cold. The hypothalamus is the central controller of thermoregulation. There is also an efferent behavioral component that responds to fluctuations in body temperature.

- For example, if a person is feeling too warm, the normal response is to remove an outer article of clothing. If a person is feeling too cold, they choose to wear more layers of clothing. Efferent responses also consist of automatic responses by the body to protect itself from extreme changes in temperature, such as sweating, vasodilation, vasoconstriction, and shivering.

ANSWER (b) factor influencing blood pressure Five factors influence blood pressure:

1. Cardiac output
2. Peripheral vascular resistance
3. Volume of circulating blood
4. Viscosity of blood
5. Elasticity of vessels walls

6. Blood pressure increases with increased cardiac output, peripheral vascular resistance, volume of blood, viscosity of blood and rigidity of vessel walls.

Blood pressure decreases with decreased cardiac output, peripheral vascular resistance, volume of blood, viscosity of blood and elasticity of vessel walls.

1. Cardiac Output

Cardiac output is the volume of blood flow from the heart through the ventricles, and is usually measured in litres per minute (L/min). Cardiac output can be calculated by the stroke volume multiplied by the heart rate. Any factor that causes cardiac output to increase, by elevating heart rate or stroke volume or both, will elevate blood pressure and promote blood flow. These factors include sympathetic stimulation, the catecholamines epinephrine and norepinephrine, thyroid hormones, and increased calcium ion levels. Conversely, any factor that decreases cardiac output, by decreasing heart rate or stroke volume or both, will decrease arterial pressure and blood flow. These factors include parasympathetic stimulation, elevated or decreased potassium ion levels, decreased calcium levels, anoxia, and acidosis.

2. Peripheral Vascular Resistance

Peripheral vascular resistance refers to compliance, which is the ability of any compartment to expand to accommodate increased content. A metal pipe, for example, is not compliant, whereas a balloon is. The greater the compliance of an artery, the more effectively it is able to expand to accommodate surges in blood flow without increased resistance or blood pressure. Veins are more compliant than arteries and can expand to hold more blood. When vascular disease causes stiffening of arteries (e.g., atherosclerosis or arteriosclerosis), compliance is reduced and resistance to blood flow is increased. The result is more turbulence, higher pressure within the vessel, and reduced blood flow. This increases the work of the heart.

3. Volume of Circulating Blood

Volume of circulating blood is the amount of blood moving through the body. Increased venous return stretches the walls of the atria where specialized baroreceptors are located. Baroreceptors are pressure-sensing receptors. As the atrial baroreceptors increase their rate of firing and as they stretch due to the increased blood pressure, the cardiac centre responds by increasing sympathetic stimulation and inhibiting parasympathetic stimulation to increase HR. The opposite is also true.

4. Viscosity of Blood

Viscosity of blood is a measure of the blood's thickness and is influenced by the presence of plasma proteins and formed elements in the blood. Blood is viscous and somewhat sticky to the touch. It has a viscosity approximately five times greater than water. Viscosity is a measure of a fluid's thickness or resistance to flow, and is influenced by the presence of the plasma proteins and formed elements within the blood. The viscosity of blood has a dramatic effect on blood pressure and flow. Consider the difference in flow between water and honey. The more viscous honey would demonstrate a greater resistance to flow than the less viscous water. The same principle applies to blood.

5. Elasticity of Vessel Walls

Elasticity of vessel walls refers to the capacity to resume its normal shape after stretching and compressing. Vessels larger than 10 mm in diameter are typically elastic. Their abundant elastic fibres allow them to expand as blood pumped from the ventricles passes through them, and then to recoil after the surge has passed. If artery walls were rigid and unable to expand and recoil, their resistance to blood flow would greatly increase and blood pressure would rise to even higher levels, which would in turn require the heart to pump harder to increase the volume of blood expelled by each pump (the stroke volume) and maintain adequate pressure and flow. Artery walls would have to become even thicker in response to this increased pressure.

ANSWER (c) functions of skin

The skin has three main functions:

1. Protection
2. Thermoregulation

3. .Sensation

1. Protection

The skin acts as a protective barrier from:

- Mechanical, thermal and other physical injury;
- Harmful agents;
- Excessive loss of moisture and protein;
- Harmful effects of UV radiation.

2. Thermoregulation

One of the skin's important functions is to protect the body from cold or heat, and maintain a constant core temperature. This is achieved by alterations to the blood flow through the cutaneous vascular bed. During warm periods, the vessels dilate, the skin reddens and beads of sweat form on the surface (vasodilatation = more blood flow = greater direct heat loss). In cold periods, the blood vessels constrict, preventing heat from escaping (vasoconstriction = less blood flow = reduced heat loss). The secretion and evaporation of sweat from the surface of the skin also helps to cool the body.

3. Sensation

Skin is the 'sense-of-touch' organ that triggers a response if we touch or feel something, including things that may cause pain. This is important for patients with a skin condition, as pain and itching can be extreme for many and cause great distress. Also touch is important for many patients who feel isolated by their skin as a result of colour, disease or the perceptions of others as many experience the fact that they are seen as dirty or contagious and should not be touched.

4. Immunological surveillance

The skin is an important immunological organ, made up of key structures and cells. Depending on the immunological response, a variety of cells and chemical messengers (cytokines) are involved. These specialised cells and their functions will be covered later.

5. Biochemical functions

The skin is involved in several biochemical processes. In the presence of sunlight, a form of vitamin D called cholecalciferol is synthesised from a derivative of the steroid cholesterol in the skin. The liver converts cholecalciferol to calcidiol, which is then converted to calcitriol (the active chemical form of the vitamin) in the kidneys. Vitamin D is essential for the normal absorption of calcium and phosphorous, which are required for healthy bones (Biga et al, 2019). The skin also contains receptors for other steroid hormones (oestrogens, progestogens and glucocorticoids) and for vitamin A.

6. Social and sexual function

How an individual is perceived by others is important. People make judgements based on what they see and may form their first impression of someone based on how that person looks. Throughout history, people have been judged because of their skin, for example, due to its colour or the presence of a skin condition or scarring. Skin conditions are visible – in this skin-, beauty- and image-conscious society, the way patients are accepted by other people is an important consideration for nurses.

Q5. Write the concept in short with the help of a diagram:

a. Contraceptive methods in humans

b.Formation of T-cells and B- cells.

c. Urinary bladder

ANSWER(a) Contraceptive methods in humans Birth Control Methods

In choosing a method of contraception, dual protection from the simultaneous risk for HIV and other STDs also should be considered. Although hormonal contraceptives and IUDs are highly effective at preventing pregnancy, they do not protect against STDs, including HIV. Consistent and correct use of the male latex condom reduces the risk for

HIV infection and other STDs, including chlamydial infection, gonococcal infection, and trichomoniasis.

Intrauterine Contraception

1. **Levonorgestrel intrauterine system (LNG IUD)**—The LNG IUD is a small T-shaped device like the Copper T IUD. It is placed inside the uterus by a doctor. It releases a small amount of progestin each day to keep you from getting pregnant. The LNG IUD stays in your uterus for up to 3 to 6 years, depending on the device. Typical use failure rate: 0.1-0.4%.
2. **Copper T intrauterine device (IUD)**—This IUD is a small device that is shaped in the form of a "T." Your doctor places it inside the uterus to prevent pregnancy. It can stay in your uterus for up to 10 years. Typical use failure rate: 0.1%

Hormonal Methods

Implant—The implant is a single, thin rod that is inserted under the skin of a women's upper arm. The rod contains a progestin that is released into the body over 3 years. Typical use failure rate: 0.1%.

Injection or "shot"—Women get shots of the hormone progestin in the buttocks or arm every three months from their doctor. Typical use failure rate: 4%.

ombined oral contraceptives—Also called "the pill," combined oral contraceptives contain the hormones estrogen and progestin. It is prescribed by a doctor. A pill is taken at the same time each day. If you are older than 35 years and smoke, have a history of blood clots or breast cancer, your doctor may advise you not to take the pill. Typical use failure rate: 7%.

Progestin only pill—Unlike the combined pill, the progestin-only pill (sometimes called the mini-pill) only has one hormone, progestin, instead of both estrogen and progestin. It is prescribed by a doctor. It is taken at the same time each day. It may be a good option for women who can't take estrogen. Typical use failure rate: 7%.

Patch—This skin patch is worn on the lower abdomen, buttocks, or upper body (but not on the breasts). This method is prescribed by a doctor. It releases hormones progestin and estrogen into the bloodstream. You put on a new patch once a week for three weeks. During the fourth week, you do not wear a patch, so you can have a menstrual period. Typical use failure rate: 7%.

Hormonal vaginal contraceptive ring—The ring releases the hormones progestin and estrogen. You place the ring inside your vagina. You wear the ring for three weeks, take it out for the week you have your period, and then put in a new ring. Typical use failure rate: 7%.

Barrier Methods

Diaphragm or cervical cap—Each of these barrier methods are placed inside the vagina to cover the cervix to block sperm. The diaphragm is shaped like a shallow cup. The cervical cap is a thimble-shaped cup. Before sexual intercourse, you insert them with spermicide to block or kill sperm. Visit your doctor for a proper fitting because diaphragms and cervical caps come in different sizes. Typical use failure rate for the diaphragm: 17%.

Sponge—The contraceptive sponge contains spermicide and is placed in the vagina where it fits over the cervix. The sponge works for up to 24 hours, and must be left in the vagina for at least 6 hours after the last act of intercourse, at which time it is removed and discarded. Typical use failure rate: 14% for women who have never had a baby and 27% for women who have had a baby.

Male condom—Worn by the man, a male condom keeps sperm from getting into a woman's body. Latex condoms, the most common type, help prevent pregnancy, and HIV and other STDs, as do the newer synthetic condoms. "Natural" or "lambskin" condoms also help prevent pregnancy, but may not provide protection against STDs, including HIV. Typical use failure rate: 13%.[1] Condoms can only be used once. You can buy condoms, KY jelly, or water-based lubricants at a drug store. Do not use oil-based lubricants such as massage oils, baby oil, lotions, or petroleum jelly with latex condoms. They will weaken the condom, causing it to tear or break.

Female condom—Worn by the woman, the female condom helps keeps sperm from getting into her body. It is packaged with a lubricant and is available at drug stores. It can be inserted up to eight hours before sexual intercourse.

Typical use failure rate: 21%,and also may help prevent STDs.

Spermicides—These products work by killing sperm and come in several forms—foam, gel, cream, film, suppository, or tablet. They are placed in the vagina no more than one hour before intercourse. You leave them in place at least six to eight hours after intercourse. You can use a spermicide in addition to a male condom, diaphragm, or cervical cap. They can be purchased at drug stores. Typical use failure rate: 21%.

Permanent Methods of Birth Control

Female Sterilization—Tubal ligation or "tying tubes"— A woman can have her fallopian tubes tied (or closed) so that sperm and eggs cannot meet for fertilization. The procedure can be done in a hospital or in an outpatient surgical center. You can go home the same day of the surgery and resume your normal activities within a few days. This method is effective immediately. Typical use failure rate: 0.5%.

Male Sterilization–Vasectomy—This operation is done to keep a man's sperm from going to his penis, so his ejaculate never has any sperm in it that can fertilize an egg. The procedure is typically done at an outpatient surgical center. The man can go home the same day. Recovery time is less than one week. After the operation, a man visits his doctor for tests to count his sperm and to make sure the sperm count has dropped to zero; this takes about 12 weeks. Another form of birth control should be used until the man's sperm count has dropped to zero. Typical use failure rate: 0.15%.

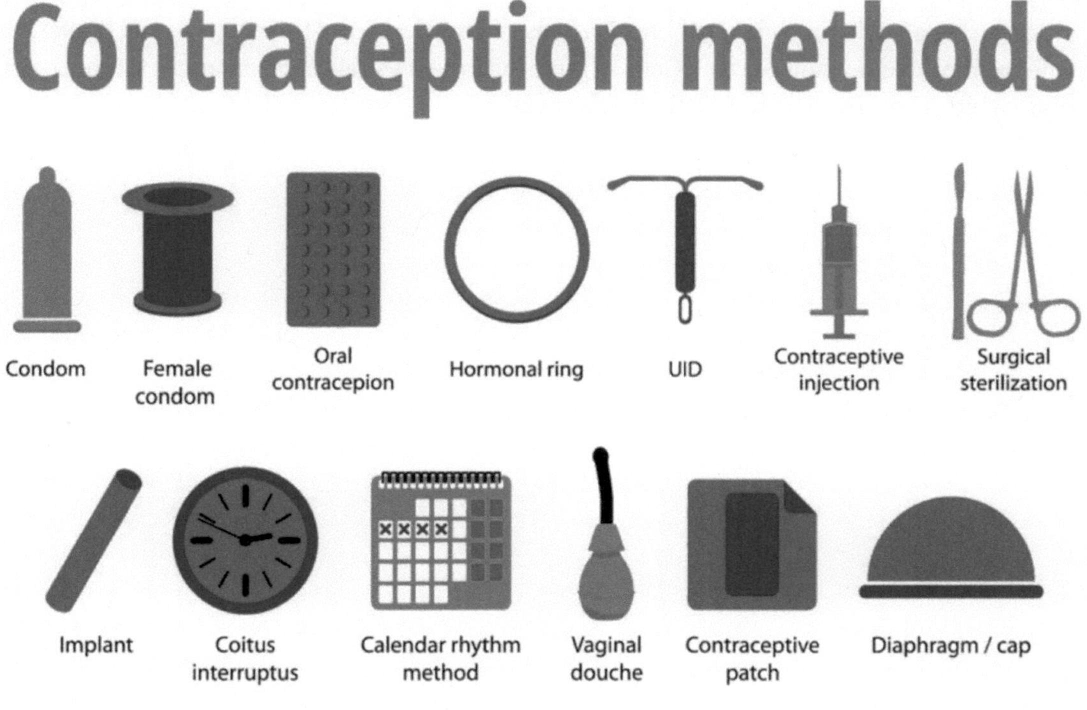

Contraceptives

ANSWER (b) Formation of T-cells and B- cells. T-cells

- The process of development and maturation of the T Cells in mammals begins with the haematopoietic stem cells (HSC) in the fetal liver and later in the bone marrow where HSC differentiate into multipotent progenitors. A subset of multipotent progenitors initiates the transcription of recombination activating gene 1 and 2 (RAG 1 and RAG2) and become lymphoid-primed multipotent progenitors and then common lymphoid progenitors (CLP).

Only a small subset of pluripotent cells migrates to the thymus and differentiates into early thymic progenitors (ETP).

- The thymus does not contain self-renewing progenitors; and therefore, long-term thymopoiesis depends on the recruitment of thymus-settling progenitors throughout the life of the individual . These progenitors must enter the thymus to become gradually reprogrammed into fully mature and functional T Cells. The T Cell's distinct developmental steps, as illustrated in are coordinated with the migration of the developing thymocytes towards specific niches in the thymus that provide the necessary stage-specific factors that are needed for further differentiation.

B- cells

- The first stages of B Cell development take place in complex microenvironments created by the stromal cells of the bone marrow known as "niches" from which come the stimuli and factors required to initiate a series of cell signals. These, in turn, activate transcription factors that induce, or repress, the expression of different target genes that modulate cell survival, proliferation, and differentiation. IL-7 is critical to the development of the B Cells and is produced by the cells of the stroma.
- The development of the B Cells initiates from a hematopoietic stem cell (HSC). This transforms into an early lymphoid progenitor (ELP) and, then, becomes a common lymphoid progenitor (CLP) from which is derived, on one hand, natural killer cells (NK) and dendritic cells (DC) and, on the other, common lymphoid progenitor-2 (CLP-2), which is responsible for the B Cell lineage. This is considered the first stage of the immature B Cells .
- A prerequisite for the development of the B Cells in bone marrow is the absence or suppression of protein Notch-1 (N1) signaling, which is necessary for T Cell development .

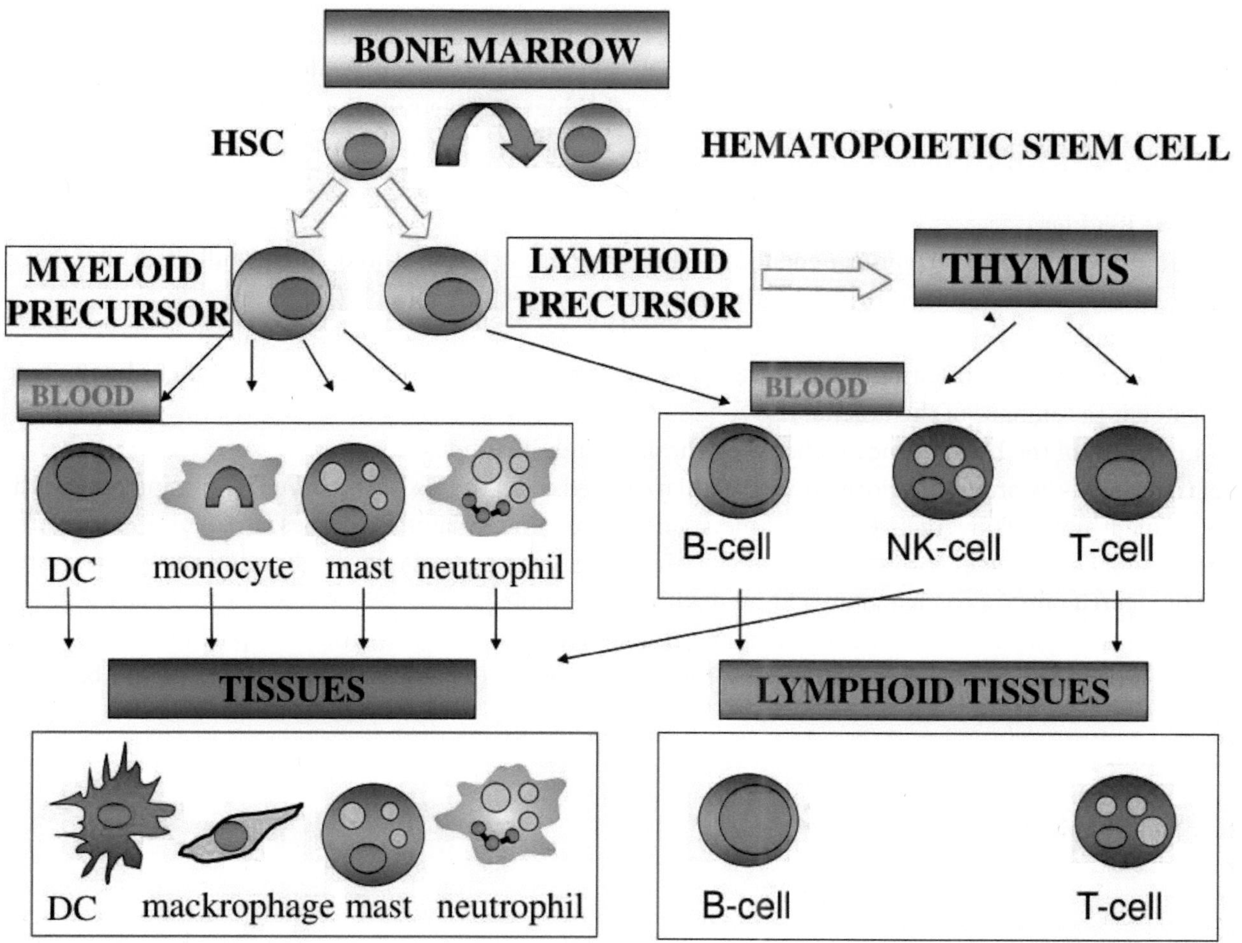

ANSWER (c) Urinary bladder

The **bladder** is an organ of the urinary system.

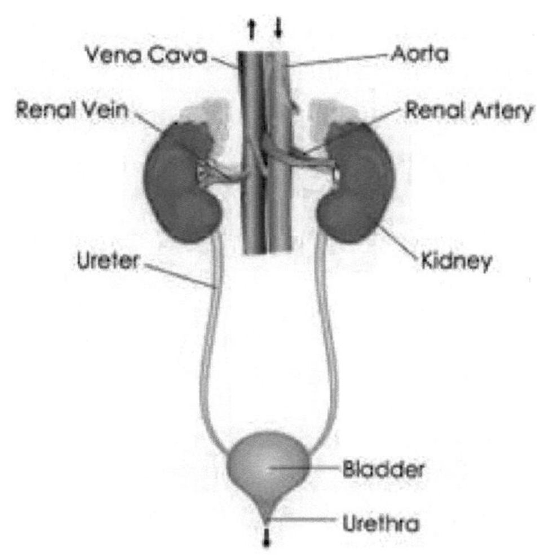

Urinary bladder

It plays two main role

- **Temporary storage of urine** – the bladder is a hollow organ with distensible walls. It has a folded internal lining (known as rugae), which allows it to accommodate up to 400-600ml of urine in healthy person.
- **Assists in the expulsion of urine** – the musculature of the bladder contracts during micturition, with concomitant relaxation of the sphincters.

Shape of the Bladder

The appearance of the bladder varies depending on the amount of urine stored. When full, it exhibits an **oval** shape, and when empty it is flattened by the overlying bowel.

The external features of the bladder are:

Apex – located superiorly, pointing towards the pubic symphysis. It is connected to the umbilicus by the median umbilical ligament (a remnant of the urachus).

Body – main part of the bladder, located between the apex and the fundus

Fundus (or base) – located posteriorly. It is triangular-shaped, with the tip of the triangle pointing backward

Neck – formed by the convergence of the fundus and the two inferolateral surfaces. It is continuous with the urethra.Urine enters the bladder through the left and right ureters, and exits via the urethra. Internally, these orifices are marked by the **trigone** – a triangular area located within the fundus.

In contrast to the rest of the internal bladder, the trigone has smooth walls (this is explained by the different embryological origin: the trigone is developed by the integration of two **mesonephric ducts** at the base of the bladder).

Q6. write features of the following:

a. Pituitary and thyroid dwarfism
b. Color blindness
c. Male fertility system

ANSWER (a) Pituitary and thyroid dwarfism

Pituitary Dwarfism

It is a condition where less amount of growth hormone results in abnormally slow growth and short stature. Growth hormone is released under the influence of hypothalamic growth hormone- releasing hormone (GHRH), and is inhibited by hypothalamic somatostatin.

Growth hormone deficiency has different negative effects if happens according to age it manifests; in newborn, the primary manifestations may be hypoglycemia, while in later infancy and childhood, growth failure is more likely. Growth hormone deficiency can be congenital or acquired. It is usually permanent, sometimes transient.

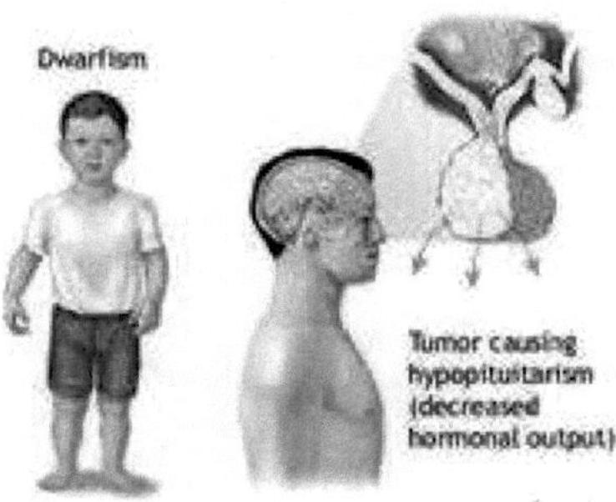

Dwarfism

Thyroid dwarfism

It is a condition arising from the deficiency of a thyroid hormone. It happens when there is lesser thyroid hormone secretion (defect of manufacturing or lesser supply of Iodine) before attaining the full development congenitally. It causes retarded growth and development of bones with disproportionate body proportions (that's dwarfism).

Answer (b) Color blindness

Color blindness

It means you see colors differently than most people. Most of the time, color blindness makes it hard to tell the difference between certain colors.

Usually, color blindness runs in families. There's no cure, but special glasses and contact lenses can help. Most people who are color blind are able to adjust and don't have problems with everyday activities.

Types of color blindness

The most common type of color blindness makes it hard to tell the difference between red and green. Another type makes it hard to tell the difference between blue and yellow. People who are completely color blind don't see color at all, but that's not very common.

Symptoms of color blindness

The main symptom of color blindness is not seeing colors the way most people do. If you're color blind, you may have trouble seeing:

- The difference between colors
- How bright colors are
- Different shades of colors

Symptoms of color blindness are often so mild that you may not notice them. And since we get used to the way we see colors, many people with color blindness don't know they have it.

People with very serious cases of color blindness might have other symptoms, too — like quick side-to-side eye movements (nystagmus) or sensitivity to light.

The treatment for color blindness

- There's no cure for color blindness that's passed down in families, but most people find ways to adjust to it. Children with color blindness may need help with some classroom activities, and adults with color blindness may not be able to do certain jobs, like being a pilot or graphic designer. Keep in mind that most of the time, color blindness doesn't cause serious problems.
- If your color blindness is happening because of another health problem, your doctor will treat the condition that's causing the problem. If you're taking a medicine that causes color blindness, your doctor may adjust how much you take or suggest you switch to a different medicine.
- If color blindness is causing problems with everyday tasks, there are devices and technology that can help, including:
- Glasses and contacts. Special contact lenses and glasses may help people who are color blind tell the difference between colors.
- Visual aids. You can use visual aids, apps, and other technology to help you live with color blindness. For example, you can use an app to take a photo with your phone or tablet and then tap on part of the photo to find out the color of that area.

ANSWER (c) Male fertility system

1. The male reproductive system consists of the internal structures: the testes, epididymis, vas deferens, prostate, and the external structures: the scrotum and penis. These structures are well- vascularized with many glands

and ducts to promote the formation, storage, and ejaculation of sperm for fertilization, and to produce important androgens for male development

2. The major male androgen is testosterone, which is produced from Leydig cells in the testes. Testosterone can be converted in the periphery to a more active form, dihydrotestosterone via 5- alpha-reductase, or estradiol via aromatase. Other key hormones include inhibin B and Mullerian inhibiting substance (MIS) hormone, both produced by the Sertoli cells in the testes.
3. Important hormones that modulate these include follicle-stimulating hormone (FSH) and luteinizing hormone (LH), which are released from the anterior pituitary gland and are regulated by gonadotropin-releasing hormone (GnRH), produced by the hypothalamus. Together, these hormones form the hypothalamic-pituitary-gonadal axis that promotes and maintains sexual development and function in the male.

FUNCTION

The function of the male reproductive system is to produce androgens such as testosterone that maintain male reproductive function and to promote spermatogenesis and transport into the female reproductive system for fertilization. The testes act as both endocrine and exocrine organs in that they are responsible for androgen production and sperm production and transport.

MECHANISM

- Spermatogenesis starts at puberty with the germ cells found in the basement membrane of the seminiferous tubules of the testes. Sertoli cells stimulated by FSH help regulate spermatogenesis.
- One cycle of spermatogenesis begins approximately every 13 days; however, spermatogenesis is not consistently synchronous throughout all seminiferous tubules. The first stage of spermatogenesis begins with mitosis of diploid spermatogonia into primary spermatocytes. These spermatocytes undergo meiosis I to produce haploid secondary spermatocytes, which undergo meiosis II to form haploid spermatids.
- The most primitive spermatocytes are found peripherally in the seminiferous tubules and mature by migrating towards the lumen. Spermatids transform into spermatozoa by reducing cytoplasm. These spermatozoa are still immotile and are released into the tubules to travel to the epididymis for maturation.
- The epididymis is a coiled structure consisting of a head, body, and tail. The tail eventually joins with the vas deferens, providing an outlet for mature sperms to ejaculate. In the epididymis, the sperm takes about twelve days to mature and develop motility. They are then stored in the tail of the epididymis until ejaculation occurs. A mature sperm consists of a head, midpiece, and tail.
- The head contains the nucleus with very little cytoplasm. An acrosome or cap covers the head and is filled with lysosomes, which aids with fertilization. The midpiece contains abundant mitochondria to provide energy for the flagellum or tail of the sperm.
- During sexual arousal (physical or psychological), vasodilation brings blood to the penis. The penis contains corpora cavernosa and a corpus spongiosum where blood flows along to enlarge and erect the penis. As sexual stimulation continues, blood continues to flow to the genitals, and the testes enlarge in preparation of ejaculation.
- When ejaculation occurs, smooth muscle contractions of the epididymis pushes sperm into the ductus deferens (vas deferens), which sits in the spermatic cord. The ductus deferens delivers the sperm to ejaculatory duct by joining with the seminal vesicle duct near the prostate. The seminal vesicles produce fructose, which provides the energy for sperm motility.
- It is released within a fluid that mixes with the sperm to form semen. Once in the ejaculatory duct, the semen passes through the prostate, which secretes an alkaline fluid that helps thicken the semen so sperm can better stay within the female reproductive system.

- The semen then passes the bulbourethral glands or Cowper's glands, which release a thick fluid that lubricates the urethral opening and clears the urethra of any urine residue. The semen then can enter the female vaginal canal, allowing the sperm to travel to and fertilize a potential egg within the female reproductive system.

CHAPTER III

Question Paper 2020

B.Sc Nursing 1st year ,annual exam, 2020
Anatomy and physiology

Note Marks 75

1. attempt all questions and draw suitable diagrams, tables, and graphs where required.

2.attempt part-1 and part-2 in separate answer book.

Part –I anatomy

Q1. Describe in detail:

a. Explain structure and function of uterus
b. Describe compact and cancellous bone
c. Describe stomach and its functions

Q2. Draw a well labeled diagram to illustrate the following:

a. Skeletal muscle
b. Thymus gland
c. Blood supply of growing long bone

Q3. **Write short note on :**
a.Coronary circulation
b.Cerebellum
c.Typical synovial joint

PART-II(Physiology)

Q4. Write short note on the following:

a. events occurring at neuro- muscular junction at skeletal muscle
b. oxygen transport
c. pathophysiology of peptic ulcer

Q5. Write on the following with the help of a diagram:

a. Spermatogenesis and the factors affecting it
b. Stretch reflex
c. ECG changes in health and disease.

Q6. Write features of the following:

a. Grave's disease.
b. Functions of middle ear
c. Iron deficiency anemia

Q1.Describe in detail:

(a) Explain structure and function of uterus

(b) Describe compact and cancellous bone

(c) Describe stomach and its functions

ANSWER(a) Explain structure and function of uterus

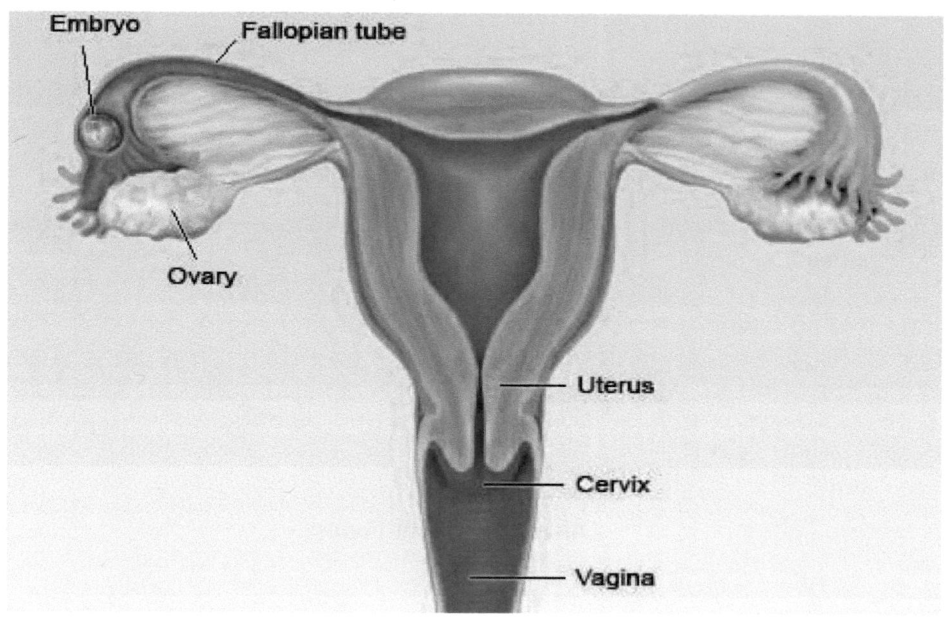

Normal uterus

Function

- The uterus performs multiple important functions in the reproductive cycle, fertility, and childbearing.

1. During a normal menstrual cycle, the endometrial lining of the uterus goes through a process called vascularization during which tiny blood vessels proliferate, leaving the lining thicker and rich with blood in the event the egg released during that cycle is fertilized. If this does not happen, the uterus sheds the lining as a menstrual period.
2. If conception occurs, the fertilized egg (the embryo) burrows into the endometrium from which the maternal portion of the placenta, the decidua basalis, will develop.
3. As a pregnancy progresses, the uterus grows and the muscular walls become thinner, like a balloon being blown up, to accommodate the developing fetus and the protective amniotic fluid produced first by the mother and later by urine and lung secretions of the baby.
4. During pregnancy, the muscular layer of the uterus begins contracting on-and-off in preparation for childbirth. These "practice" contractions, Braxton-Hicks contractions, resemble menstrual cramps; some women don't even notice them. They are not the increasingly powerful and regular contractions that are strong enough to squeeze the baby out of the uterus and into the vagina.
5. After a baby is born, the uterus continues to contract in order to expel the placenta. It will continue to contract in the coming weeks to return the uterus to its normal size and to stop the bleeding that occurs in the uterus during childbirth.

ANSWER(b) Describe compact and cancellous bone

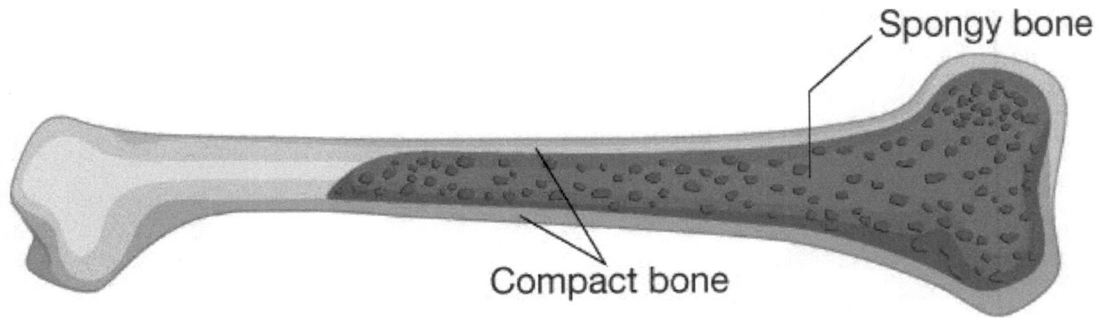

SPONGY BONE

- Spongy bone is also called cancellous or trabecular bone. It is found in the long bones and it is surrounded by compact bone.

COMPACT BONE

- Compact bone, also called cortical bone, surrounds spongy bone. They are heavy, tough and compact in nature

Different Type of bones

Spongy Bones

1. Spongy Bones are also called cancellous bones.
2. They light, spongy and soft in nature.
3. They are made up of trabeculae.
4. They fill the inner layer of most bones.
5. Bone-marrow cavity absent.
6. Bone marrow produces red corpuscles and white granular corpuscles.
7. It forms the ends or epiphyses of long bones.

Compact Bones

1. Compact bones are also called cortical bones
2. They are heavy, tough and compact in nature
3. They are made up of osteons
4. They fill the outer layer of most bones
5. Bone-marrow cavity present in the centre
6. Bone marrow stores fat
7. It forms the shaft or diaphysis of long bones

ANSWER(c) Describe stomach and its functions

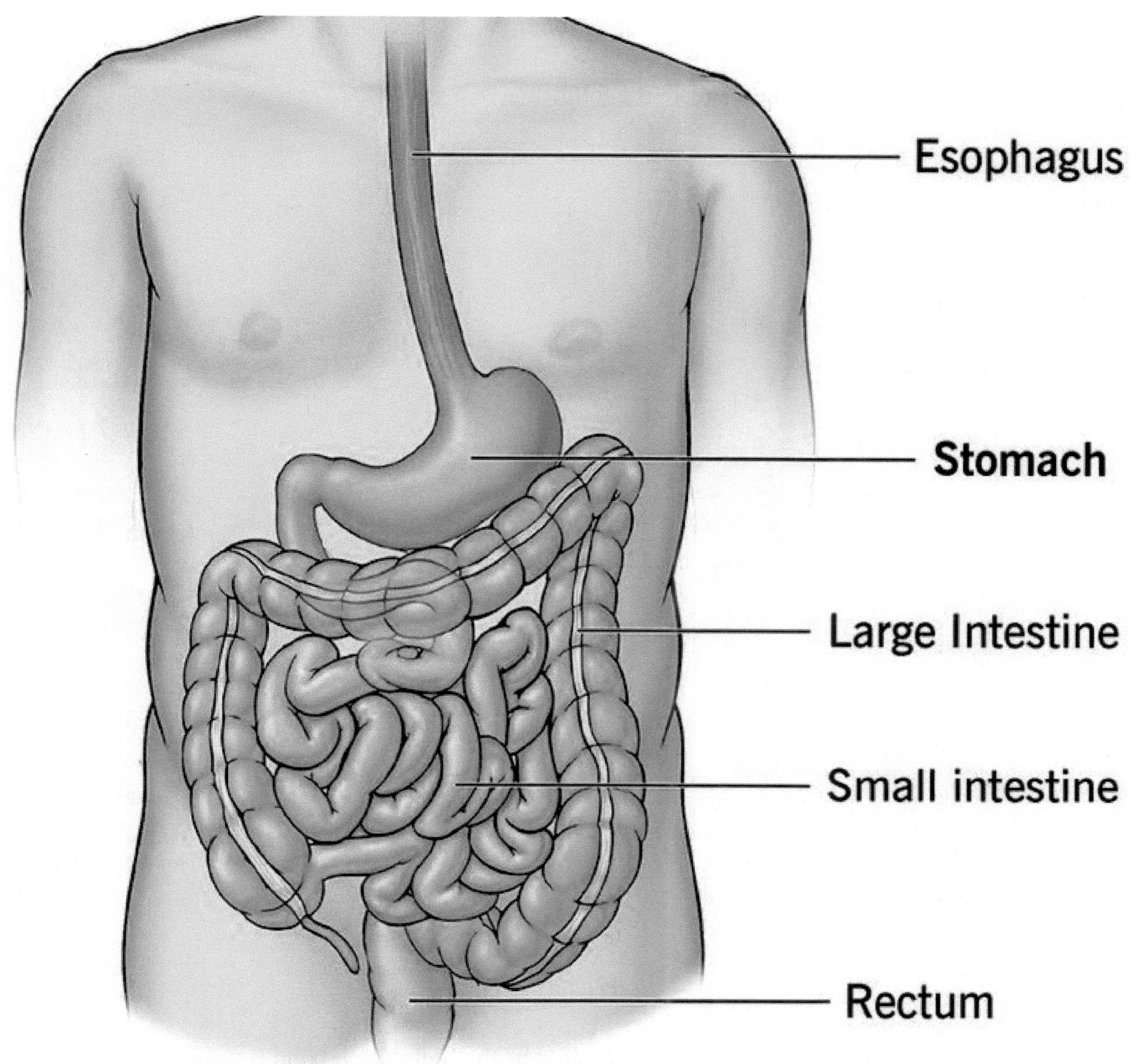

Stomach

Stomach:

- The stomach is a J-shaped organ that digests food. It produces enzymes (substances that create chemical reactions) and acids (digestive juices). This mix of enzymes and digestive juices breaks down food so it can pass to your small intestine.
- Your stomach is part of the gastrointestinal (GI) tract. The GI tract is a long tube that starts at your mouth. It runs to your anus, where stool (poop) leaves your body.

FUNCTIONS:-

Our stomach's purpose is to digest food and send it to your small intestine. It has three functions:

- Temporarily store food.

- Contract and relax to mix and break down food.
- Produce enzymes and other specialized cells to digest food.

Q2. Draw a well labeled diagram to illustrate the following:

(a) Skeletal muscle

(b) Thymus gland

(c) Blood supply of growing long bone

ANSWER (a) Skeletal muscle

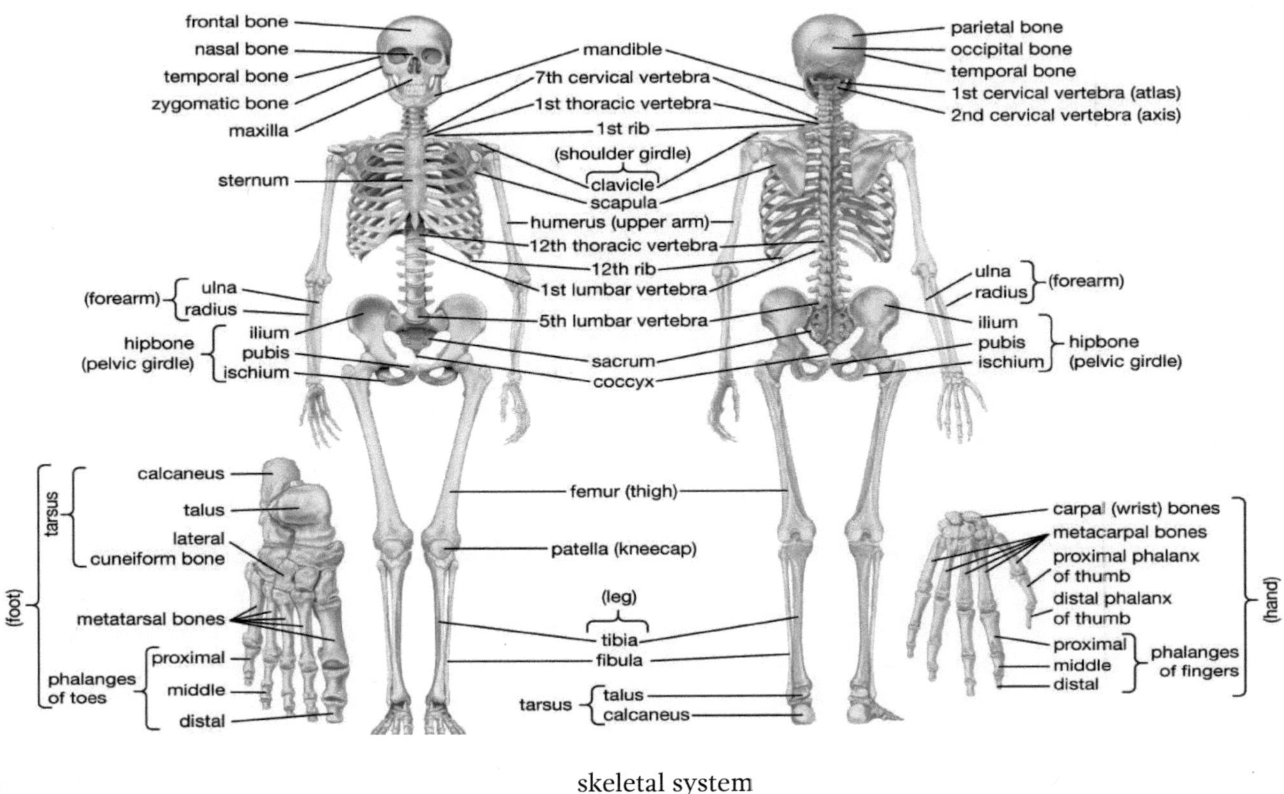

skeletal system

The skeletal system **includes all of the bones and joints in the body**. Each bone is a complex living organ that is made up of many cells, protein fibers, and minerals. The skeleton acts as a scaffold by providing support and protection for the soft tissues that make up the rest of the body.

ANSWER (b) Thymus gland

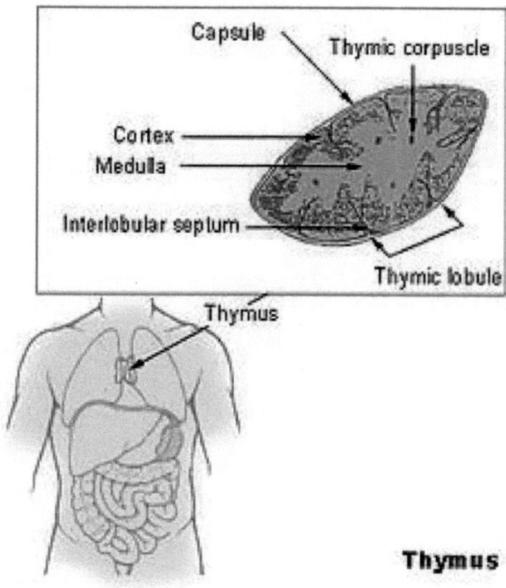

Thymus gland

Thymus gland

A lymphoid organ situated in the neck of vertebrates which produces T-lymphocytes for the immune system. The human thymus becomes much smaller at the approach of puberty.

ANSWER(c) Blood supply of growing long bone

BASIC ANATOMY OF THE LONG BONE

The elongated central part of the long bone is called the diaphysis. The enlarged area of the bone at the ends is called the epiphysis and the intermediate bone segment between the two is called the metaphysics. The articular ends of the epiphyseal surface is covered by articular cartilage .The rest of the bone is covered by tough connective tissue called the periosteum. The nutrient foramen is an oblique canal usually situated in the diaphysis of the long bone.

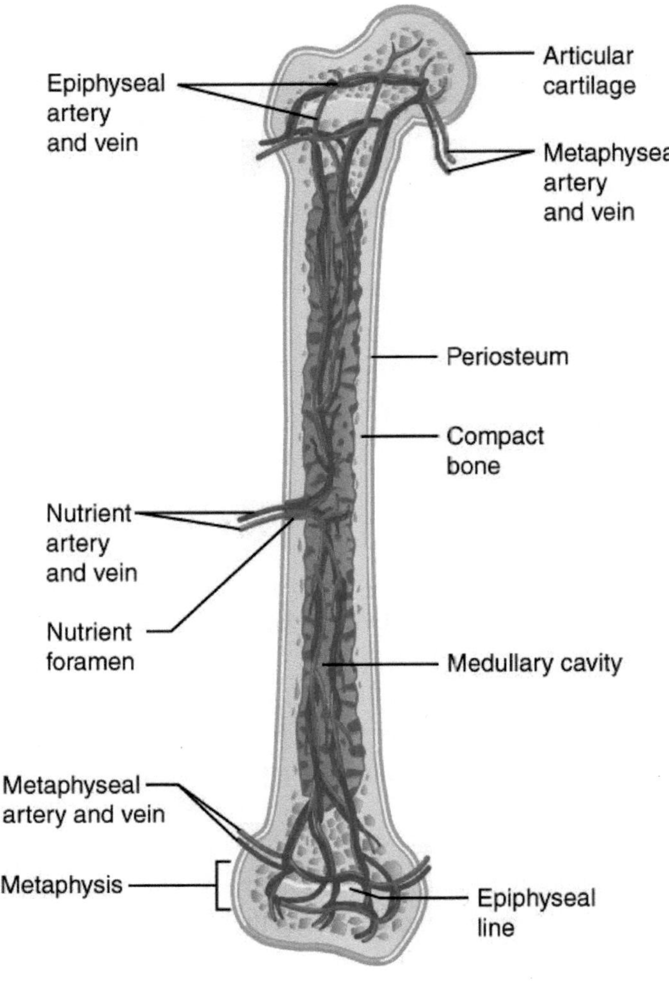

Anatomy of Bone

ARTERIAL SUPPLY OF THE LONG BONE:-

Blood supply of the long bone accounts for 5-10% of the cardiac output. A typical long bone receives blood supply from various sources. They are the Nutrient arteries , Epiphyseal arteries , Metaphyseal arteries and periosteal arteries .

THE NUTRIENT ARTERY:-

The nutrient artery supplies directly from major systemic arteries. It enters the long bone through the nutrient foramen. It then divides into ascending and descending branches. These branches gives of smaller parallel arteries called the radial branches .These branches supply the bone marrow and inner third of the compact bone of the diaphysis. The ascending and descending branches at the metaphysis divides into smaller spiral branches which anastomoses with the metaphyseal and epiphyseal arteries.

THE METAPHYSEAL ARTERY:-

Metaphyseal arteries arising from the anastomosis around the joint enters the metaphysis at the margin of the capsule attachment. These anastomose with the spiral arteries making the metaphysic the most vascular area of the long bone.

THE EPIPHYSEAL ARTERY:-

Epiphyseal arteries are derived from periarticular vascular arcades. The epiphysis has openings that allows arteries to go in and out. In children the epiphyseal arteries are separated from the metaphyseal arteries due to the presence of an epiphyseal plate. In adults the epiphysis and metaphysis is fused together following the arrest of growth plate. Here the epiphyseal arteries freely anastomose with metaphyseal and nutrient arteries.

When epiphyseal cartilage and articular cartilage are continuous, the epiphyseal artery pierces the epiphyseal cartilage and supplies the epiphysis. If these arteries are damaged in epiphyseal separation, avascular necrosis may occur. In other bones where the epiphyseal cartilage is not continuous with the articular cartilage, the epiphyseal vessels enters the bone without piercing the growth plate. This helps in preventing avascular necrosis on epiphyseal separation.

THE PERIOSTEAL ARTERY:-

The periosteum has rich blood supply from the blood vessels that anastomose beneath the periosteum. Periosteal arteries act as a low pressure system and penetrate bone at the sides of attachment of the facial sheath or aponeurosis. They enter the Volksmann canal and supply roughly the outer one third of the compact bone of the diaphysis.

VENOUS DRAINAGE:-

Long bones drain into central venous sinus , then drains to nutrient veins ,then to periosteal vein and to emissary veins successively.

Q3. Write short note on :4×3=12

(a) Coronary circulation

(b) Cerebellum

(c) Typical synovial joint

ANSWER (a)Coronary circulation

1. **Coronary circulation**, part of the systemic circulatory system that supplies blood to and provides drainage from the tissues of the heart. In the human heart, two coronary arteries arise from the aorta just beyond the semilunar valves; during diastole, the increased aortic pressure above the valves forces blood into the coronary arteries and thence into the musculature of the heart.

2. Deoxygenated blood is returned to the chambers of the heart via coronary veins; most of these converge to form the coronary venous sinus, which drains into the right atrium.

3. The heart normally extracts 70 to 75 percent of the available oxygen from the blood in coronary circulation, which is much more than the amount extracted by other organs from their circulations—e.g., 40 percent by resting skeletal muscle and 20 percent by the liver.

4. Obstruction of a coronary artery, depriving the heart tissue of oxygen-rich blood, leads to death of part of the heart muscle (myocardial infarction) in severe cases, and total heart failure and death may ensue.

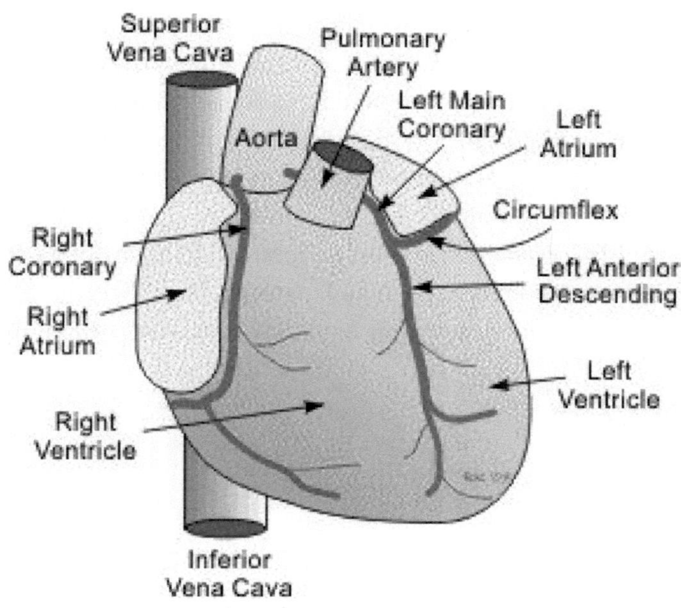

Coronary artery

ANSWER (b) Cerebellum

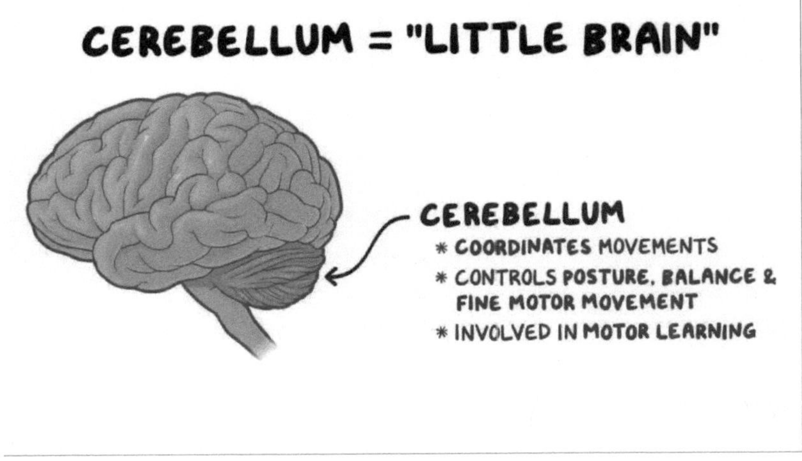

Cerebellum

The **cerebellum** ("little brain") is a structure that is located at the back of the brain, underlying the occipital and temporal lobes of the cerebral cortex . Although the cerebellum accounts for approximately 10% of the brain's volume, it contains over 50% of the total number of neurons in the brain. Historically, the cerebellum has been considered a motor structure, because cerebellar damage leads to impairments in motor control and posture and because the majority of the cerebellum's outputs are to parts of the motor system. Motor commands are not initiated in the cerebellum; rather, the cerebellum modifies the motor commands of the descending pathways to make movements more adaptive and accurate. The cerebellum is involved in the following functions:

Maintenance of balance and posture. The cerebellum is important for making postural adjustments in order to maintain balance. Through its input from vestibular receptors and proprioceptors, it modulates commands to motor neurons to compensate for shifts in body position or changes in load upon muscles. Patients with cerebellar damage suffer from balance disorders, and they often develop stereotyped postural strategies to compensate for this problem (e.g., a wide-based stance).

Coordination of voluntary movements. Most movements are composed of a number of different muscle groups acting together in a temporally coordinated fashion. One major function of the cerebellum is to coordinate the timing and force of these different muscle groups to produce fluid limb or body movements.

Motor learning. The cerebellum is important for motor learning. The cerebellum plays a major role in adapting and fine-tuning motor programs to make accurate movements through a trial-and-error process (e.g., learning to hit a baseball).

Cognitive functions. Although the cerebellum is most understood in terms of its contributions to motor control, it is also involved in certain cognitive functions, such as language. Thus, like the basal ganglia, the cerebellum is historically considered as part of the motor system, but its functions extend beyond motor control in ways that are not yet well understood.

ANSWER (c) Typical synovial joint

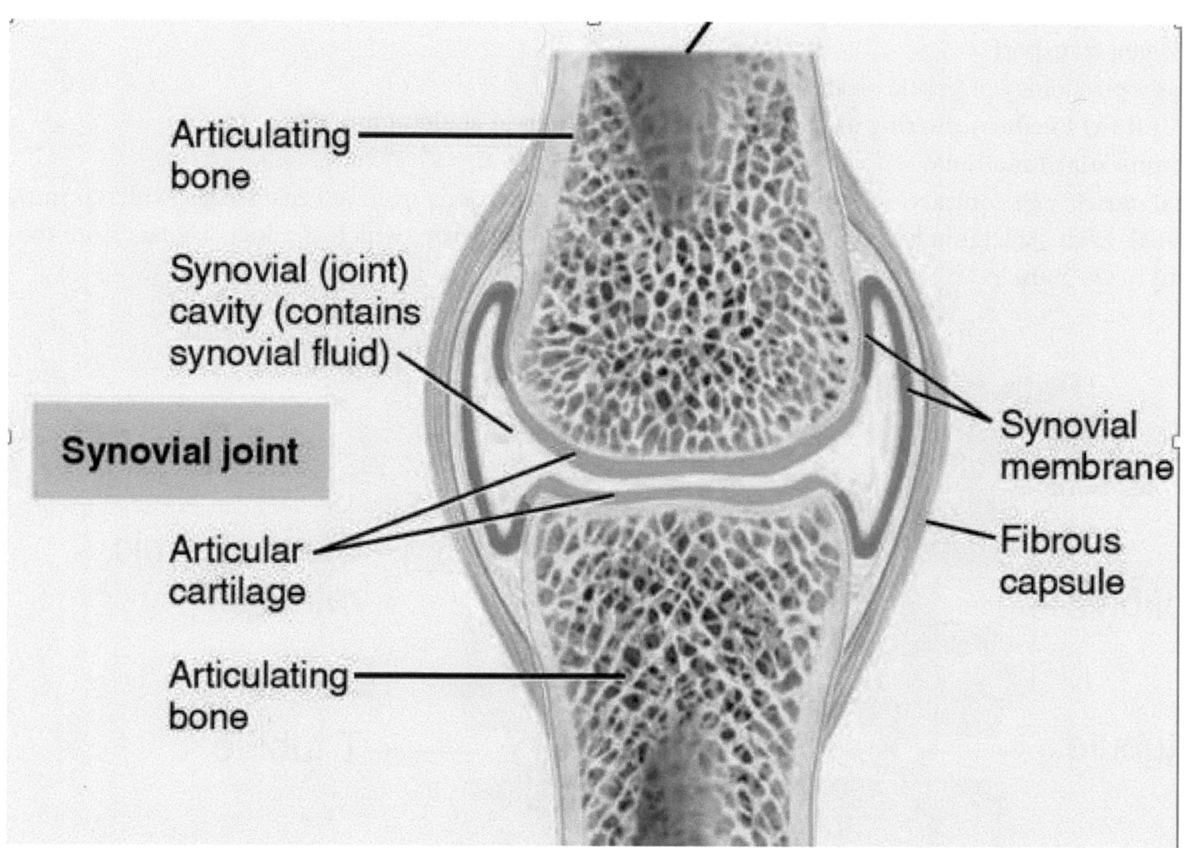

Synovial joint

Joint is the place where two bones come together and it is further three types:
(I) Fibrous (fixed): Sutures, Gomphosis and Syndesmosis.
(II) Cartilaginous (slightly movable): Primary and secondary cartilage.
(III) Synovial joint (movable): Plane, hinge, pivot, saddle, ellipsoid, bicondylar and ball and socket.

- The two bones are joined by connective tissues which help in the movement of the bones is known as the synovial joint.
- Synovial joint found between the long bones. The two bones are held with fibrous tissue of the ligament.
- Articular cartilage is present at the end of the long bones. There is a capsular structure which is formed by the synovial membrane. This cavity which is formed by synovial membrane is filled with the synovial fluid. Synovial fluid is secreted by membranes which helps to prevent abrasion between the cartilages,

Synovial joint are of various type according to the structure:

- Plane: Slightly curved articular surface e.g. carpals
- Ball and socket: Most moveable type e.g. shoulder and hip joints
- Hinge: Uniaxial e.g. elbow, knee and finger
- Pivot: Rotation e.g. radioulnar and atlas
- Saddle: concave and convex surface e.g. base of thumb
- Condyloid: Rounded articular surface e.g. base of finger
- Ellipsoid: Ovoid shaped joint e.g. wrist joint
- Compound: made by two types of joint e.g. temporomandibular joint (Hinge and gliding)

PART-II(Physiology)

Q4. Write short note on the following:

(a) Events occurring at neuro- muscular junction at skeletal muscle

(b) Oxygen transport

(c) Pathophysiology of peptic ulcer

ANSWER (a) Events occurring at neuro- muscular junction at skeletal muscle

Neuromuscular Junctions

Skeletal muscle cell contraction occurs after a release of calcium ions from internal stores, which is initiated by a neural signal. Each skeletal muscle fiber is controlled by a motor neuron, which conducts signals from the brain or spinal cord to the muscle.

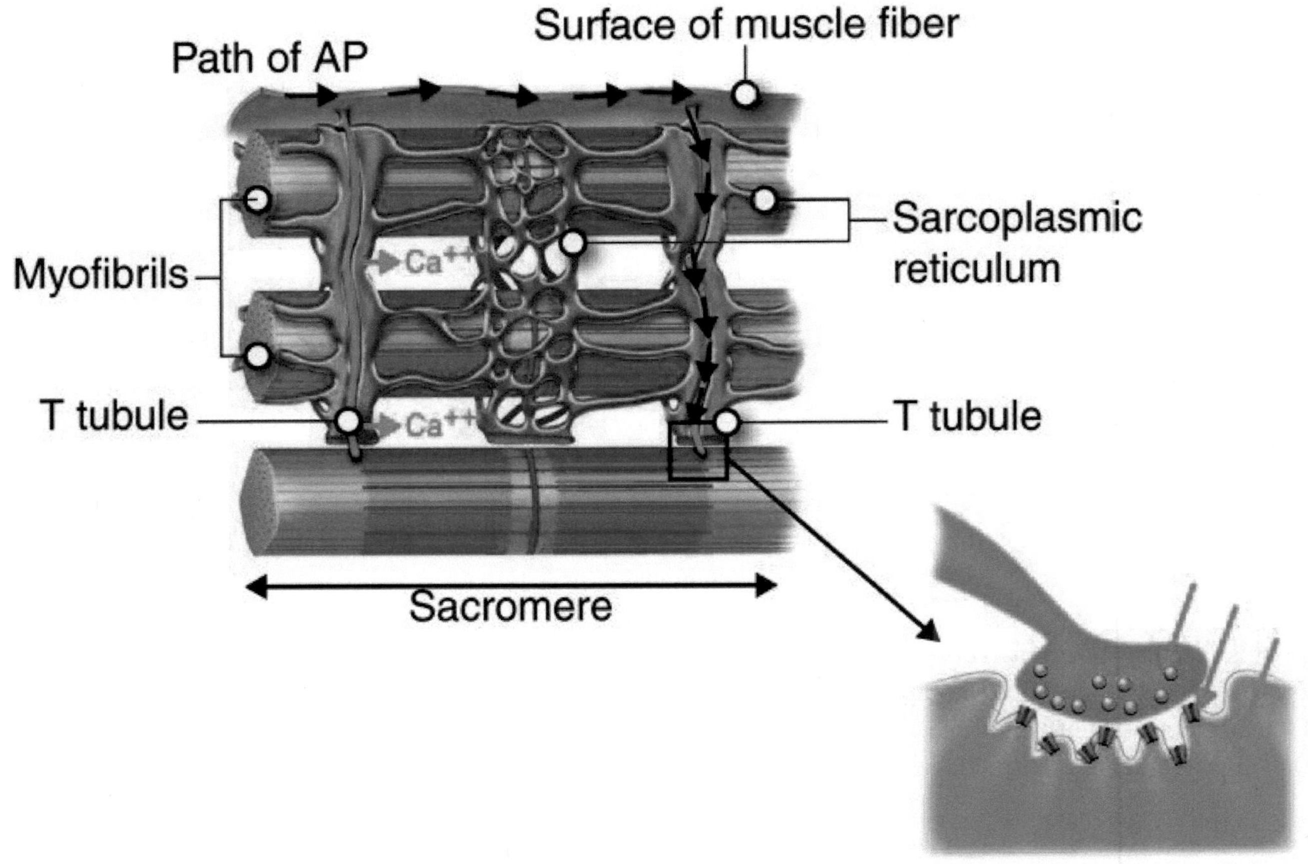

Skeltal muscle

The following list presents an overview of the sequence of events involved in the contraction cycle of skeletal muscle:

1. The action potential travels down the neuron to the presynaptic axon terminal.
2. Voltage-dependent calcium channels open and Ca^{2+} ions flow from the extracellular fluid into the presynaptic neuron's cytosol.
3. The influx of Ca^{2+} causes neurotransmitter (acetylcholine)-containing vesicles to dock and fuse to the presynaptic neuron's cell membrane.
4. Vesicle membrane fusion with the nerve cell membrane results in the emptying of the neurotransmitter into the synaptic cleft; this process is called exocytosis.
5. Acetylcholine diffuses into the synaptic cleft and binds to the nicotinic acetylcholine receptors in the motor end-plate.
6. The nicotinic acetylcholine receptors are ligand-gated cation channels, and open when bound to acetylcholine.

7. The receptors open, allowing sodium ions to flow into the muscle's cytosol.
8. The electrochemical gradient across the muscle plasma membrane causes a local depolarization of the motor end-plate.
9. The receptors open, allowing sodium ions to flow into and potassium ions to flow out of the muscle's cytosol.
10. The electrochemical gradient across the muscle plasma membrane (more sodium moves in than potassium out) causes a local depolarization of the motor end-plate.
11. This depolarization initiates an action potential on the muscle fiber cell membrane (sarcolemma) that travels across the surface of the muscle fiber.
12. The action potentials travel from the surface of the muscle cell along the membrane of T tubules that penetrate into the cytosol of the cell.
13. Action potentials along the T tubules cause voltage-dependent calcium release channels in the sarcoplasmic reticulum to open, and release Ca^{2+} ions from their storage place in the cisternae.
14. Ca^{2+} ions diffuse through the cytoplasm where they bind to troponin, ultimately allowing myosin to interact with actin in the sarcomere; this sequence of events is called excitation-contraction coupling.
15. As long as ATP and some other nutrients are available, the mechanical events of contraction occur.
16. Meanwhile, back at the neuromuscular junction, acetylcholine has moved off of the acetylcholine receptor and is degraded by the enzyme acetylcholinesterase (into choline and acetate groups), causing termination of the signal.
17. The choline is recycled back into the presynaptic terminal, where it is used to synthesize new acetylcholine molecules.

ANSWER (b) Oxygen transport

Transport of Oxygen

Oxygen is transported in the blood in two ways:

- **Dissolved** in the blood (1.5%).
- Bound to **haemoglobin** (98.5%).

Bound to Haemoglobin

Once oxygen has entered the blood from the lungs, it is taken up by haemoglobin **(Hb)** in the red blood cells.

Haemoglobin is a protein found in red blood cells that is comprised of four subunits: two alpha subunits and two beta subunits. Each subunit has a heme group in the centre that contains iron and binds one oxygen molecule. This means each haemoglobin molecule can bind four oxygen molecules, forming oxyhaemoglobin. Haemoglobin molecules with a greater number of oxygen molecules bound are brighter red, hence why oxygenated arterial blood is brighter red and deoxygenated venous blood is darker red.

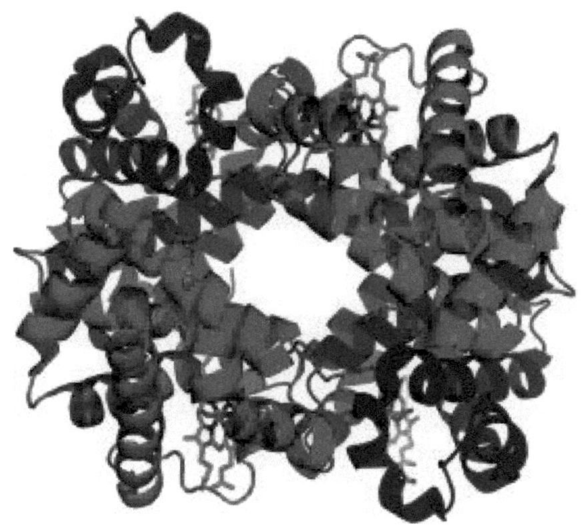

oxygen binding to haemoglobin

Oxygen Binding to Haemoglobin

Haemoglobin changes shape based on how many oxygen molecules are bound to it. The change in shape also causes a change in affinity to oxygen. As the number of oxygen molecules bound to haemoglobin increases, the affinity of haemoglobin for oxygen increases. This is known as **cooperativity**.

When no oxygen is bound, the haemoglobin is said to be in the Tense State **(T-state)**, with a low affinity for oxygen. At the point where oxygen first binds, the haemoglobin alters its shape into the Relaxed State **(R-state)**, which has a higher affinity for oxygen. We can plot this change on a graph of oxygen saturation over partial pressure of oxygen.

Oxygen Delivery at Tissues

As shown on the diagram above, the percentage of oxygen bound to haemoglobin is related to the partial pressure of oxygen (pO_2) at a given site. When **oxyhaemoglobin** reaches a tissue that has a low pO_2 (e.g. skeletal muscle), it will dissociate into oxygen and haemoglobin, resulting in an increase in local pO_2. Inversely, when it reaches a tissue that has a high pO_2 (e.g. in the pulmonary circulation), haemoglobin will continue to take up more oxygen, resulting in a lowered pO_2.

ANSWER (c) pathophysiology of peptic ulcer:

- The peptic ulcer disease (PUD) mechanism results from an imbalance between gastric mucosal protective and destructive factors.
- Risk factors predisposing to the development of PUD:

- *H. pyl*ori infection
- NSAID use
- First-degree relative with PUD
- Emigrant from a developed nation
- African American/Hispanic ethnicity

- With peptic ulcers, there is usually a defect in the mucosa that extends to the muscularis mucosa. Once the protective superficial mucosal layer is damaged, the inner layers are susceptible to acidity. Further, the ability of the mucosal cells to secrete bicarbonate is compromised.
- H. pylori are known to colonize the gastric mucosa and causes inflammation. The H. pylori also impair the secretion of bicarbonate, promoting the development of acidity and gastric metaplasia.

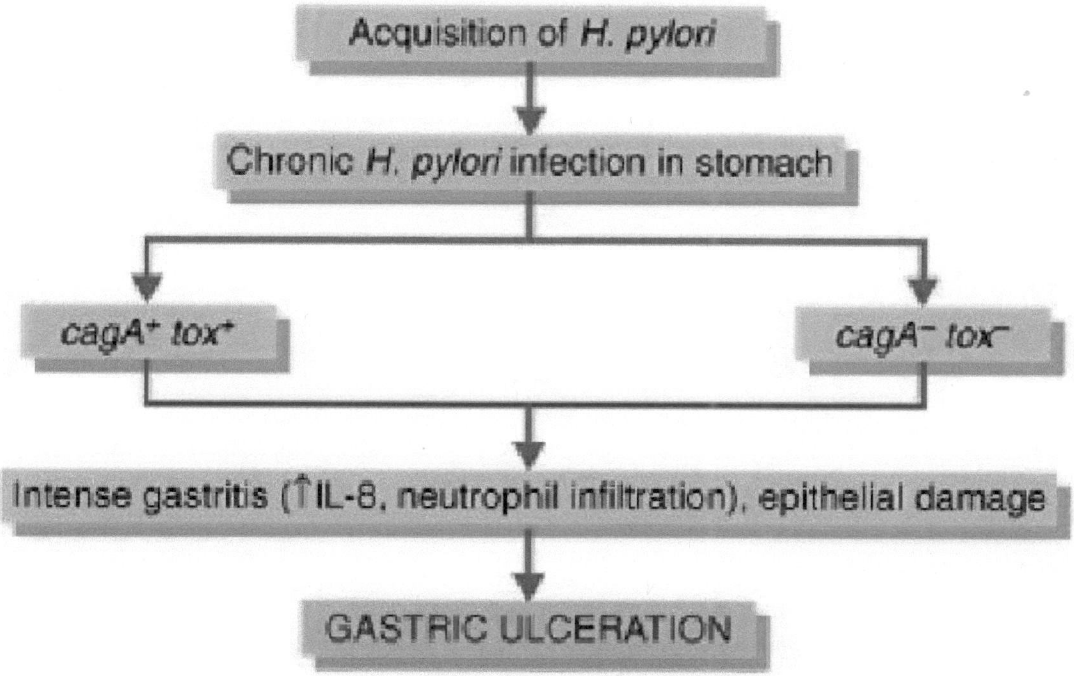

<u>**Q5. Write on the following with the help of a diagram :**</u>(a) Spermatogenesis and the factors affecting it
(b) Stretch reflex
(c) ECG changes in health and disease.
ANSWER (a) Spermatogenesis and the factors affecting it

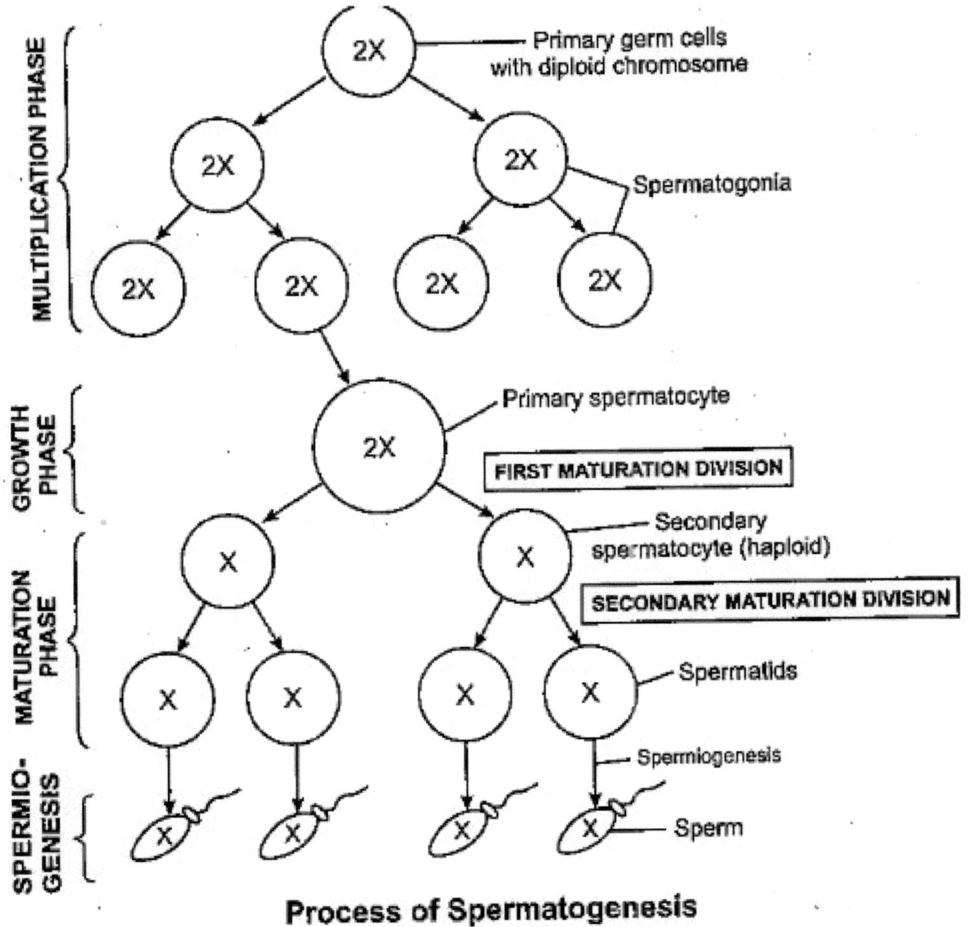

Process of Spermatogenesis

The factors affecting spermatogenesis

- The process of spermatogenesis is highly sensitive to fluctuations in the environment, particularly hormones and temperature.
- Dietary deficiencies (such as vitamins B, E and A), anabolic steroids, metals (cadmium and lead), x-ray exposure, alcohol, and infectious diseases will also adversely affect the rate of spermatogenesis. In addition, the male germ line is susceptible to DNA damage caused by oxidative stress, and this damage likely has a significant impact on fertilization and pregnancy. Exposure to pesticides also affects spermatogenesis.

ANSWER (b) Stretch reflex

A reflex is defined as an involuntary, unlearned, repeatable, automatic reaction to a specific stimulus which does not require input from the brain. The muscle stretch reflex is the most basic reflex pathway in the body and as such, understanding this allows understanding of more complex reflexes.

Reflex Arc Components

A reflex arc is a neural pathway that controls a reflex. Most sensory neurones have a synapse within the spinal cord, allowing for reflexes to take place without the involvement of the central nervous system (CNS) – speeding up the process. The pathway can be described as a **'reflex arc'** which is made up of 5 components:

- A receptor – muscle spindle
- An afferent fibre – muscle spindle afferent
- An integration centre – lamina IX of spinal cord

- An efferent fibre – α-motoneurones
- An effector – muscle

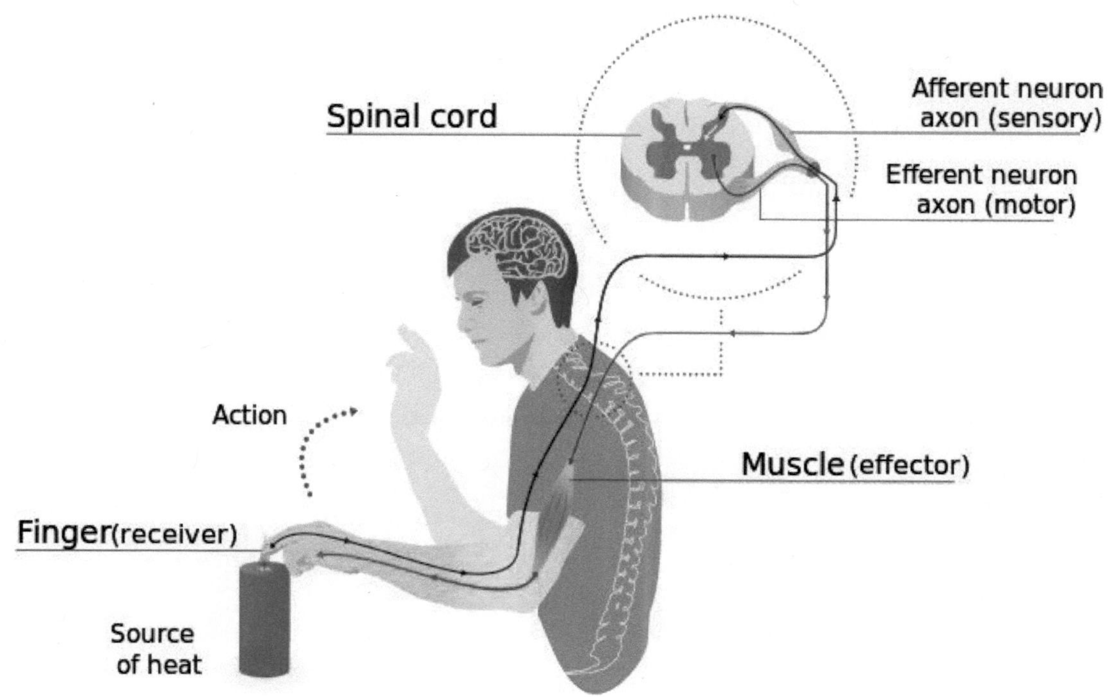

Reflex arc

ANSWER (c) ECG changes in health and disease.

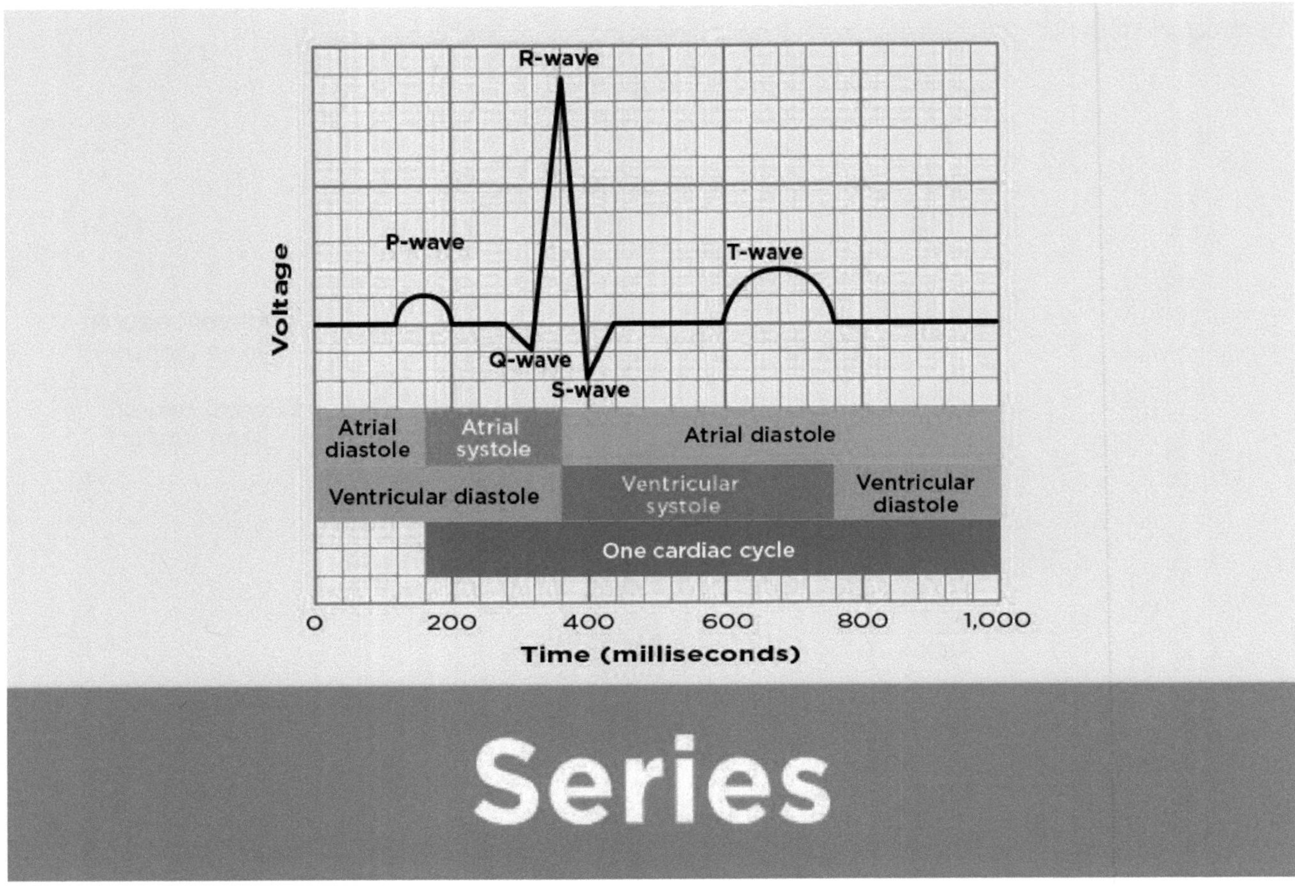

ECG

Interpretation of Abnormal ECGs
Abnormal results can signify several issues. These include:

- **Defects or abnormalities in the heart's shape and size:** An abnormal ECG can signal that one or more aspects of the heart's walls are larger than another meaning that the heart is working harder than normal to pump blood.
- **Electrolyte imbalances:** Electrolytes are electricity-conducting particles in the body that help keep the heart muscle beating in rhythm. If your electrolytes are imbalanced, you may have an abnormal ECG reading.
- Heart attack **or ischemia:** During a heart attack, blood flow in the heart is affected and heart tissue can begin to lose oxygen. This tissue will not conduct electricity as well, which can cause an abnormal ECG. Ischemia, or lack of blood flow, may also cause an abnormal ECG.
- Heart rhythm **abnormalities:** A heart typically beats in a steady rhythm. An EKG can reveal if the heart is beating out of rhythm or sequence.
- **Medication side effects:** Taking certain medications can impact a heart's rate and rhythm. Sometimes, medications given to improve the heart's rhythm can have the reverse effect and cause arrhythmias. Such as beta-blockers, sodium channel blockers, and calcium channel blockers.

Q6. Write features of the following:
(a) Grave's disease.
(b) Functions of middle ear
(c) Iron deficiency anaemia
ANSWER (a) Grave's disease.

- Graves‘ disease is an immune system disorder that results in the overproduction of thyroid hormones (hyperthyroidism). Although a number of disorders may result in hyperthyroidism, Graves' disease is a common cause.
- Thyroid hormones affect many body systems, so signs and symptoms of Graves‘ disease can be wide ranging. Although Graves' disease may affect anyone, it's more common among women and in people younger than age 40.
- The primary treatment goals are to reduce the amount of thyroid hormones that the body produces and lessen the severity of symptoms.

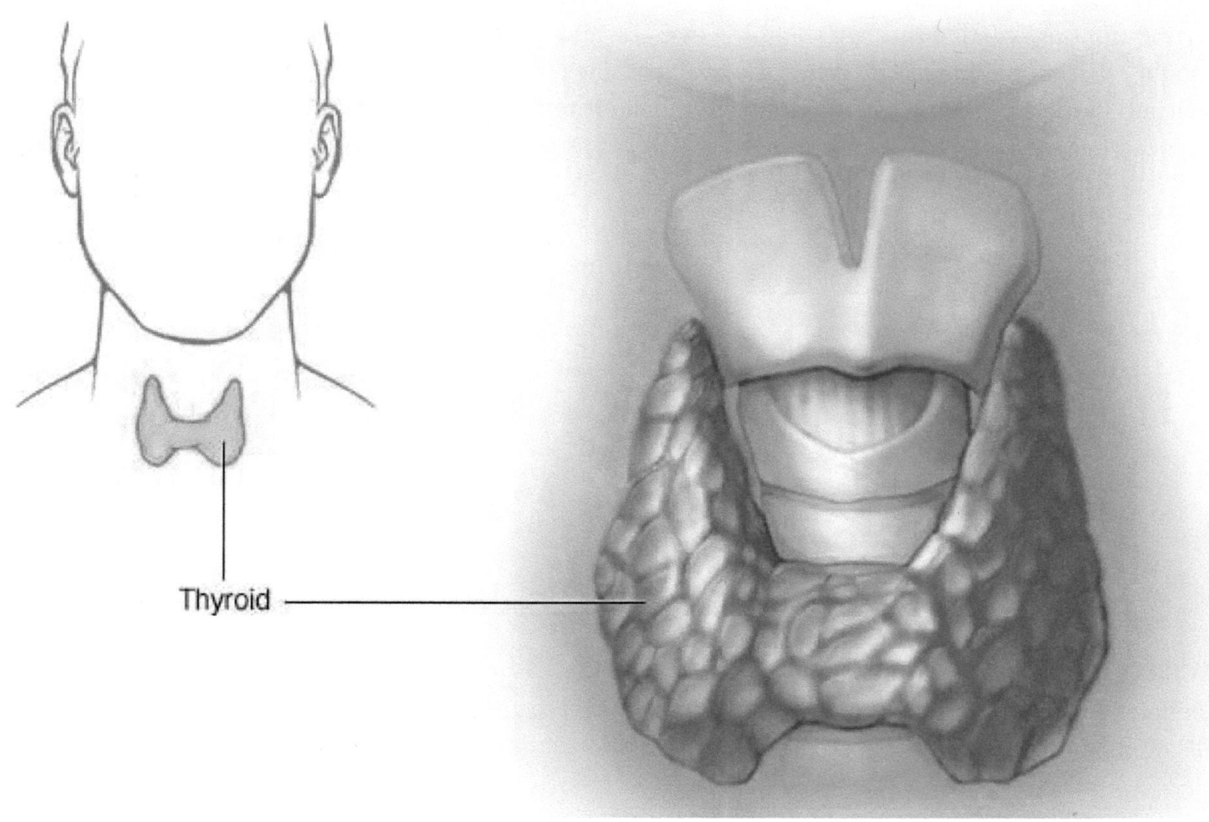

Thyroid gland

Common signs and symptoms of Graves‘ disease include:

- Anxiety and irritability
- A fine tremor of the hands or fingers
- Heat sensitivity and an increase in perspiration or warm, moist skin
- Weight loss, despite normal eating habits
- Enlargement of the thyroid gland (goiter)
- Change in menstrual cycles
- Erectile dysfunction or reduced libido
- Frequent bowel movements

- Bulging eyes (Graves' ophthalmopathy)
- Fatigue
- Thick, red skin usually on the shins or tops of the feet (Graves' dermopathy)
- Rapid or irregular heartbeat (palpitations)
- Sleep disturbance

ANSWER (b) Functions of middle ear

- The main function of the middle ear is to carry sound waves from the outer ear to the inner ear, which contains the cochlea and where sound input can be communicated to the brain. Sound waves are funneled into the outer ear and strike the tympanic membrane, causing it to vibrate.
- These vibrations are carried through the three ossicles, and the stapes strikes the oval window, which separates the middle ear from the inner ear. When the oval window is hit, it causes waves in the fluid inside the inner ear and sets into motion a chain of events leading to the interpretation of sound as we know it.

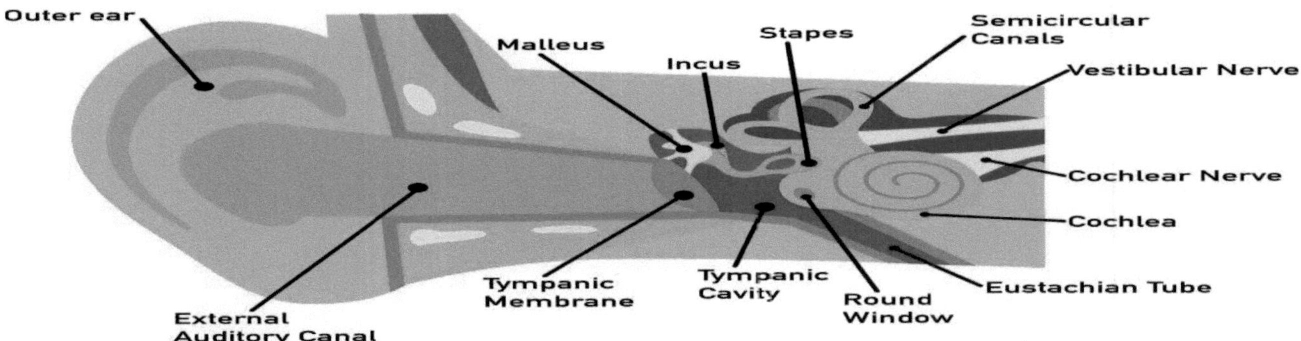

Middle ear

ANSWER (c) Iron deficiency anaemia

Iron deficiency anemia is a common type of anemia — a condition in which blood lacks adequate healthy red blood cells. Red blood cells carry oxygen to the body's tissues.

- As the name implies, iron deficiency anemia is due to insufficient iron. Without enough iron, your body can't produce enough of a substance in red blood cells that enables them to carry oxygen (hemoglobin). As a result, iron deficiency anemia may leave you tired and short of breath.
- You can usually correct iron deficiency anemia with iron supplementation. Sometimes additional tests or treatments for iron deficiency anemia are necessary, especially if your doctor suspects that you're bleeding internally.

Symptoms

Initially, iron deficiency anemia can be so mild that it goes unnoticed. But as the body becomes more deficient in iron and anemia worsens, the signs and symptoms intensify.

Iron deficiency anemia signs and symptoms may include:

- Extreme fatigue
- Weakness

- Pale skin
- Chest pain, fast heartbeat or shortness of breath
- Headache, dizziness or lightheadedness
- Cold hands and feet
- Inflammation or soreness of your tongue
- Brittle nails
- Unusual cravings for non-nutritive substances, such as ice, dirt or starch
- Poor appetite, especially in infants and children with iron deficiency anemia

CHAPTER IV

Question Paper 2019

B.Sc Nursing 1st year ,annual exam, 2019
Anatomy and physiology

Note Marks 75

1. attempt all questions and draw suitable diagrams, tables, and graphs where required.

2.attempt part-1 and part-2 in separate answer book.

Part –I anatomy

Q1. **Describe in detail:**
(a) Bronchopulmonary segments
(b) Describe different parts of the brain
(c) Classify synovial joint with suitable example

Q2. **Draw a well labelled diagram to illustrate the following:**
(a) Difference between large intestine and small intestine
(b) Neurons
(C) Anterior relations of right kidney

Q3. Write short note on
(a) Support of uterus
(b) Blood supply of heart
(c) Functions of Pituitary gland

Part-II (Physiology)

Q4. Write short notes on:
(a) Regulation of Tone and Posture
(b) Regulation of body temperature
(c) Carbohydrate metabolism.

Q5. Write the concept, in short, with the help of a diagram:
(a) Physiology of Haemostasis
(b) Cerebrospinal fluid formation and functions
(c) Short term regulation of blood pressure

Q6. Write Features of:
(a) Lung volume and capacity
(b) Growth Hormone excess
(c) Cellular Immunity

Part –I anatomy

Q1. **Describe in detail**
(a) Bronchopulmonary segments
(b) Describe different parts of the brain
(c) Classify synovial joint with suitable example

Answer(a) Bronchopulmonary segments

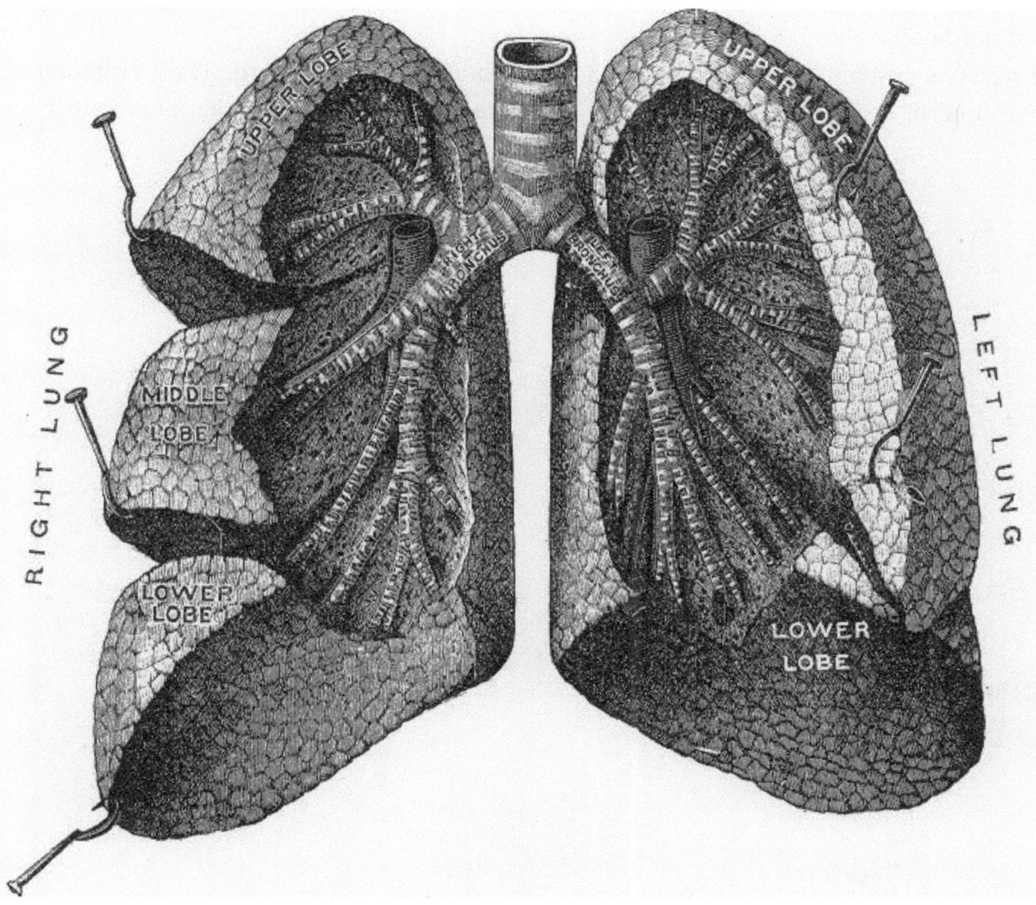

Lungs

- A bronchopulmonary segment is a portion of lung supplied by a specific segmental bronchus and its vessels. These arteries branch from the pulmonary and bronchial arteries, and run together through the center of the segment. Veins and lymphatic vessels drain along the edges of the segment.
- The segments are separated from each other by layers of connective tissue that forms them into discrete anatomical and functional units.
- This separation means that a bronchopulmonary segment can be surgically removed without affecting the function of the others.
- There are ten bronchopulmonary segments in the right lung: three in the superior lobe, two in the middle lobe, and five in the inferior lobe. Some of the segments may fuse in the left lung to form usually eight to nine segments (four to five in the upper lobe and four to five in the lower lobe.

ANSWER (b) Describe different parts of the brain

- The brain is an amazing three-pound organ that controls all functions of the body, interprets information from the outside world, and embodies the essence of the mind and soul. Intelligence, creativity, emotion, and memory are a few of the many things governed by the brain. Protected within the skull, the brain is composed of the cerebrum, cerebellum, and brainstem.
- The brain receives information through our five senses: sight, smell, touch, taste, and hearing - often many at one time. It assembles the messages in a way that has meaning for us, and can store that information in our memory.

- The brain controls our thoughts, memory and speech, movement of the arms and legs, and the function of many organs within our body.
- The central nervous system (CNS) is composed of the brain and spinal cord. The peripheral nervous system (PNS) is composed of spinal nerves that branch from the spinal cord and cranial nerves that branch from the brain.

Brain

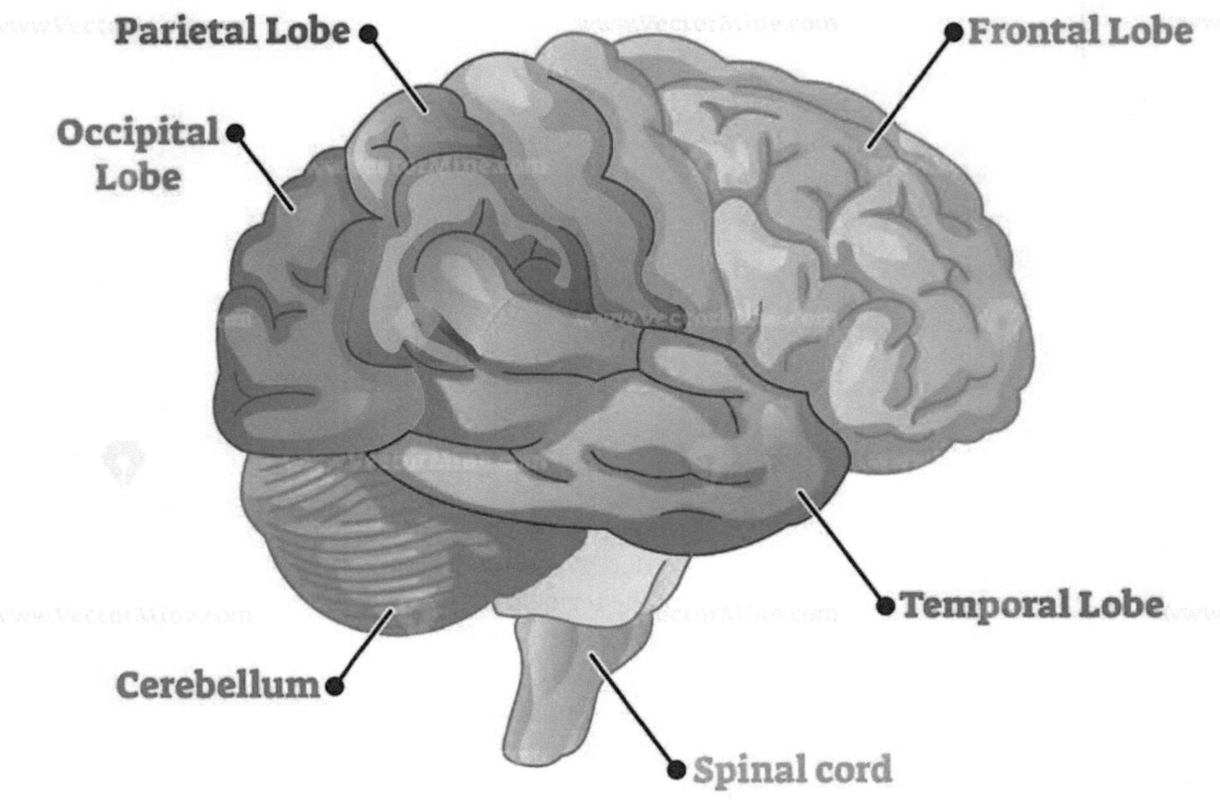

Human brain

The brain has three main parts: the cerebrum, cerebellum and brainstem.

Cerebrum: is the largest part of the brain and is composed of right and left hemispheres. It performs higher functions like interpreting touch, vision and hearing, as well as speech, reasoning, emotions, learning, and fine control of movement.

Cerebellum: is located under the cerebrum. Its function is to coordinate muscle movements, maintain posture, and balance.

Brainstem: acts as a relay center connecting the cerebrum and cerebellum to the spinal cord. It performs many automatic functions such as breathing, heart rate, body temperature, wake and sleep cycles, digestion, sneezing, coughing, vomiting, and swallowing.

Answer (c) Classify synovial joint with suitable example

Synovial joints are the most common type of joint in the body. A key structural characteristic for a synovial joint that is not seen at fibrous or cartilaginous joints is the presence of a joint cavity. This fluid-filled space is the site at which the articulating surfaces of the bones contact each other. At synovial joints, the articular surfaces of bones are covered with smooth articular cartilage. This gives the bones of a synovial joint the ability to move smoothly against each other, allowing for increased joint mobility.

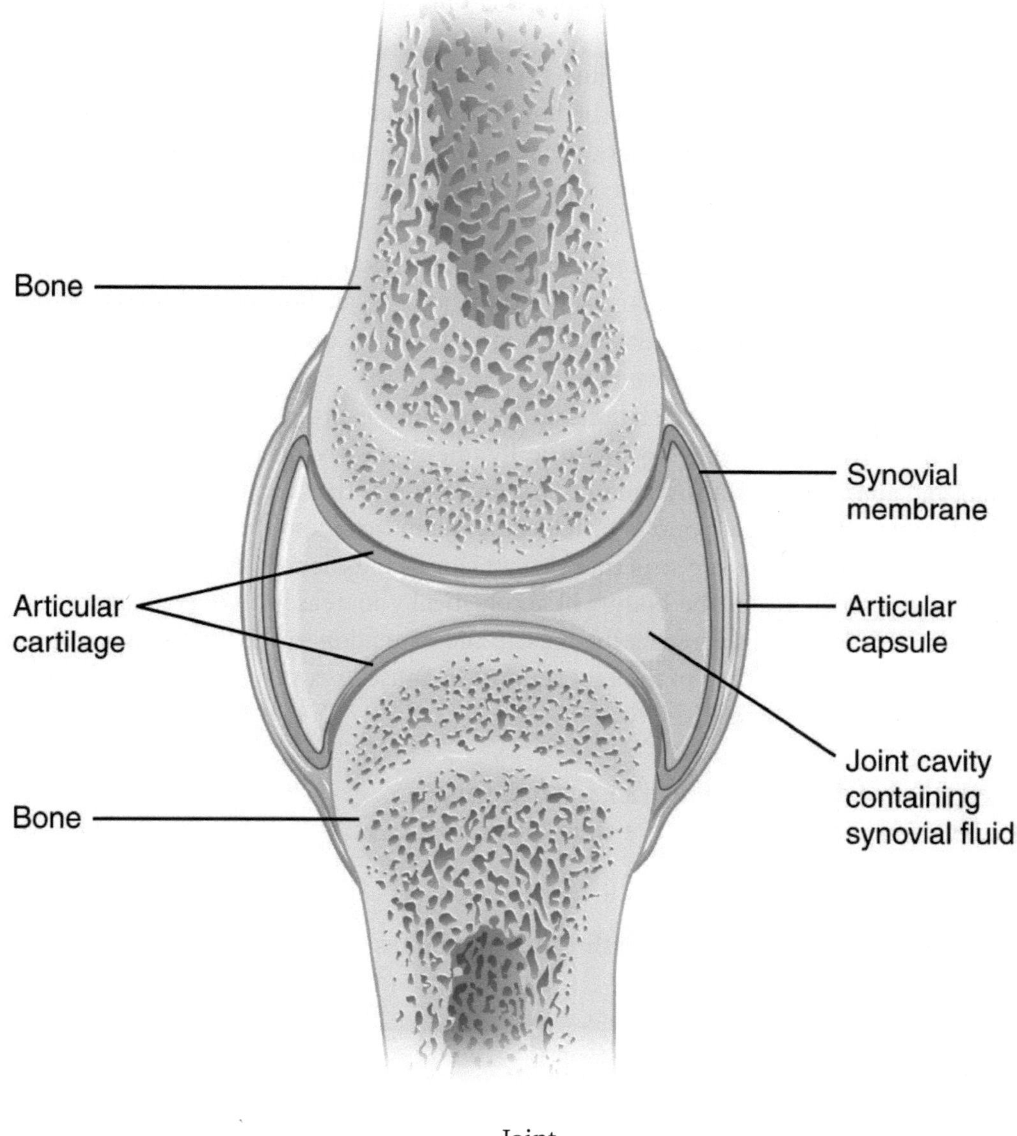

Joint

Joints: Synovial joints allow for smooth movements between the adjacent bones. The joint is surrounded by an articular capsule that defines a joint cavity filled with synovial fluid. The articulating surfaces of the bones are covered by a thin layer of articular cartilage. Ligaments support the joint by holding the bones together and resisting excess or abnormal joint motions.

Structural Features of Synovial Joints

- Synovial joints are characterized by the presence of a joint cavity. The walls of this space are formed by the **articular capsule**, a fibrous connective tissue structure that is attached to each bone just outside the area of the bone's articulating surface. The bones of the joint articulate with each other within the joint cavity.
- Friction between the bones at a synovial joint is prevented by the presence of the **articular cartilage**, a thin layer of hyaline cartilage that covers the entire articulating surface of each bone. However, unlike at a cartilaginous joint, the articular cartilages of each bone are not continuous with each other. Instead, the articular cartilage acts like a Teflon coating over the bone surface, allowing the articulating bones to move smoothly against each other without damaging the underlying bone tissue. Lining the inner surface of the articular capsule is a thin **synovial membrane**.
- The cells of this membrane secrete **synovial fluid** (synovia = "a thick fluid"), a thick, slimy fluid that provides lubrication to further reduce friction between the bones of the joint. This fluid also provides nourishment to the articular cartilage, which does not contain blood vessels. The ability of the bones to move smoothly against each other within the joint cavity, and the freedom of joint movement this provides, means that each synovial joint is functionally classified as a diarthrosis.
- Outside of their articulating surfaces, the bones are connected together by ligaments, which are strong bands of fibrous connective tissue. These strengthen and support the joint by anchoring the bones together and preventing their separation. Ligaments allow for normal movements at a joint, but limit the range of these motions, thus preventing excessive or abnormal joint movements.
- Ligaments are classified based on their relationship to the fibrous articular capsule. An **extrinsic ligament** is located outside of the articular capsule, an **intrinsic ligament** is fused to or incorporated into the wall of the articular capsule, and an **intracapsular ligament** is located inside of the articular capsule.
- At many synovial joints, additional support is provided by the muscles and their tendons that act across the joint. A **tendon** is the dense connective tissue structure that attaches a muscle to bone.
- As forces acting on a joint increase, the body will automatically increase the overall strength of contraction of the muscles crossing that joint, thus allowing the muscle and its tendon to serve as a "dynamic ligament" to resist forces and support the joint. This type of indirect support by muscles is very important at the shoulder joint, for example, where the ligaments are relatively weak.

Q2. Draw a well labelled diagram to illustrate the following:
(a) Difference between large intestine and small intestine
(b) Neurons
(C) Anterior relations of right kidney

ANSWER (a) Difference between large intestine and small intestine

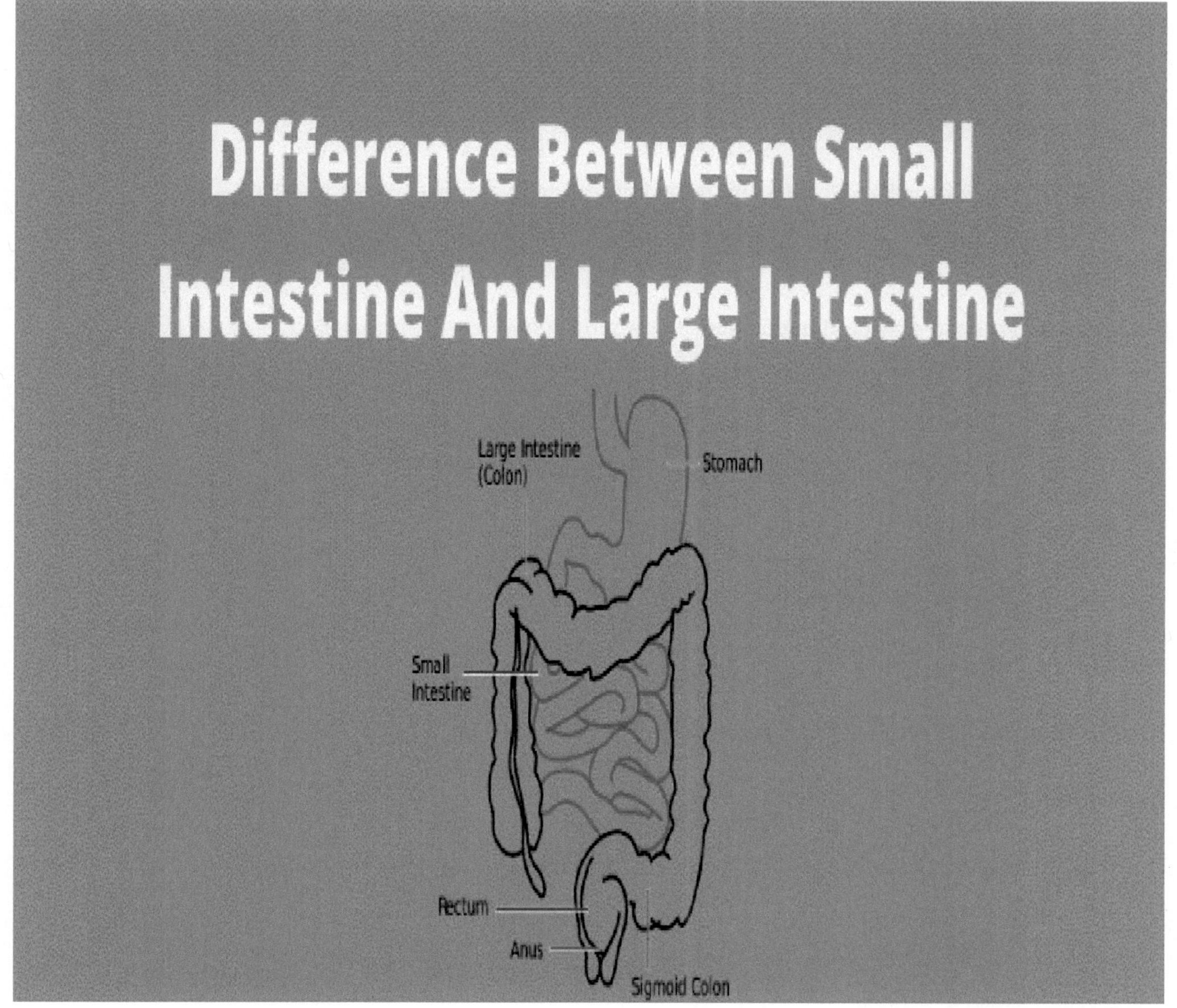

Intestines

Difference Between Small Intestine And Large Intestine
Small Intestine
Digestion

- Small intestine helps in completing digestion.

Length

- It is measured around 4.5 – 7.0 m in size.

Width

- Small intestine is narrow in width of around 3.5 – 4.5 cm.

Villi

- Villi is present in small intestine.

Motility

- Small intestine shows small movements in the abdominal cavity.

Parts

- Small intestine has three parts, jejunum, duodenum and ileum.

Muscle bands

- Small intestine is capable to forms the layer of continuous bands of muscles around it.

Taeniae Coli

- Taenia coli is absent in small intestine.

Hormones

- Various hormones are secreted by small intestine.

Circular folds

- Internal surface of small intestine has circular folds. These folds are also known as 'palicae circulares'.

Hastura

- It is absent in small intestine.

Activity

- Small intestine absorb the nutrients from the digested food.

Peyers Patches

- Peyers Patches are present in small intestine.

Large Intestine

- Large intestine does not play any role in digestion.
- It is measured around 1.5 m in size.
- Large intestine has width of around 4 – 6 cm in diameter.
- Villi is absent in large intestine.
- It is fixed or show very little mobility.
- Large intestine has four parts, which are, rectum, colon, caecum and anal canal.

- Large intestine is reduced to three types of muscles bands. These bands are known as taeniae coli.
- Taenia Coli are present in large intestine.
- No hormones are secretedby large intestine.
- Circular folds are absent in large intestine.
- It is present in large intestine.
- Large intestine helps in the absorption of water and electrolytes and in production of vitamins.
- Peyers patches are absent in large intestine.

ANSWER (b) Neurons

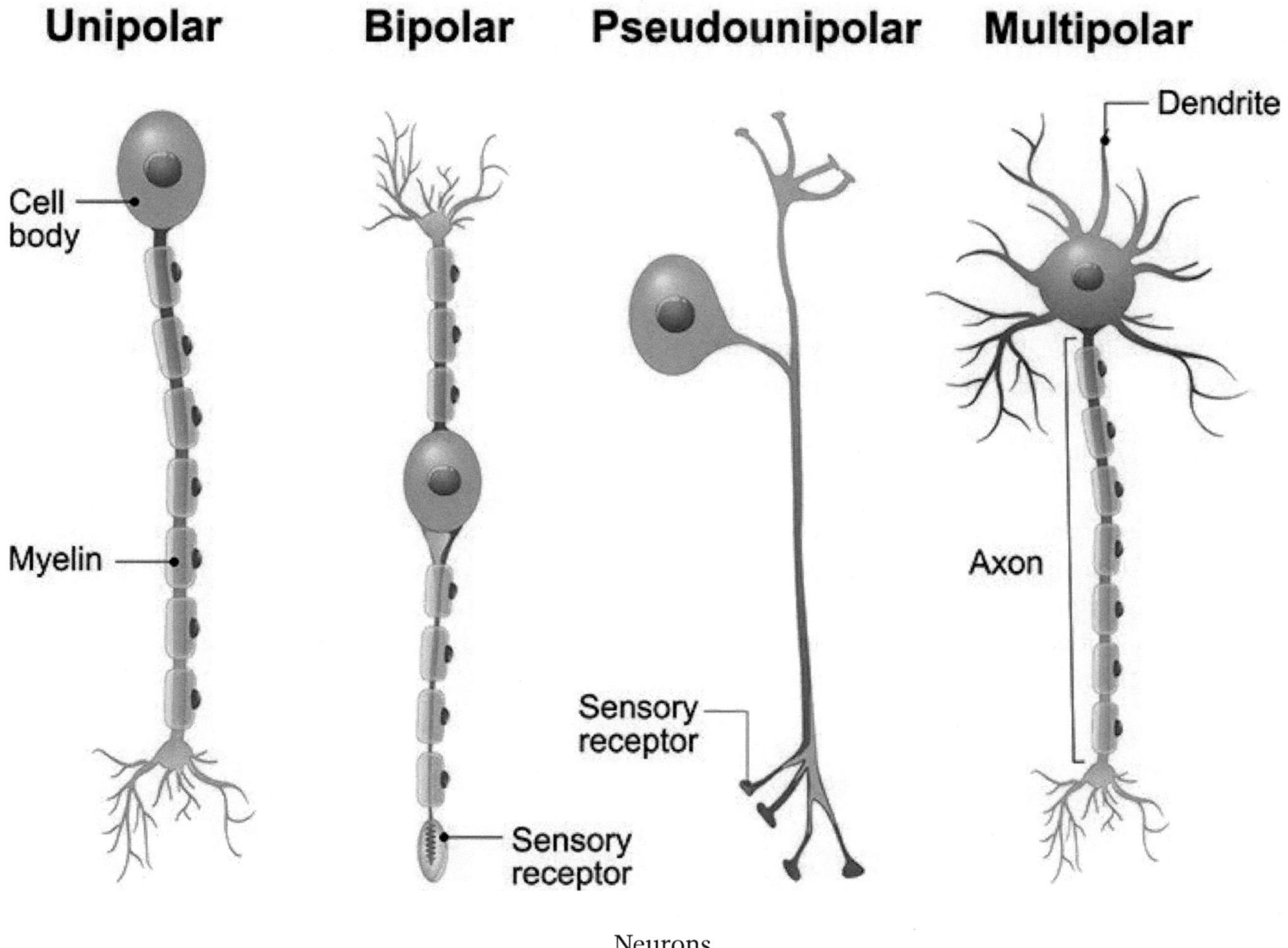

Neurons

Neurons are the cells that make up the brain and the nervous system. They are the fundamental units that send and receive signals which allow us to move our muscles, feel the external world, think, form memories and much more.

There are three types of neurons: sensory, motor, and interneurons.

Sensory neurons:

- Sensory neurons are the nerve cells that are activated by sensory input from the environment - for example, when you touch a hot surface with your fingertips, the sensory neurons will be the ones firing and sending off signals to the rest of the nervous system about the information they have received.

- The inputs that activate sensory neurons can be physical or chemical, corresponding to all five of our senses. Thus, a physical input can be things like sound, touch, heat, or light. A chemical input comes from taste or smell, which neurons then send to the brain.
- Most sensory neurons are pseudounipolar, which means they only have one axon which is split into two branches.

Motor neurons:

Motor neurons of the spinal cord are part of the central nervous system (CNS) and connect to muscles, glands and organs throughout the body. These neurons transmit impulses from the **spinal cord** to skeletal and smooth muscles (such as those in your stomach), and so directly control all of our muscle movements. There are in fact two types of motor neurons: those that travel from spinal cord to muscle are called *lower* motor neurons, whereas those that travel between the brain and spinal cord are called *upper* motor neurons.

Motor neurons have the most common type of 'body plan' for a nerve cell - they are multipolar, each with one axon and several dendrites.

Interneurons:

As the name suggests, interneurons are the ones in between - they connect spinal motor and sensory neurons. As well as transferring signals between sensory and motor neurons, interneurons can also communicate with each other, forming circuits of various complexity. They are multipolar, just like motor neurons.

Neurons in the brain:

In the brain, the distinction between types of neurons is much more complex.Whereas in the spinal cord we could easily distinguish neurons based on their function, that isn't the case in the brain. Certainly, there are brain neurons involved in sensory processing – like those in visual or auditory cortex – and others involved in motor processing – like those in the cerebellum or motor cortex.

ANSWER(C) Anterior relations of right kidney

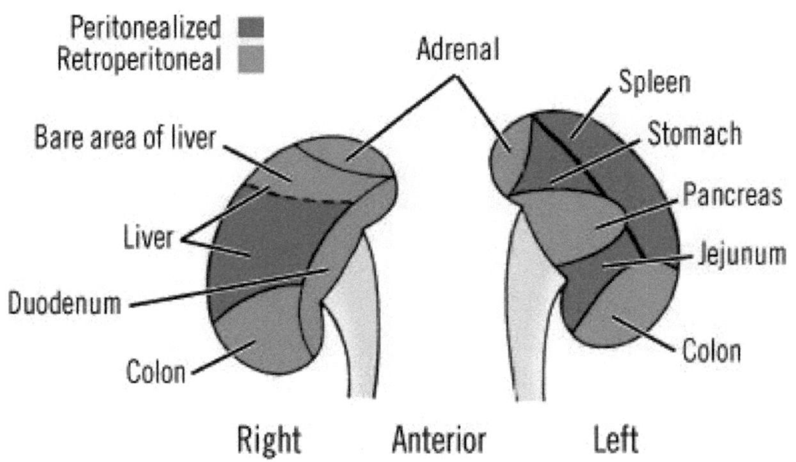

Anterior relation of kidney

1. **Anteriorly the right kidney** is related to the Liver, duodenum and hepatic flexure of ascending colon.
2. **Anteriorly the left kidney** is related to Stomach, Jejunum, Pancreas, Spleen and descending Colon. .
3. Right Kidney is related to the 12th rib posteriorly resting on diaphragm.

Q3. Write short note on
(a) Support of uterus
(b) Blood supply of heart
(c) Functions of Pituitary gland
ANSWER (a) Support of uterus
Ligaments

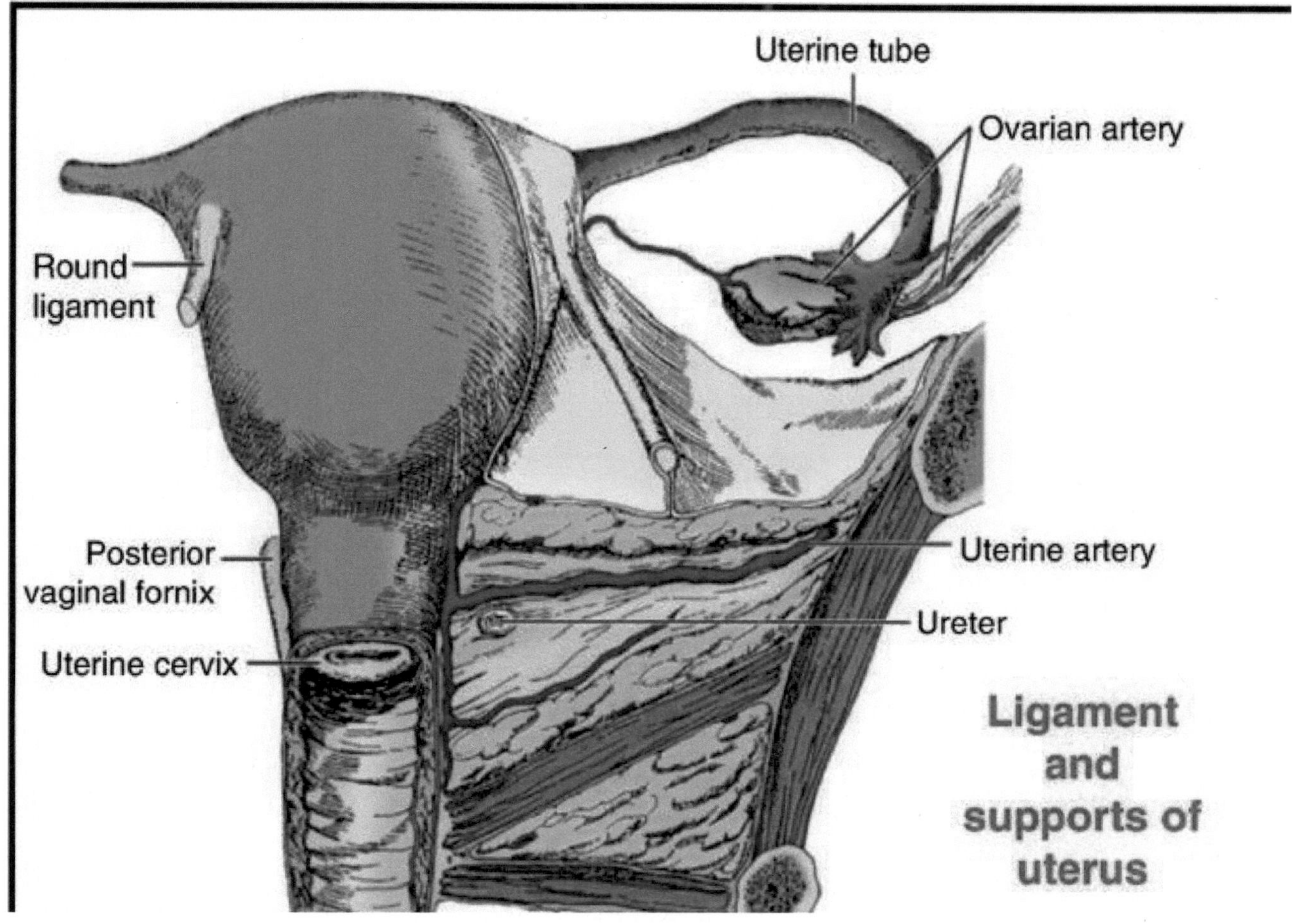

The tone of the pelvic floor provides the primary support for the uterus. Some ligaments provide further support, securing the uterus in place.

They are:

- **Broad Ligament:**This is a double layer of peritoneum attaching the sides of the uterus to the pelvis. It acts as a mesentery for the uterus and contributes to maintaining it in position.
- **Round Ligament:**A remnant of the gubernaculum extending from the uterine horns to the labia majora via the inguinal canal. It functions to maintain the anteverted position of the uterus.
- **Ovarian Ligament:**Joins the ovaries to the uterus.
- **Cardinal Ligament:**Located at the base of the broad ligament, the cardinal ligament extends from the cervix to the lateral pelvic walls. It contains the uterine artery and vein in addition to providing support to the uterus.

- **Uterosacral Ligament:**Extends from the cervix to the sacrum. It provides support tothe uterus.

ANSWER (b) Blood supply of heart

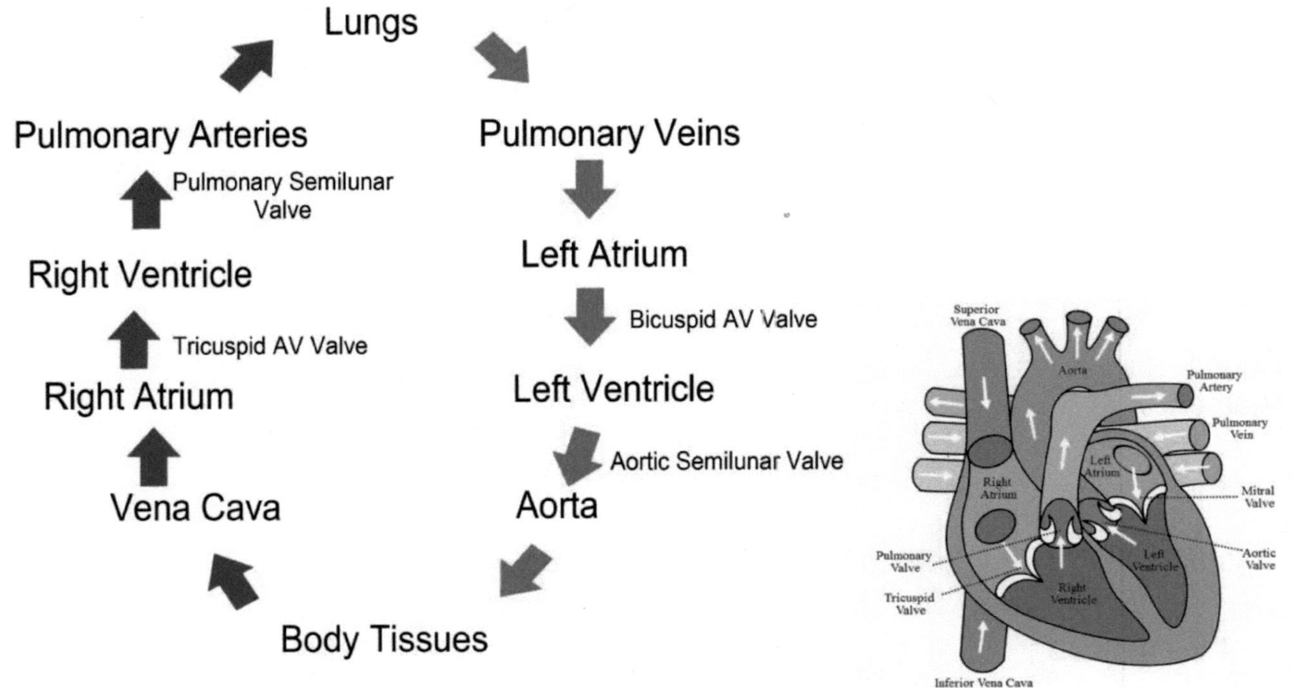

Enter Caption

- The above figure shows how blood circulates through the chambers of the heart. The right atrium collects blood from two large veins, the superior vena cava (from the upper body) and the inferior vena cava (from the lower body).
- The blood that collects in the right atrium is pumped through the tricuspid valve into the right ventricle. From the right ventricle, the blood is pumped through the pulmonary valve into the pulmonary artery.
- The pulmonary artery carries the blood to the lungs, where it enters the pulmonary circulation, gives up carbon dioxide, and picks up oxygen. The oxygenated blood travels back from the lungs through the pulmonary veins (of which there are four), and enters the left atrium of the heart.
- From the left atrium, the blood is pumped through the mitral valve into the left ventricle. From the left ventricle, the blood is pumped through the aortic valve into the aorta, which subsequently branches into smaller arteries that carry the blood throughout the rest of the body.
- After passing through capillaries and exchanging substances with cells, the blood returns to the right atrium via the superior vena cava and inferior vena cava, and the process begins anew.

ANSWER (c) Functions of Pituitary gland

Pituitary (hypophysis) is a pea-sized endocrine gland at the base of your brain, behind the bridge of your nose and directly below your hypothalamus. It sits in an indent in the sphenoid bone called the sella turcica. The pituitary gland is one of eight interrelated major endocrine glands.

The major hormones produced by the pituitary gland are:

- **ACTH:** Adrenocorticotrophic hormone. Stimulates the production of cortisol, a "stress hormone" that maintains blood pressure and blood sugar levels.
- **FSH:** Follicle-stimulating hormone. Promotes sperm production and stimulates the ovaries to produce estrogen.
- **LH:** Luteinizing hormone. Stimulates ovulation in women and testosterone production in men.
- **GH:** Growth hormone. Helps maintain healthy muscles and bones and manage fat distribution.
- **PRL**: Prolactin. Causes breast milk to be produced after childbirth. It also affects hormones that control the ovaries and testes, which can affect menstrual periods, sexual functions and fertility.
- **TSH:** Thyroid-stimulating hormone. Stimulates the thyroid gland, which regulates metabolism, energy and the nervous system.
- Oxytocin: Helps labor to progress, causes breast milk to flow, affects labor, breastfeeding, behavior and social interaction and the bonding between a mother and child.
- **ADH:** Anti-diuretic hormone, or vasopressin. Regulates water balance and sodium levels.

Hormones are not released from the pituitary gland in a steady stream. They come in bursts, every one to three hours, and alternate between periods of activity and periods of inactivity.

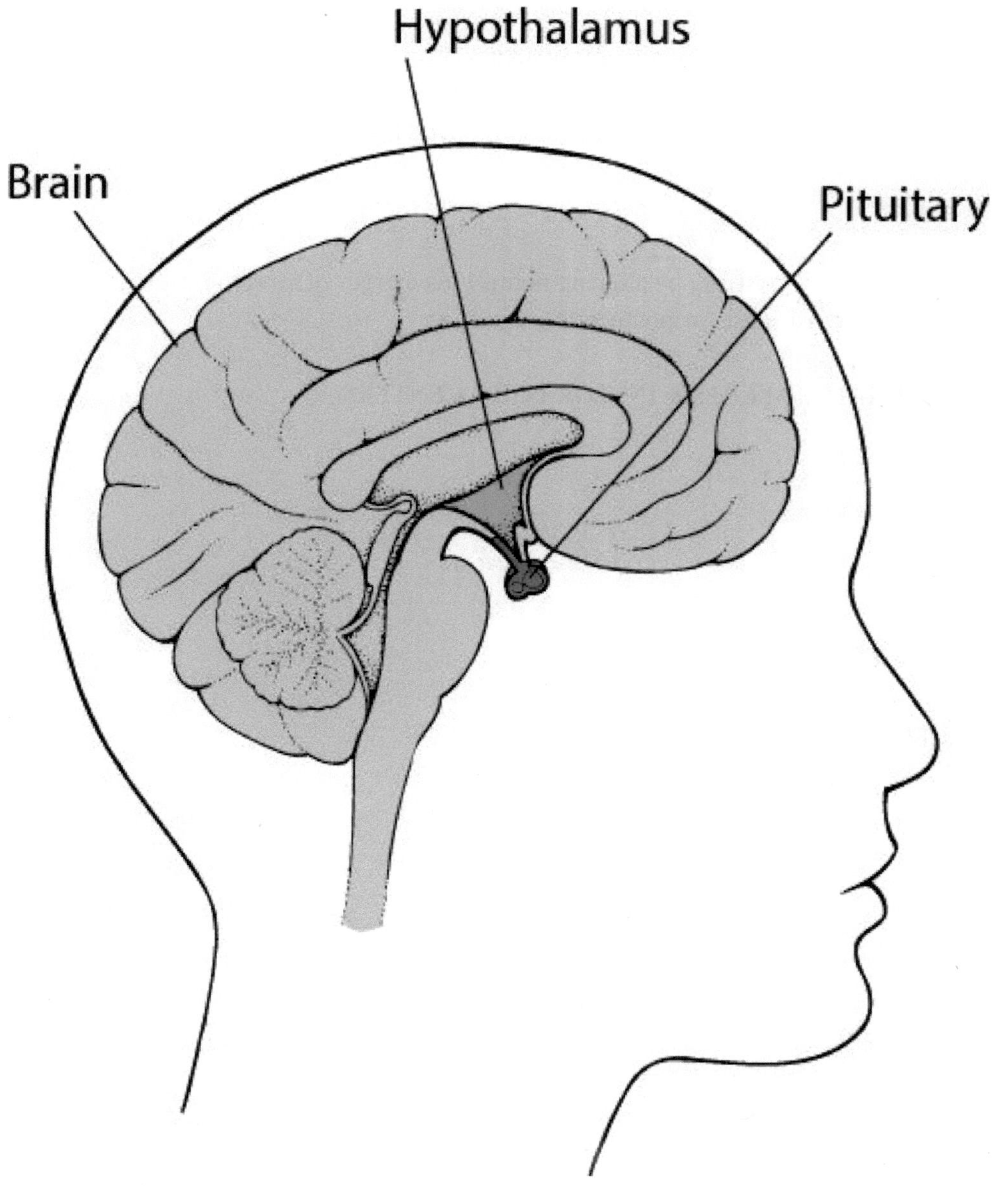

Q4. Write short notes on:

(a) Regulation of Tone and Posture

(b) Regulation of body temperature

(c) Carbohydrate metabolism.

ANSWER (a) Regulation of Tone and Posture

REGULATION OF POSTURE

- Posture – Stable equilibrium adopted by an individual.

MECHANISMS OF POSTURE:

- Muscle tone distribution.
- Postural reflexes.

MUSCLE TONE DISTRIBUTION:

- Posture is maintained by reflex adjustments of tone in anti-gravity muscles.
- Anti-gravity muscles – Flexors of upper extremity & extensors of lower extremity.
- Muscle tone is controlled by basic postural reflex mainly, stretch reflex.

POSTURAL REFLEXES:

- Responsible for maintaining a posture, by altering neutral discharges of stretch reflexes.
- Stretch reflex arc integrity is a must for posture maintenance.

IMPORTANT POSTURAL REFLEXES & INTEGRATING CENTERS:

POSTURAL REFLEX

- Tonic labyrinthine reflexes
- Tonic neck reflex
- Righting reflex
- Long-loop stretch reflex
- Hopping & placing reactions

INTEGRATING CENTER

- Medulla oblongata
- Medulla oblongata
- midbrain
- cerebral cortex
- cerebral cortex

VESTIBULAR REFLEXES:

- **Inputs from vestibular reflexes are used for reflex adjustment of posture & eye movements.**

Includes,

- Tonic labyrinthine reflex.
- Labyrinthine **righting reflex.**
- Visual reflex (vestibulo-ocular reflex).

ANSWER (b) Regulation of body temperature

- Thermoregulation is a mechanism by which mammals maintain body temperature with tightly controlled self-regulation independent of external temperatures. Temperature regulation is a type of homeostasis and a means of preserving a stable internal temperature in order to survive. Ectotherms are animals that depend on their external environment for body heat, while endotherms are animals that use thermoregulation to maintain a somewhat consistent internal body temperature even when their external environment changes.
- Humans and other mammals and birds are endotherms. Human beings have a normal core internal temperature of around 37 degrees Celsius (98.6 degrees Fahrenheit) measured most accurately via a rectal probe thermometer.
- This is the optimal temperature at which the human body's systems function. Thermoregulation is crucial to human life; without thermoregulation, the human body would cease to function. Thermoregulation also plays an adaptive role in the body's response to infectious pathogens.

DEVELOPMENT

- The brain, more specifically the hypothalamus, controls thermoregulation. If the hypothalamus senses internal temperatures growing too hot or too cold, it will automatically send signals to the skin, glands, muscles, and organs.
- For example, if the body is generating heat during high-level exercise or if the external ambient temperature is elevated enough to cause a rise in the core temperature, afferent signals to the hypothalamus result in efferent signals to the cells of the skin to produce sweat. Sweating is one mechanism the body can use to cool itself as heat is lost through the process of sweat evaporation.
- In contrast, when the body experiences a cold environment, a shivering reflex results in skeletal muscles contracting and generating heat; additionally, the arrector pili muscles (a type of smooth muscle) raise the bodily hair follicles to trap the heat generated.

MECHANISM

- Thermoregulation has three mechanisms: afferent sensing, central control, and efferent responses. There are receptors for both heat and cold throughout the human body. Afferent sensing works through these receptors to determine if the body core temperature is too hold or cold. The hypothalamus is the central controller of thermoregulation. There is also an efferent behavioral component that responds to fluctuations in body temperature.
- For example, if a person is feeling too warm, the normal response is to remove an outer article of clothing. If a person is feeling too cold, they choose to wear more layers of clothing. Efferent responses also consist of automatic responses by the body to protect itself from extreme changes in temperature, such as sweating, vasodilation, vasoconstriction, and shivering.

ANSWER (c) Carbohydrate metabolism.

1.Carbohydrate digestion (in the intestine)

2.Fructose metabolism (in the liver)

3.Galactose metabolism (in the liver)

4.Glucose oxidation via glycolysis (in the cytoplasm), oxidative decarboxylation reaction (in the mitochondria), citric acid cycle (in the mitochondria) and the electron transport chain (ETC) (in the inner mitochondrial membrane

(IMM))

5.Glycogenesis (in the liver and skeletal muscle)

6.Glycogenolysis (in the liver, skeletal muscle and kidney)

7.Pentose phosphate pathway (in the liver, adipose tissue, adrenal cortex, testis, milk glands, phagocyte cells and red blood cells (RBCs))

8.Gluconeogenesis (in the liver, kidney, brain, testes and erythrocytes)

Carbohydrate digestion

Dietary carbohydrates of greatest importance are composed of hexoses such as sucrose (saccharose or table sugar), lactose (milk sugar), galactose (derived from fermented products) and maltose (derived from hydrolysis of starch) and also pentoses such as xylose and arabinose (from fruits) [2]. Food digestion starts in the mouth through secretion of salivary alpha-amylase (or ptyalin) that hydrolyses alpha-1,4 (α-1,4) linkage of starch (or amylum) and converts it to maltose. The next enzyme is

Fructose metabolism

Glucose is the main source of energy in cells; however, with high consumption of sucrose (composed of glucose and fructose) cells can use fructose as well. In the muscles, adipose tissue and kidney, which contain hexokinase (HK), fructose gets phosphorylated to become fructose-6-phosphate (F6P) to be directly used in the glycolysis pathway. However, in the liver, which contains glucokinase (GK), fructose must first be converted to glucose for consumption in the glycolysis pathway. Therefore,

Galactose metabolism

Galactose enters the body following consumption of milk. Milk sugar or lactose is composed of galactose and glucose. Lactose is converted to its constituents with lactase activity in the brush border of the small intestine. Galactose enters the blood stream following absorption by enterocytes and enters the liver through the portal vein to be metabolized and converted to glucose for consumption as energy. Glucose and galactose are the sugars whose active forms are transferred by the uridine

Glucose oxidation

There are two non-oxidative and oxidative pathways that oxidize glucose to prepare the energy source of cells. Oxidative decarboxylation reaction is the linker reaction between these two pathways.

Glycolysis (Embden–Meyerhof–Parnas pathway)

Degradation of glucose for releasing its energy for the anabolic pathways starts from glycolysis and continues to the Krebs or tricarboxylic acid (TCA) cycle in the mitochondria. Glycolysis is a cytoplasmic non-oxidative reaction for glucose degradation that is composed of 9 processes. A non-specific HK enzyme by using ATP phosphorylates glucose following entrance to the cell and converts it to G6P. In the liver both HK as well as GK (the specific kinase for glucose substrate) exist. Therefore,

Pyruvate dehydrogenase (PDH) or oxidative decarboxylation reaction

This mitochondrial reaction is the process that happens following glycolysis and preceding the Krebs cycle. PDH reaction utilizes coenzyme A (CoA or CoASH), thiamine pyrophosphate (TPP) and PDC to oxidize cytoplasmic pyruvate, which is transferred to the mitochondria by a carrier protein, to acetyl-CoA and CO2. In this reaction, one molecule NAD^+ is reduced to NADH2 (Fig. 3/6). In the absence of TPP, pyruvate is concentrated in the cytoplasm and converted to lactate (Fig. 10).

Krebs cycle (citric acid or tricarboxylic acid (TCA) cycle)

The Krebs cycle is an aerobic biodegradation process that starts from catabolism of acetyl-CoA to produce the reduced coenzymes (NADH2 and FADH2) and CO_2. OAA (derived from pyruvate carboxylation) is the first substrate of the Krebs cycle. OAA joins to acetyl-CoA to form citric acid (CA). Therefore, the source of OAA is sugar. In diabetic patients, who have less sugar and pyruvate in their cells, the level of OAA and consequently the activity of the Krebs cycle is low.In the higher energy

Glycogenesis

Glycogenesis is the process of glycogen synthesis. Glycogen is a polymer of glucose residues that is linked by α-1,4 and α-1,6 glycosidic bonds. Therefore, it is the glucose storage molecule in the hepatocytes and skeletal muscle cells.

The total amount of glycogen storage among these two tissues depends on the mass of the hepatocytes and skeletal muscle cells. Glycogen amount per mass unit of the liver is higher than the skeletal muscle; however, since in body the total mass of the skeletal.

Glycogenolysis

Glycogenolysis is the process of glycogen degradation. Glycogenolysis happens in the liver and kidney to produce glucose for balancing the blood sugar; however, it produces G6P in muscle cells to be used as the energy supplier of myocytes.

Glycogen phosphorylase using inorganic phosphate group (P_i) hydrolyzes the α-1,4 glycosidic linkages of glycogen and produces G1P (or glucose in the heart). G1P is converted to G6P and thereafter to glucose using G6Pase in the liver and kidney. In the skeletal

Pentose phosphate pathway (PPP), phosphogluconate pathway or hexose monophosphate shunt

In the liver, adipose tissue, adrenal cortex, testis, milk glands, phagocyte cells and RBCs another glucose oxidation pathway exists that is called pentose phosphate pathway (PPP). G6P is the substrate of PPP to produce ribose-5-phosphate (R5P), riboluse-5-phosphate (Ru5P) and reduced coenzyme NADPH2. R5P is either used for nucleotide synthesis of nucleic acids or is recycled in the PPP for more production of NADPH2. The reduced equivalent (NADPH2) is consumed for the reductive biosynthesis

Gluconeogenesis

Gluconeogenesis is the process in which non-carbohydrate molecules (pyruvate, lactate, glycerol, alanine and glutamine) are converted to glucose in the liver, kidneys, brain, testes and erythrocytes. Gluconeogenesis is the reverse process of glycolysis and happens mostly in the cytoplasm. It starts from conversion of pyruvate to oxalate in the mitochondria using PC and biotin as its coenzyme.

Q5. Write the concept, in short, with the help of a diagram:

(a) Physiology of Haemostasis.

(b) Cerebrospinal fluid formation and functions.

(c) Short term regulation of blood pressure .

ANSWER (a) Physiology of Haemostasis.

Definition.

Hemostasis is the mechanism that leads to cessation of bleeding from a blood vessel. It is a process that involves multiple interlinked steps. This cascade culminates into the formation of a "plug" that closes up the damaged site of the blood vessel controlling the bleeding. It begins with trauma to the lining of the blood vessel.

Stages.

The mechanism of hemostasis can divide into four stages. 1) Constriction of the blood vessel. 2) Formation of a temporary "platelet plug." 3) Activation of the coagulation cascade. 4) Formation of "fibrin plug" or the final clot.

Purpose.

Hemostasis facilitates a series of enzymatic activations that lead to the formation of a clot with platelets and fibrin polymer.This clot seals the injured area, controls and prevents further bleeding while the tissue regeneration process takes place. Once the injury starts to heal, the plug slowly remodels, and it dissolves with the restoration of normal tissue at the site of the damage.

FUNCTIONS

Hemodynamic Stability:-

- Under normal circumstances, there exists a fine balance between the procoagulant and anticoagulant pathway. This mechanism ensures control of hemorrhage as needed and cessation of pro-coagulant pathway activation beyond the injury site/or without any bleeding.
- When this equilibrium becomes compromised under any condition, this may lead to thrombotic/bleeding complications. The hemostatic system also helps in wound healing.

Cardiovascular System:-

- PGA1 and PGA2 cause peripheral arteriolar dilation. Prostacyclin produces vasodilation, and thromboxane A2 causes vasoconstriction. Prostacyclin inhibits platelet aggregation and produces vasodilation whereas thromboxane A2 and endoperoxides promote platelet aggregation and cause vasoconstriction.
- The balance between the prostacyclin and thromboxane A2 determines the degree of platelet plug formation. Thus, prostaglandins greatly influence temporary hemostasis.

CELLULAR

There are various cellular components in the process of coagulation. Most notably are those processes associated with the endothelium, platelets, and hepatocytes.

- **Endothelium.** Clotting factors III and VIII originate from the endothelial cells while the clotting factor IV comes from the plasma. Factor III, IV, and VIII all undergo K dependent gamma-carboxylation of their glutamic acid residues, which allows for binding with calcium and other ions while in the coagulation pathway.
- **Platelets.** These are non-nucleated disc-like cells created from megakaryocytes that arise from the bone marrow. They are about 2 to 3 microns in size. Some of their unique structural elements include plasma membrane, open canalicular system, spectrin and actin cytoskeleton, microtubules, mitochondria, lysosomes, granules, and peroxisomes. These cells release proteins involved in clotting and platelet aggregation.
- **Hepatocytes.** The liver produces the majority of the proteins that function as clotting factors and as anticoagulants.

Hemostasis

Vasoconstriction

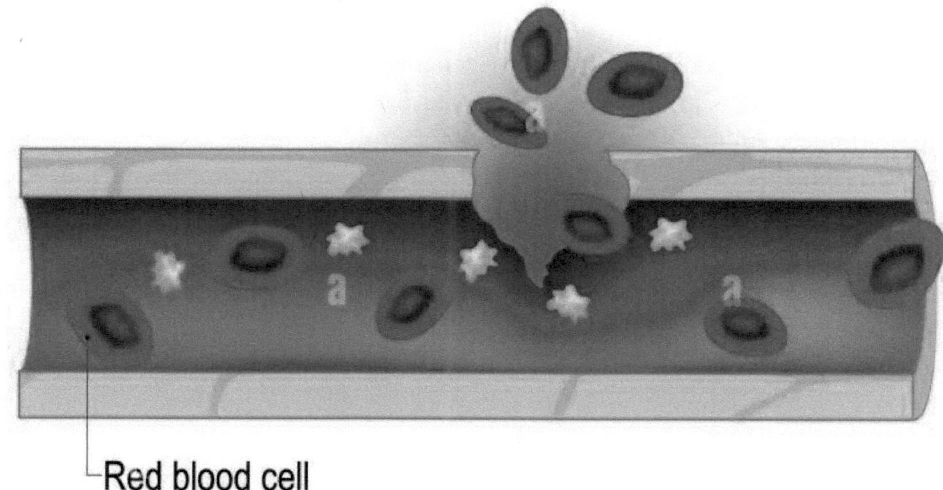

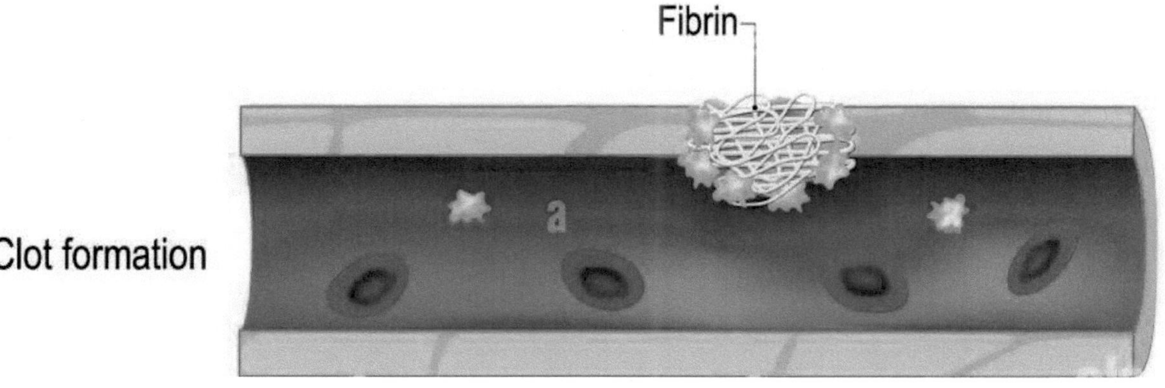

Enter Caption

ANSWER (b) Cerebrospinal fluid formation and functions

Cerebrospinal fluid (CSF) is an ultra-filtrate of plasma contained within the ventricles of the brain and the subarachnoid spaces of the cranium and spine. It performs vital functions, including providing nourishment, waste removal, and protection to the brain. Adult CSF volume is estimated to be 150 ml, with a distribution of 125 ml within the subarachnoid spaces and 25 ml within the ventricles.

MECHANISM

- CSF is continuously secreted with an unchanging composition, functioning to maintain a stable environment within the brain. CSF is propelled along the neuroaxis from the site of secretion to the site of absorption, mainly by the rhythmic systolic pulse wave within the choroidal arteries.
- Lesser determinants of CSF flow are frequency of respiration, posture, venous pressure of the jugular vein, the physical effort of the individual, and time of day.
- CSF is secreted by the CPs located within the ventricles of the brain, with the two lateral ventricles being the primary producers. CSF flows throughout the ventricular system unidirectionally in a rostral to caudal manner.
- CSF produced in the lateral ventricles travel through the interventricular foramina to the third ventricle, through the cerebral aqueduct to the fourth ventricle, and then through the median aperture (also known as the foramen of Magendie) into the subarachnoid space at the base of the brain. Once in the subarachnoid space, the CSF begins to have a gentle multidirectional flow that creates an equalization of composition throughout the CSF. The CSF flows over the surface of the brain and down the length of the spinal cord while in the subarachnoid space.
- It leaves the subarachnoid space through arachnoid villi found along the superior sagittal venous sinus, intracranial venous sinuses, and around the roots of spinal nerves.
- Arachnoid villi are protrusions of arachnoid mater through the dura mater into the lumen of a venous sinus. A 3 to 5 mmHg pressure gradient between the subarachnoid space and venous sinus pulls CSF into the venous outflow system through the arachnoid villi that help in its absorption.
- CSF may also enter into the lymphatic system via the nasal cribriform plate or spinal nerve roots. The clearance of CSF is dependent upon the posture of the individual, pressure differentials, and pathophysiology.

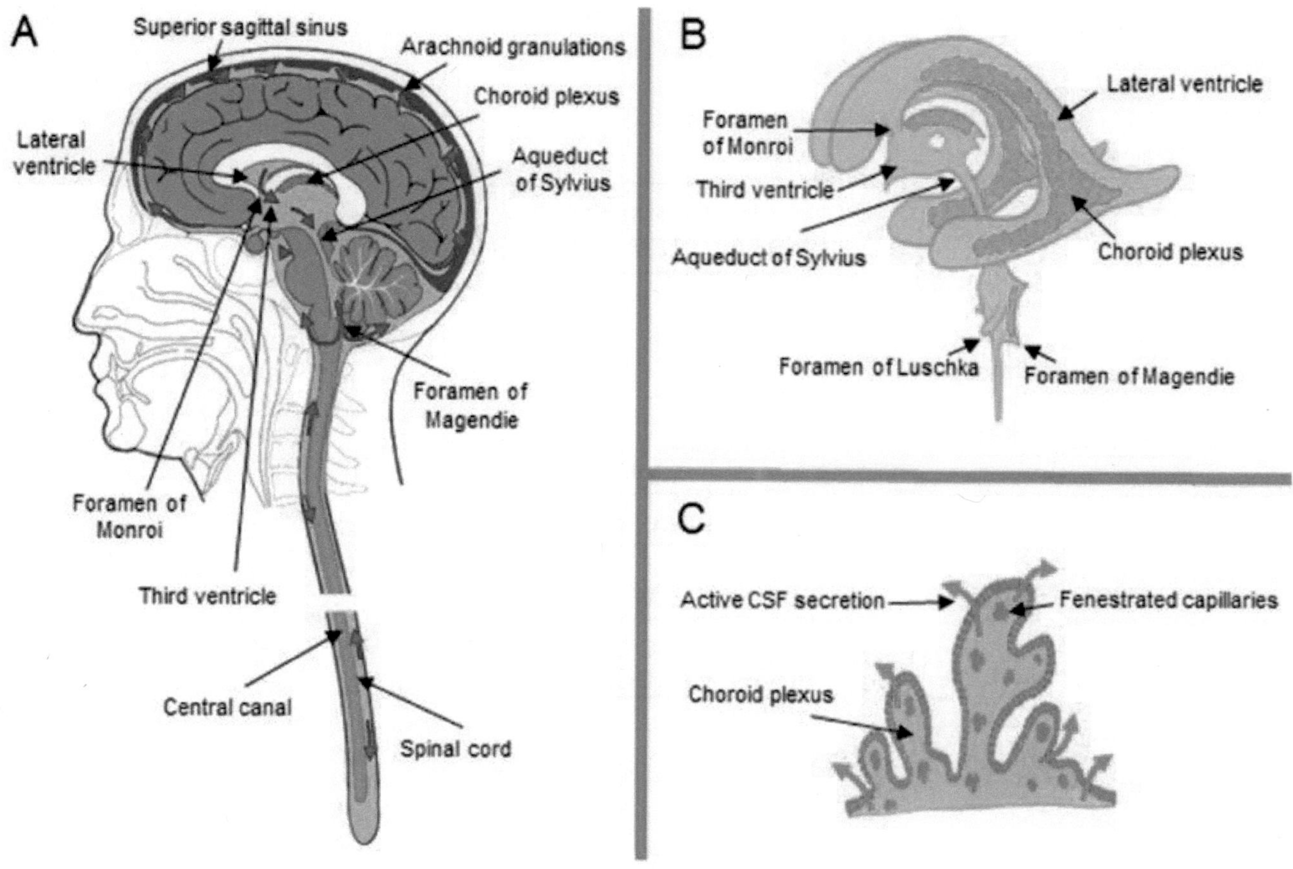

Cerebro spinal fluid

ANSWER (c) Short term regulation of blood pressure

Short-term regulation of blood pressure is controlled by the **autonomic nervous system** (ANS).

Changes in blood pressure are detected by **baroreceptors**. These are located in the arch of the aorta and the carotid sinus.

- Increased arterial pressure stretches the wall of the blood vessel, triggering the baroreceptors. These baroreceptors then feedback to the autonomic nervous system. The ANS then acts to reduce the heart rate via the efferent **parasympathetic fibres** (vagus nerve). This reduces the blood pressure.
- Decreased arterial pressure is detected by baroreceptors, which trigger a **sympathetic response.** This stimulates an increase in heart rate and cardiac contractility leading to increased blood pressure.
- Baroreceptors cannot regulate blood pressure long-term. This is because the mechanism that triggers baroreceptors resets itself once a more adequate blood pressure is restored.

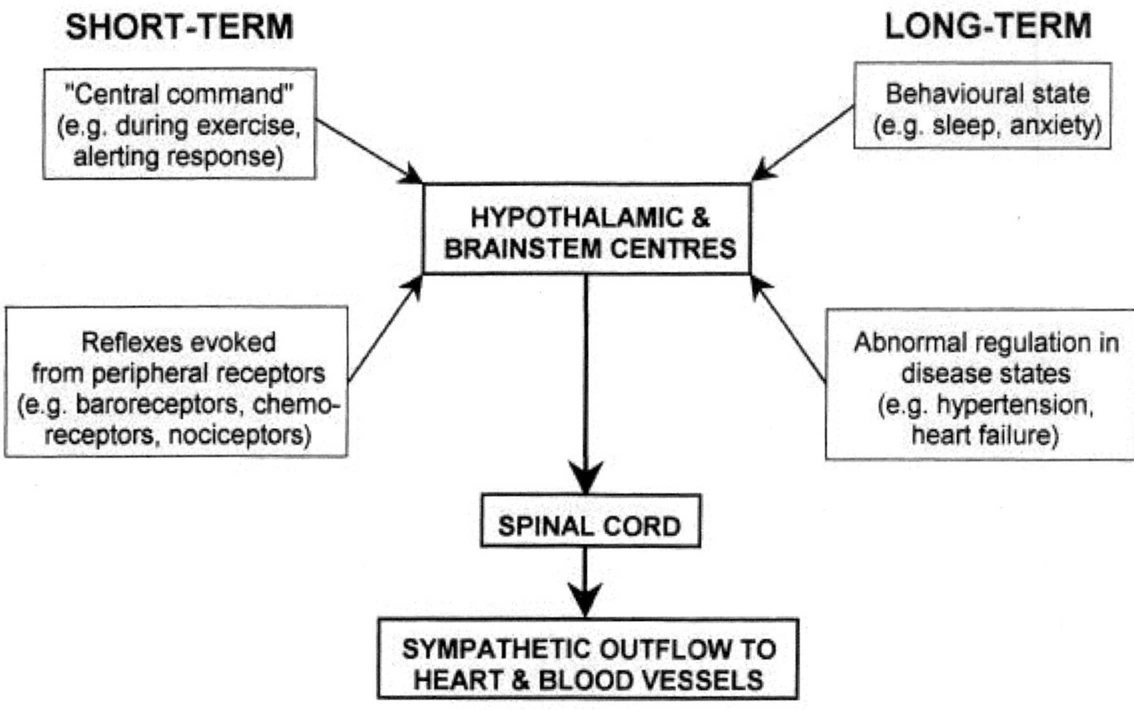

Rgulation of blood pressure

Q6. Write Features of:

(a) Lung volume and capacity

(b) Growth Hormone excess

(c) Cellular Immunity

ANSWER (a) Lung volume and capacity

Lung Volumes and Capacities

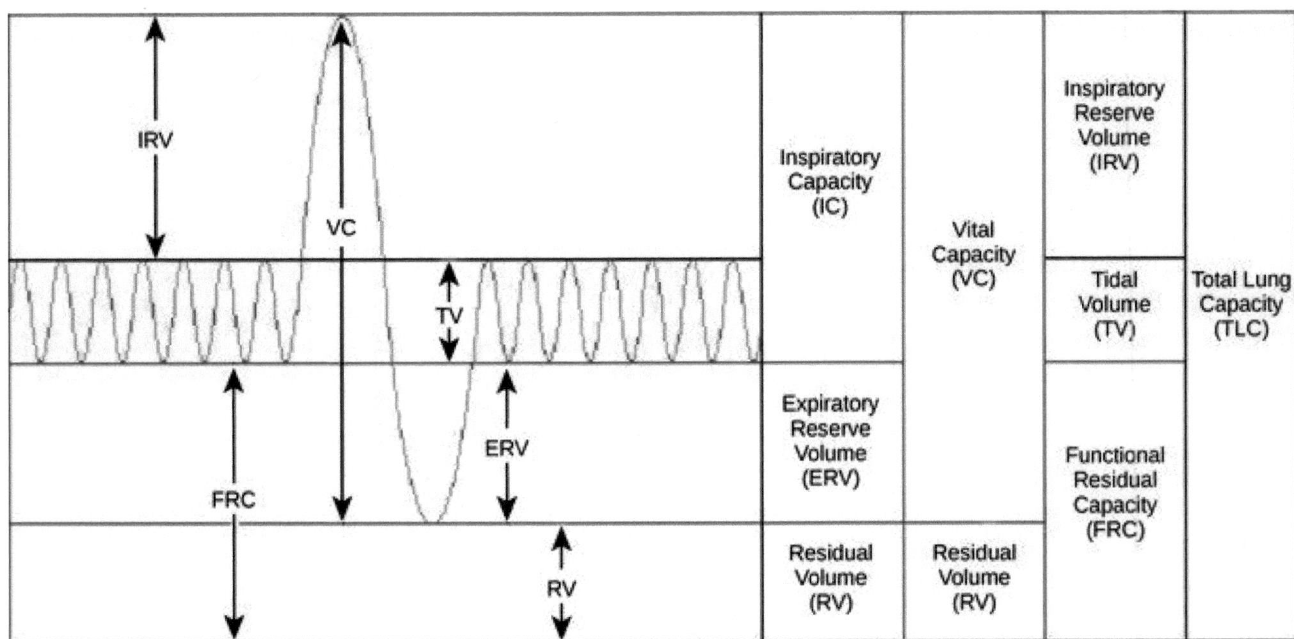

Lung Volume capacity

Human lung volumes and capacities: The total lung capacity of the adult male is six liters. Tidal volume is the volume of air inhaled in a single, normal breath. Inspiratory capacity is the amount of air taken in during a deep breath, while residual volume is the amount of air left in the lungs after forceful respiration.

Lung Volumes

- The volume in the lung can be divided into four units: tidal volume, expiratory reserve volume, inspiratory reserve volume, and residual volume. Tidal volume (TV) measures the amount of air that is inspired and expired during a normal breath. On average, this volume is around one-half liter, which is a little less than the capacity of a 20-ounce drink bottle.
- The expiratory reserve volume (ERV) is the additional amount of air that can be exhaled after a normal exhalation. It is the reserve amount that can be exhaled beyond what is normal. Conversely, the inspiratory reserve volume (IRV) is the additional amount of air that can be inhaled after a normal inhalation.
- The residual volume (RV) is the amount of air that is left after expiratory reserve volume is exhaled. The lungs are never completely empty; there is always some air left in the lungs after a maximal exhalation. If this residual volume did not exist and the lungs emptied completely, the lung tissues would stick together. The energy necessary to re-inflate the lung could be too great to overcome. Therefore, there is always some air remaining in the lungs.
- Residual volume is also important for preventing large fluctuations in respiratory gases (O_2 and CO_2). The residual volume is the only lung volume that cannot be measured directly because it is impossible to completely empty the lung of air. This volume can only be calculated rather than measured..
- Lung volumes are measured by a technique called spirometry. An important measurement taken during spirometry is the forced expiratory volume (FEV), which measures how much air can be forced out of the lung over a specific period, usually one second (FEV1). In addition, the forced vital capacity (FVC), which is the total amount of air that can be forcibly exhaled, is measured.
- The ratio of these values (FEV1/FVC ratio) is used to diagnose lung diseases including asthma, emphysema, and fibrosis. If the FEV1/FVC ratio is high, the lungs are not compliant (meaning they are stiff and unable to bend properly); the patient probably has lung fibrosis. Patients exhale most of the lung volume very quickly.
- Conversely, when the FEV1/FVC ratio is low, there is resistance in the lung that is characteristic of asthma. In this instance, it is difficult for the patient to get the air out of his or her lungs. It takes a long time to reach the maximal exhalation volume. In either case, breathing is difficult and complications arise.

Lung Capacities

- The lung capacities are measurements of two or more volumes. The vital capacity (VC) measures the maximum amount of air that can be inhaled or exhaled during a respiratory cycle. It is the sum of the expiratory reserve volume, tidal volume, and inspiratory reserve volume.
- The inspiratory capacity (IC) is the amount of air that can be inhaled after the end of a normal expiration. It is, therefore, the sum of the tidal volume and inspiratory reserve volume. The functional residual capacity (FRC) includes the expiratory reserve volume and the residual volume. The FRC measures the amount of additional air that can be exhaled after a normal exhalation.
- The total lung capacity (TLC) is a measurement of the total amount of air that the lung can hold. It is the sum of the residual volume, expiratory reserve volume, tidal volume, and inspiratory reserve volume.

ANSWER(b) Growth Hormone excess

Acromegaly is a hormonal disorder that develops when your pituitary gland produces too much growth hormone during adulthood.

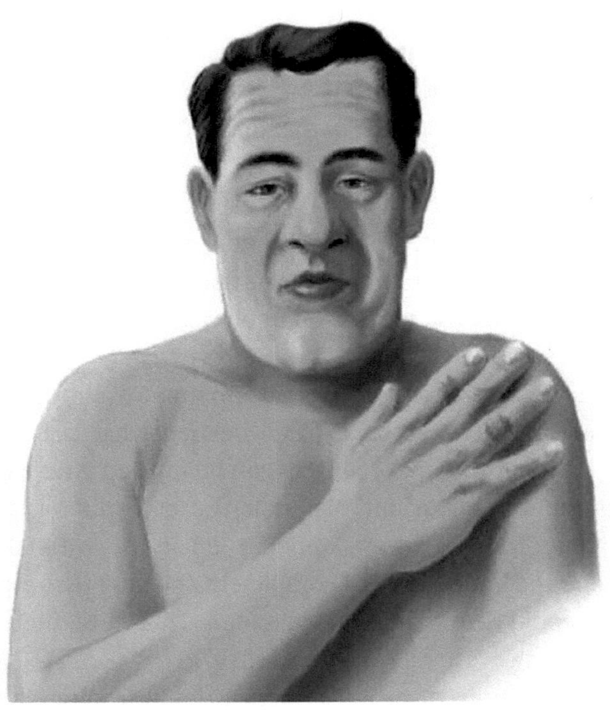

Acromegaly

Symptoms

A common sign of acromegaly is enlarged hands and feet. For example, you may notice that you aren't able to put on rings that used to fit, and that your shoe size has progressively increased.

Acromegaly may also cause gradual changes in your face's shape, such as a protruding lower jaw and brow bone, an enlarged nose, thickened lips, and wider spacing between your teeth.

Because acromegaly tends to progress slowly, early signs may not be obvious for years. Sometimes, people notice the physical changes only by comparing old photos with newer ones.

Overall, acromegaly signs and symptoms tend to vary from one person to another, and may include any of the following:

- Enlarged hands and feet
- Enlarged facial features, including the facial bones, lips, nose and tongue
- Coarse, oily, thickened skin
- Excessive sweating and body odor
- Small outgrowths of skin tissue (skin tags)
- Fatigue and joint or muscle weakness
- Pain and limited joint mobility
- A deepened, husky voice due to enlarged vocal cords and sinuses
- Severe snoring due to obstruction of the upper airway
- Vision problems
- Headaches, which may be persistent or severe
- Menstrual cycle irregularities in women
- Erectile dysfunction in men
- Loss of interest in sex

CAUSES

Acromegaly occurs when the pituitary gland produces too much growth hormone (GH) over a long period of time.

The pituitary gland is a small gland at the base of your brain, behind the bridge of your nose. It produces GH and a number of other hormones. GH plays an important role in managing your physical growth.

When the pituitary gland releases GH into your bloodstream, it triggers your liver to produce a hormone called insulin-like growth factor-1 (IGF-1) — sometimes also called insulin-like growth factor-I, or IGF-I. IGF-1 is what causes your bones and other tissues to grow. Too much GH leads to too much IGF-1, which can cause acromegaly signs, symptoms and complications.

In adults, a tumor is the most common cause of too much GH production:

- **Pituitary tumors.** Most acromegaly cases are caused by a noncancerous (benign) tumor (adenoma) of the pituitary gland. The tumor produces excessive amounts of growth hormone, causing many of the signs and symptoms of acromegaly. Some of the symptoms of acromegaly, such as headaches and impaired vision, are due to the tumor pressing on nearby brain tissues.
- **Nonpituitary tumors.** In a few people with acromegaly, tumors in other parts of the body, such as the lungs or pancreas, cause the disorder. Sometimes, these tumors secrete GH. In other cases, the tumors produce a hormone called growth hormone-releasing hormone (GH-RH), which signals the pituitary gland to make more GH.

Complications

If left untreated, acromegaly can lead to major health problems. Complications may include:

- High blood pressure (hypertension)
- High cholesterol
- Heart problems, particularly enlargement of the heart (cardiomyopathy)
- Osteoarthritis
- Type 2 diabetes
- Enlargement of the thyroid gland (goiter)
- Precancerous growths (polyps) on the lining of your colon
- Sleep apnea, a condition in which breathing repeatedly stops and starts during sleep
- Carpal tunnel syndrome
- Increased risk of cancerous tumors
- Spinal cord compression or fractures
- Vision changes or vision loss

Early treatment of acromegaly can prevent these complications from developing or becoming worse. Untreated, acromegaly and its complications can lead to premature death.

ANSWER(c) Cellular Immunity

- Cellular immunity is mediated by *T lymphocytes*, also called T cells. Their name refers to the organ from which they're produced: the thymus. This type of immunity promotes the destruction of microbes residing in phagocytes, or the killing of infected cells to eliminate reservoirs of infection.
- T cells do not produce antibody molecules. They have antigen receptors that are structurally related to antibodies. These structures help recognize antigens only in the form of peptides displayed on the surface of antigen-presenting cells.
- T cells consist of functionally distinct populations. These include naive T cells that recognize antigens and are activated in peripheral lymphoid organs. This activation results in the expansion of the antigen-specific lymphocyte pool and the differentiation of these cells into effector and memory cells. Effector cells include helper

T cells, and cytolytic or cytotoxic T cells.

- In response to antigenic stimulation, helper T cells (characterized by the expression of CD4 marker on their surface) secrete proteins called cytokines, whose function is to stimulate the proliferation and differentiation of the T cells themselves, as well as other cells, including B cells, macrophages, and other leukocytes. Cytolytic or cytotoxic T cells (characterized by the expression of CD8 marker on their surface) kill cells that produce foreign antigens, such as cells infected by viruses and other intracellular microbes.

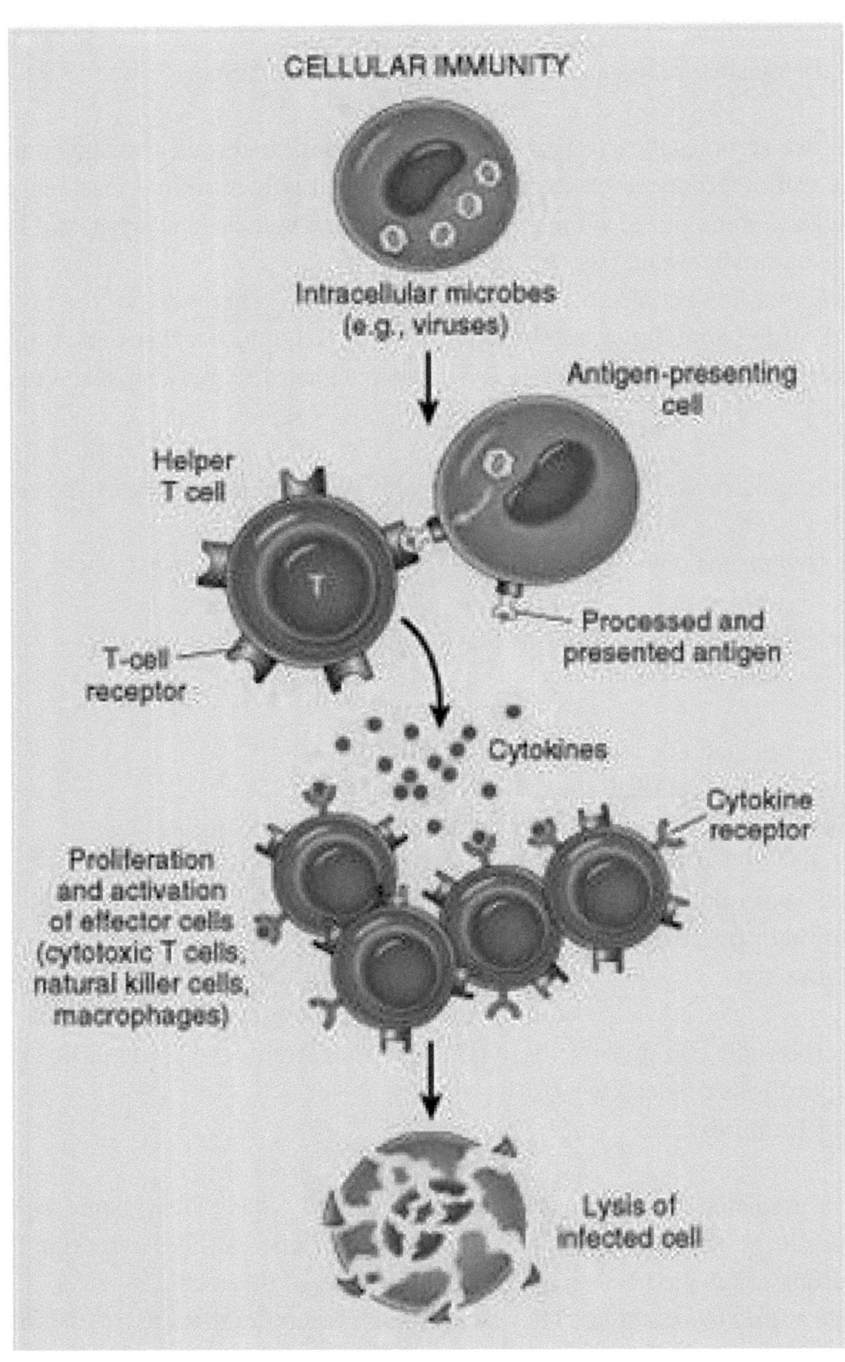

CHAPTER V

Question Paper2018

B.Sc Nursing 1st year ,annual exam, 2018
Anatomy and physiology

Note Marks 75

1. attempt all questions and draw suitable diagrams, tables, and graphs where required.

2.attempt part-1 and part-2 in separate answer book.

Part –I anatomy

Q1. Describe in detail:

(a) Describe the formation of long bone. Discuss its blood supply.

(b) Describe different parts of the brain

(c) Classify joints with one example of each. Discuss salient Features of a typical synovial joint

Q2. Draw a well labelled diagram to illustrate the following:

(a) Thyroid gland

(b) Cerebrospinal fluid (CSF) circulation

(C) Urinary Bladder

Q3. Write short note on

(a) Stomach

(b) Bronchopulmonary segments

(c) Kidney

Part-II (Physiology)

Q4. Write short notes on:

(a) Spermatogenesis

(b) Factors regulating cardiac output4

(c) Juxta glomerular apparatus

Q5. Write the concept, in short, with the help of a diagram:

(a) Visual pathway

(b) Regulation of ovarian hormones

(c) Structure of neuron

Q6. Write Features of:

(a) Hyperthyroidism

(b) Gigantism

(c) Plasma proteins

Q1. Describe in detail:

(a) Describe the formation of long bone. Discuss its blood supply.

(b) Describe different parts of the brain

(c) Classify joints with one example of each. Discuss salient Features of a typical synovial joint

ANSWER(a)Describe the formation of long bone. Discuss its blood supply.

BASIC ANATOMY OF THE LONG BONE

The elongated central part of the long bone is called the diaphysis. The enlarged area of the bone at the ends is called the epiphysis and the intermediate bone segment between the two is called the metaphysics. The articular ends of the epiphyseal surface is covered by articular cartilage .The rest of the bone is covered by tough connective tissue called the periosteum. The nutrient foramen is an oblique canal usually situated in the diaphysis of the long bone.

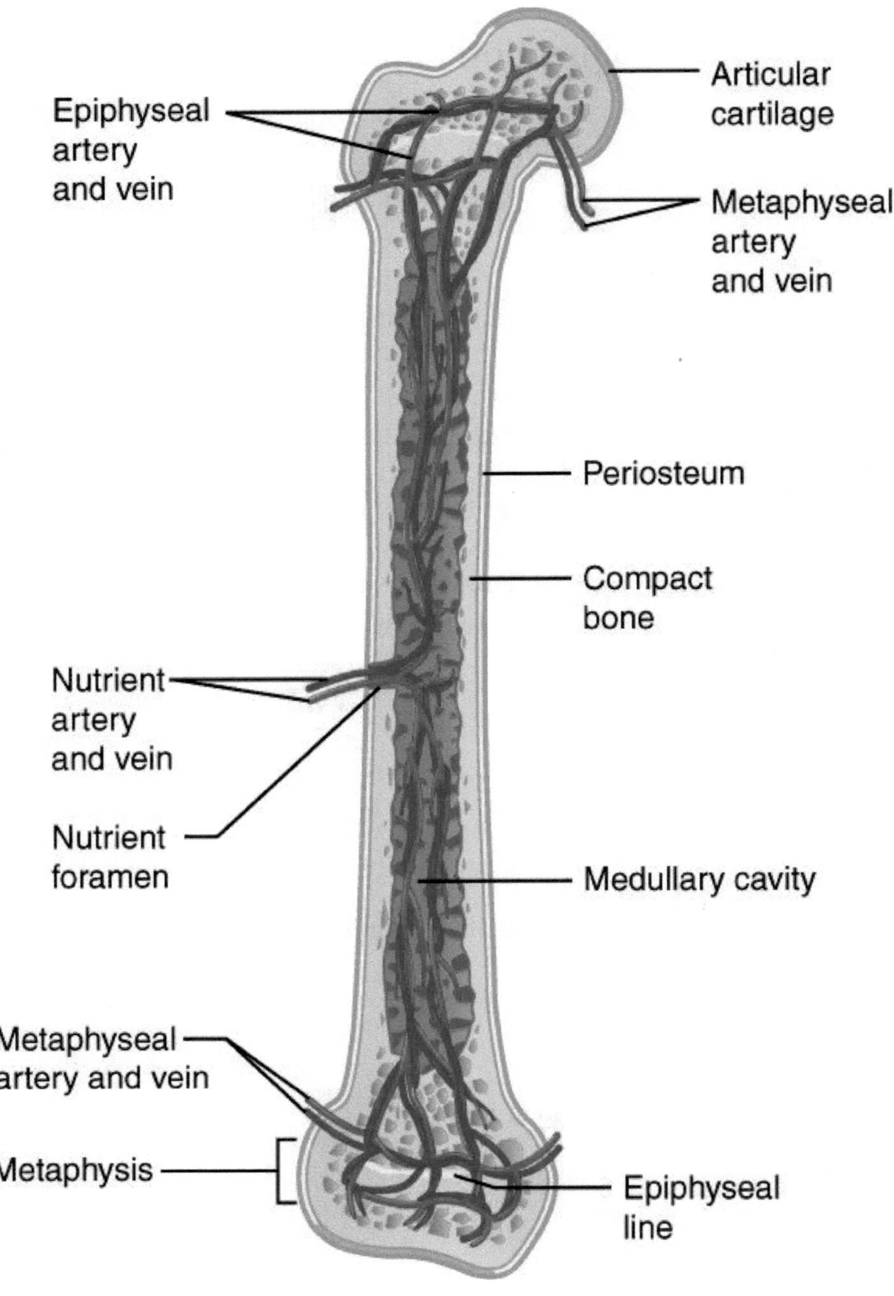

Long bone

ARTERIAL SUPPLY OF THE LONG BONE:-

Blood supply of the long bone accounts for 5-10% of the cardiac output. A typical long bone receives blood supply from various sources. They are the Nutrient arteries , Epiphyseal arteries , Metaphyseal arteries and periosteal arteries .

THE NUTRIENT ARTERY:-

The nutrient artery supplies directly from major systemic arteries. It enters the long bone through the nutrient foramen. It then divides into ascending and descending branches. These branches gives of smaller parallel arteries called the radial branches .These branches supply the bone marrow and inner third of the compact bone of the diaphysis. The ascending and descending branches at the metaphysis divides into smaller spiral branches which anastomoses with the metaphyseal and epiphyseal arteries.

THE METAPHYSEAL ARTERY:-

Metaphyseal arteries arising from the anastomosis around the joint enters the metaphysis at the margin of the capsule attachment. These anastomose with the spiral arteries making the metaphysic the most vascular area of the long bone.

THE EPIPHYSEAL ARTERY:-

Epiphyseal arteries are derived from periarticular vascular arcades. The epiphysis has openings that allows arteries to go in and out. In children the epiphyseal arteries are separated from the metaphyseal arteries due to the presence of an epiphyseal plate. In adults the epiphysis and metaphysis is fused together following the arrest of growth plate. Here the epiphyseal arteries freely anastomose with metaphyseal and nutrient arteries.

When epiphyseal cartilage and articular cartilage are continuous, the epiphyseal artery pierces the epiphyseal cartilage and supplies the epiphysis. If these arteries are damaged in epiphyseal separation, avascular necrosis may occur. In other bones where the epiphyseal cartilage is not continuous with the articular cartilage, the epiphyseal vessels enter the bone without piercing the growth plate. This helps in preventing avascular necrosis on epiphyseal separation.

THE PERIOSTEAL ARTERY:-

The periosteum has rich blood supply from the blood vessels that anastomose beneath the periosteum. Periosteal arteries act as a low-pressure system and penetrate bone at the sides of attachment of the facial sheath or aponeurosis. They enter the Volksmann canal and supply roughly the outer one third of the compact bone of the diaphysis.

VENOUS DRAINAGE: -

Long bones drain into central venous sinus, then drains to nutrient veins, then to periosteal vein and to emissary veins successively.

ANSWER(b) Describe different parts of the brain

- The brain is an amazing three-pound organ that controls all functions of the body, interprets information from the outside world, and embodies the essence of the mind and soul. Intelligence, creativity, emotion, and memory are a few of the many things governed by the brain. Protected within the skull, the brain is composed of the cerebrum, cerebellum, and brainstem.
- The brain receives information through our five senses: sight, smell, touch, taste, and hearing - often many at one time. It assembles the messages in a way that has meaning for us, and can store that information in our memory.
- The brain controls our thoughts, memory and speech, movement of the arms and legs, and the function of many organs within our body.
- The central nervous system (CNS) is composed of the brain and spinal cord. The peripheral nervous system (PNS) is composed of spinal nerves that branch from the spinal cord and cranial nerves that branch from the brain.

Brain

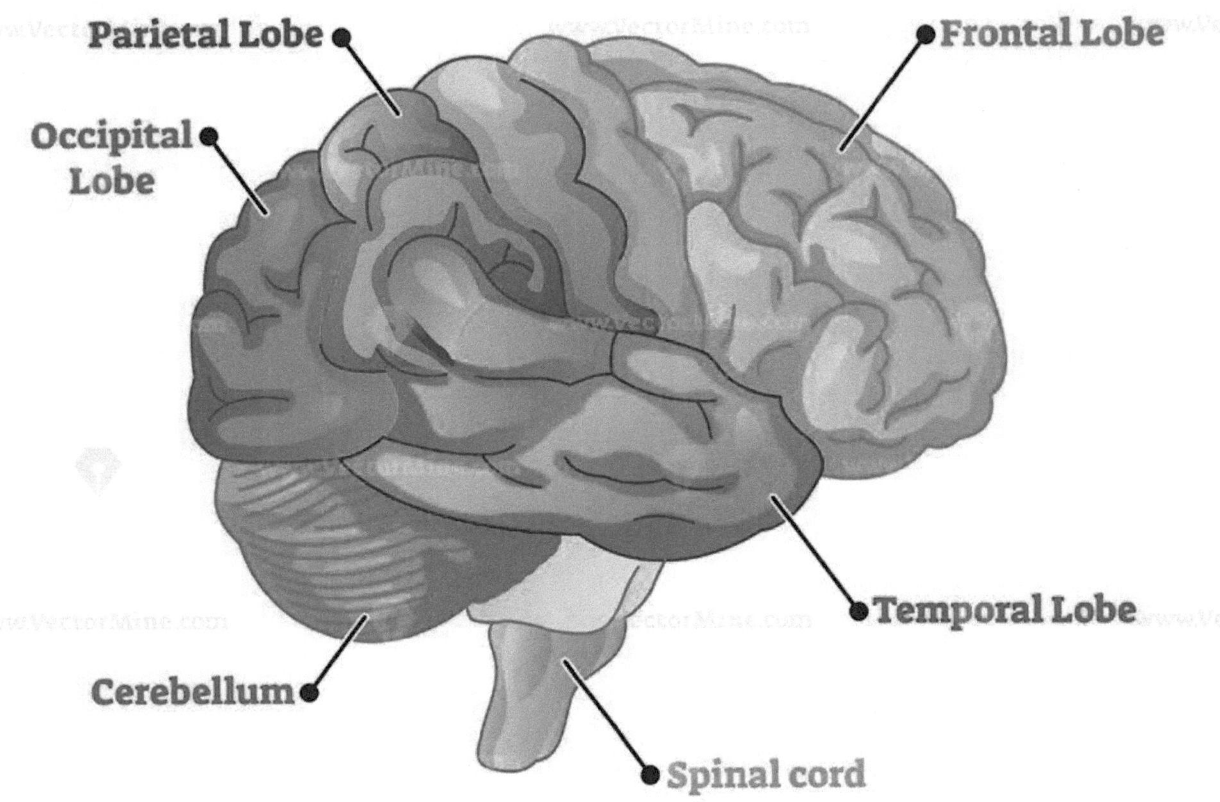

Human Brain

The brain has three main parts: the cerebrum, cerebellum and brainstem.

Cerebrum: is the largest part of the brain and is composed of right and left hemispheres. It performs higher functions like interpreting touch, vision and hearing, as well as speech, reasoning, emotions, learning, and fine control of movement.

Cerebellum: is located under the cerebrum. Its function is to coordinate muscle movements, maintain posture, and balance.

Brainstem: acts as a relay center connecting the cerebrum and cerebellum to the spinal cord. It performs many automatic functions such as breathing, heart rate, body temperature, wake and sleep cycles, digestion, sneezing, coughing, vomiting, and swallowing.

ANSWER (c) Classify joints with one example of each. Discuss salient Features of a typical synovial joint

According to the structural classification of joints, they are divided into 3 types, namely:

Fibrous Joints

Fixed joints, also called immovable joints, are found where bones are not flexible. In such joints, bones have been fused together in such a way that they are fixed to that part, most commonly to create a structure. A prominent example of a fixed joint is the skull, which is made up of a number of fused bones.

Other examples include the upper jaw, rib cage, backbone, and pelvic bone, etc.

Cartilaginous Joints

Cartilaginous joints are partly movable joints comprising of symphysis or synchondrosis joints. These joints occur only in those regions where the connection between the articulating bones is made up of cartilage. Synchondrosis are temporary cartilaginous joints which are present in young children and last until the end of their puberty.

For example, the epiphyseal plates present at each end of the long bones is responsible for bone growth in children. The symphysis or the secondary cartilaginous joints (the place where bones join) is permanent. Examples include the pubic symphysis. Other examples of cartilaginous types of joints include the spinal column and the ribcage.

Synovial Joints

The synovial joints are the most common type of joint because this joint helps us to perform a wide range of motion such as walking, running, typing and more. Synovial joints are flexible, movable, can slide over one another, rotatable and so on. These joints are found in our shoulder joint, neck joint, knee joint, wrist joint, etc.

Synovial joints are the most common type of joint in the body. A key structural characteristic for a synovial joint that is not seen at fibrous or cartilaginous joints is the presence of a joint cavity. This fluid-filled space is the site at which the articulating surfaces of the bones contact each other. At synovial joints, the articular surfaces of bones are covered with smooth articular cartilage. This gives the bones of a synovial joint the ability to move smoothly against each other, allowing for increased joint mobility.

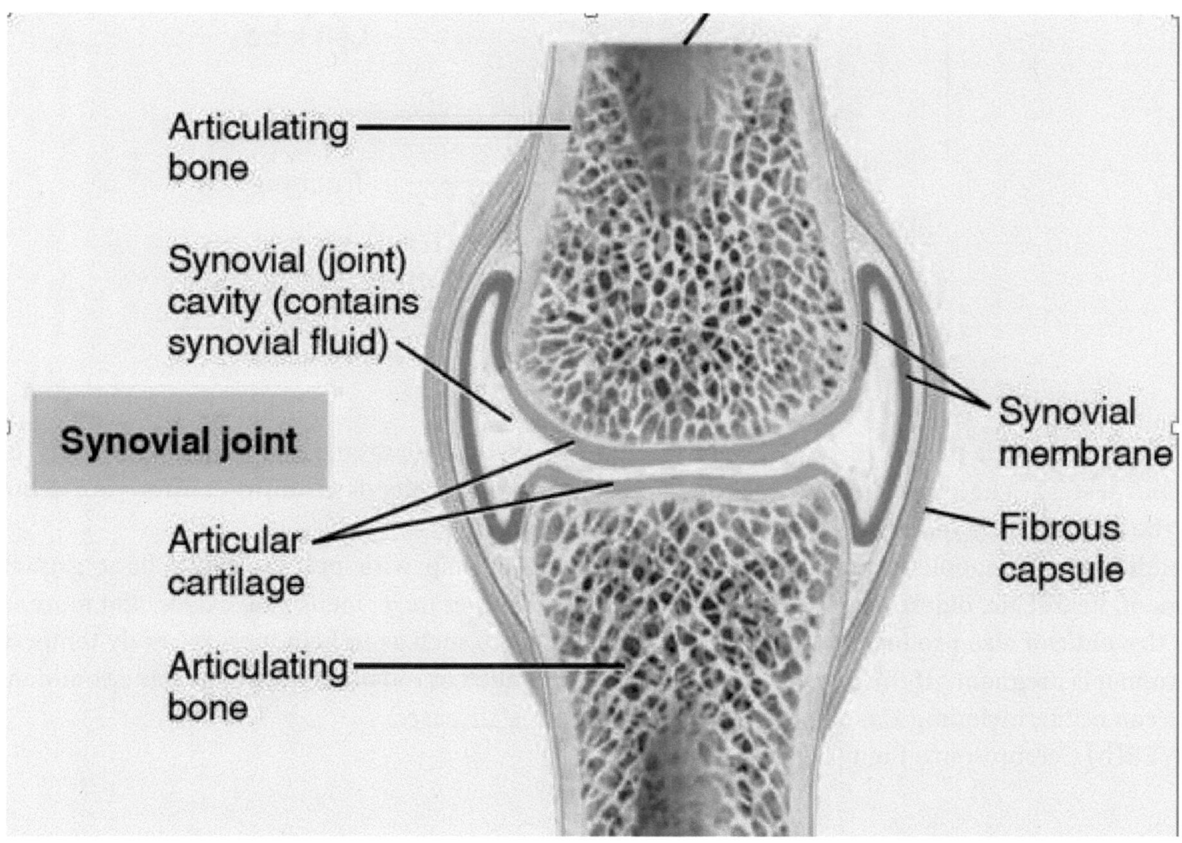

Joints: Synovial joints allow for smooth movements between the adjacent bones. The joint is surrounded by an articular capsule that defines a joint cavity filled with synovial fluid. The articulating surfaces of the bones are covered by a thin layer of articular cartilage. Ligaments support the joint by holding the bones together and resisting excess or abnormal joint motions.

Q2. <u>Draw a well labelled diagram to illustrate the following</u>

(a) Thyroid gland

(b) Cerebrospinal fluid (CSF) circulation

(C) Urinary Bladder

ANSWER(a) Thyroid gland

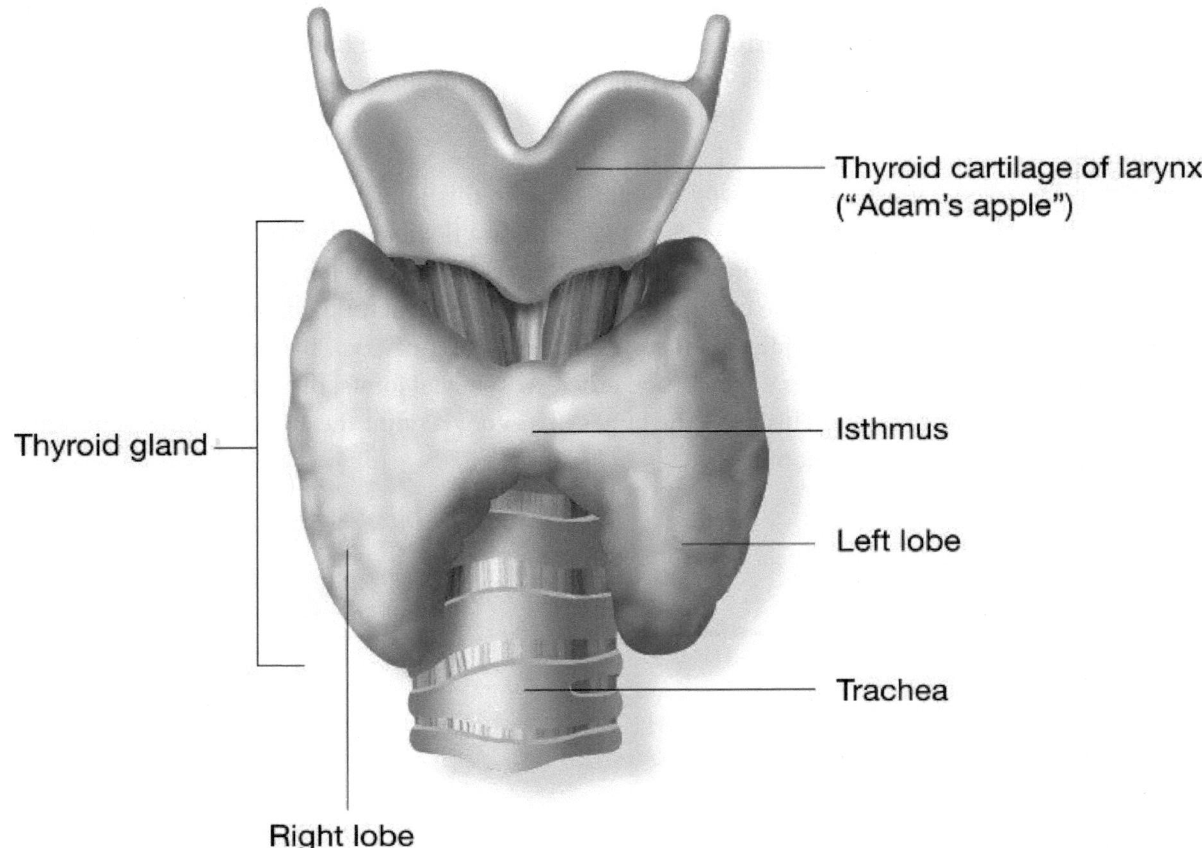

1.The thyroid gland is part of the endocrine system (along with the adrenal glands, hypothalamus, pituitary, ovaries, and testes). The thyroid gland releases hormones into the bloodstream to control your metabolism, which is the primary way your body uses energy.

2.In addition to metabolism, the hormones it releases also help with processes like bone growth, brain development, heart rate, digestion, muscle functioning, body temperature, menstrual cycles, and more.

3.The thyroid can also produce more hormones when needed, such as to help increase body temperature or when a woman is pregnant.[1] If the thyroid gland produces too much or too little hormones some common thyroid disorders can occur, including Hashimoto's disease and Graves' disease.

ANSWER(b) Cerebrospinal fluid (CSF) circulation

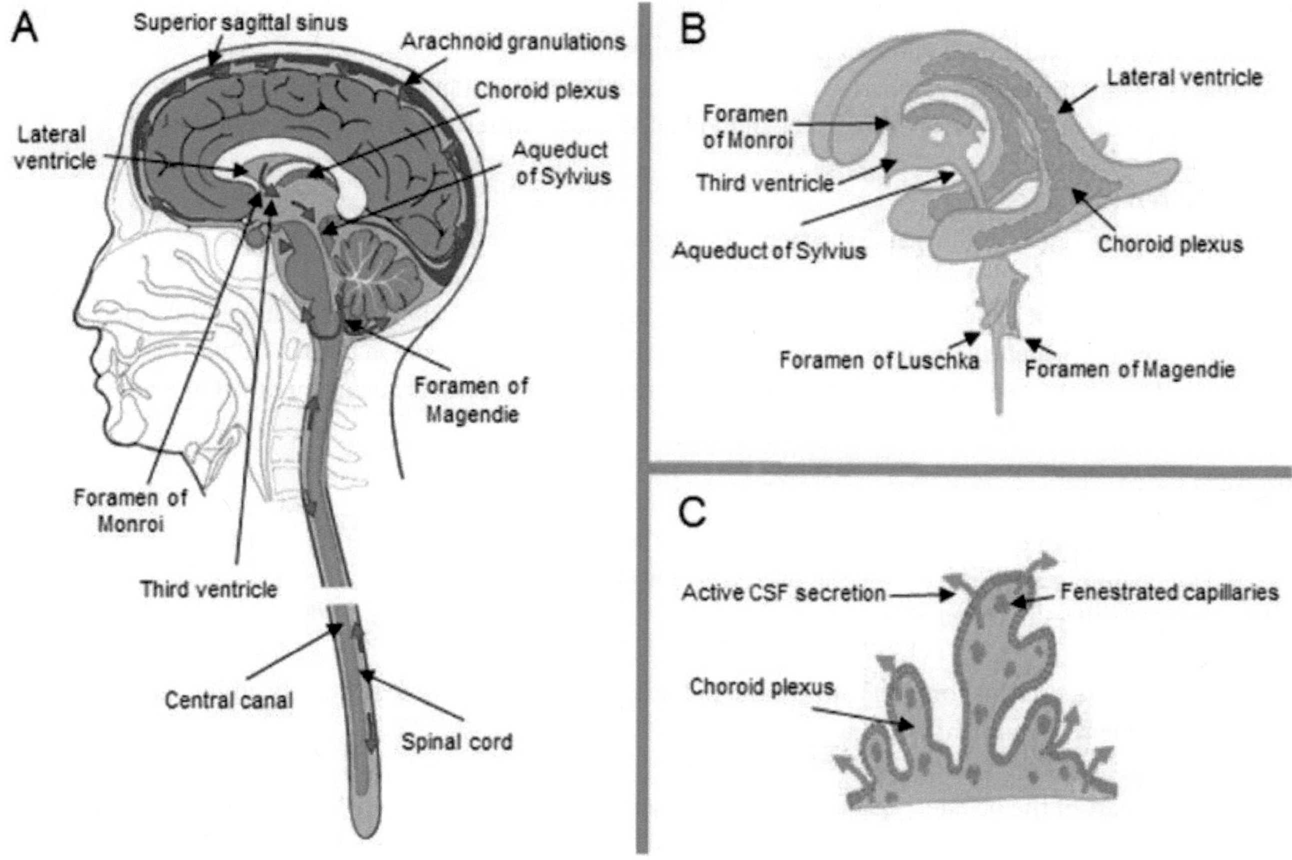

Cerebro Spinal fluid

Cerebrospinal fluid (CSF) is an ultra-filtrate of plasma contained within the ventricles of the brain and the subarachnoid spaces of the cranium and spine. It performs vital functions, including providing nourishment, waste removal, and protection to the brain. Adult CSF volume is estimated to be 150 ml, with a distribution of 125 ml within the subarachnoid spaces and 25 ml within the ventricles.

MECHANISM

- CSF is continuously secreted with an unchanging composition, functioning to maintain a stable environment within the brain. CSF is propelled along the neuroaxis from the site of secretion to the site of absorption, mainly by the rhythmic systolic pulse wave within the choroidal arteries.
- Lesser determinants of CSF flow are frequency of respiration, posture, venous pressure of the jugular vein, the physical effort of the individual, and time of day.
- CSF is secreted by the CPs located within the ventricles of the brain, with the two lateral ventricles being the primary producers. CSF flows throughout the ventricular system unidirectionally in a rostral to caudal manner.
- CSF produced in the lateral ventricles travel through the interventricular foramina to the third ventricle, through the cerebral aqueduct to the fourth ventricle, and then through the median aperture (also known as the foramen of Magendie) into the subarachnoid space at the base of the brain. Once in the subarachnoid space, the CSF begins to have a gentle multidirectional flow that creates an equalization of composition throughout the CSF. The CSF flows over the surface of the brain and down the length of the spinal cord while in the subarachnoid space.
- It leaves the subarachnoid space through arachnoid villi found along the superior sagittal venous sinus, intracranial venous sinuses, and around the roots of spinal nerves.

- Arachnoid villi are protrusions of arachnoid mater through the dura mater into the lumen of a venous sinus. A 3 to 5 mmHg pressure gradient between the subarachnoid space and venous sinus pulls CSF into the venous outflow system through the arachnoid villi that help in its absorption.
- CSF may also enter into the lymphatic system via the nasal cribriform plate or spinal nerve roots. The clearance of CSF is dependent upon the posture of the individual, pressure differentials, and pathophysiology.

ANSWER (C) Urinary Bladder

The **bladder** is an organ of the urinary system. It plays two main roles:

- **Temporary storage of urine** – the bladder is a hollow organ with distensible walls. It has a folded internal lining (known as rugae), which allows it to accommodate up to 400-600ml of urine in healthy adults.
- **Assists in the expulsion of urine** – the musculature of the bladder contracts during micturition, with concomitant relaxation of the sphincters.

Shape of the Bladder

The appearance of the bladder varies depending on the amount of urine stored. When full, it exhibits an **oval** shape, and when empty it is flattened by the overlying bowel.

The external features of the bladder are:

- **Apex** – located superiorly, pointing towards the pubic symphysis. It is connected to the umbilicus by the median umbilical ligament (a remnant of the urachus).

- **Body** – main part of the bladder, located between the apex and the fundus

- **Fundus (orbase)**– located posteriorly. It is triangular-shaped, with the tip of the triangle pointing backwards.

- **Neck** – formed by the convergence of the fundus and the two inferolateral surfaces. It is continuous with the urethra.

Urine enters the bladder through the left and right ureters, and exits via the urethra. Internally, these orifices are marked by the **trigone** – a triangular area located within the fundus.

In contrast to the rest of the internal bladder, the trigone has smooth walls (this is explained by the different embryological origin: the trigone is developed by the integration of two **mesonephric ducts** at the base of the bladder).

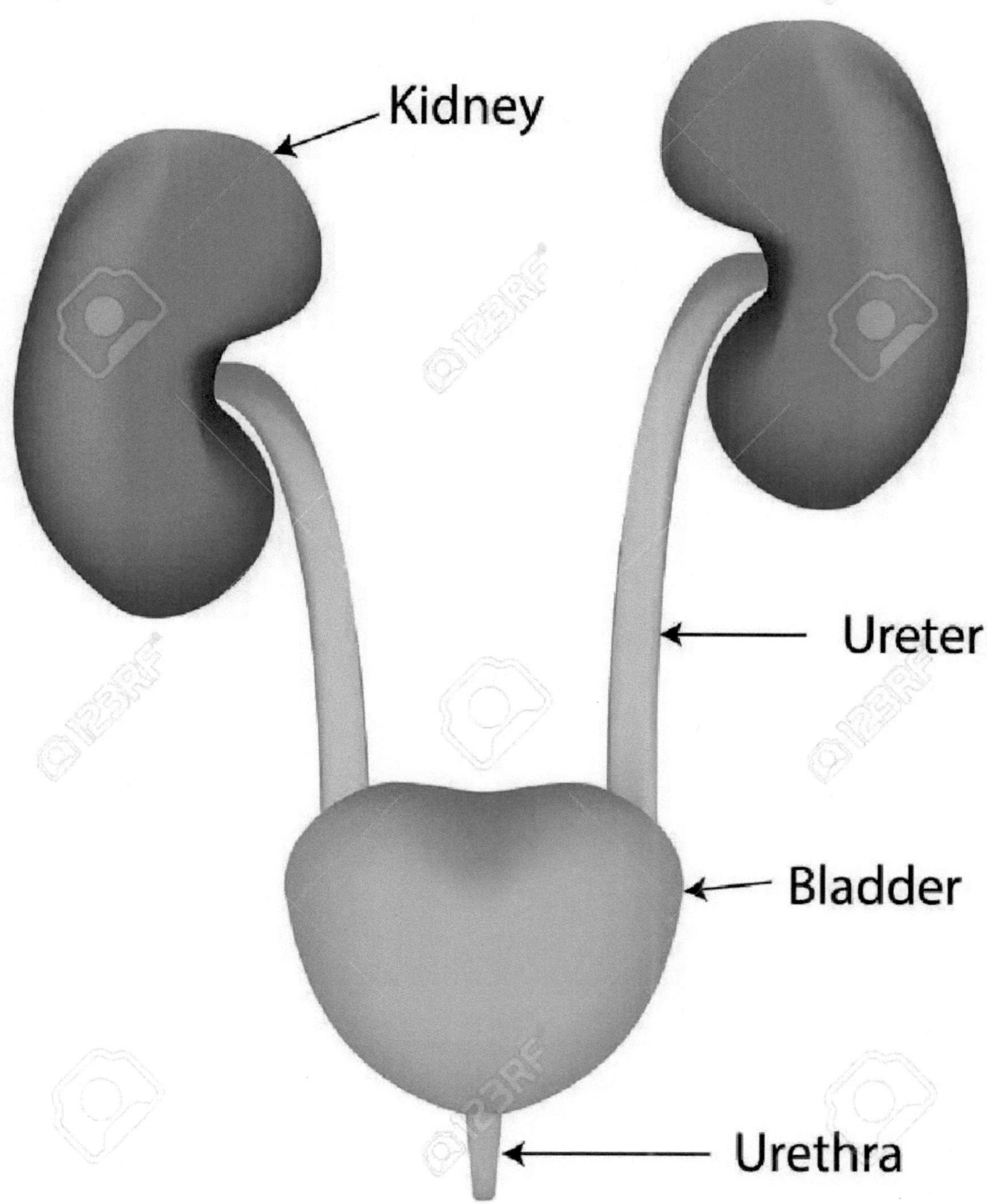

Q3. Write short note on

(a) Stomach

(b) Bronchopulmonary segments

(c) Kidney

Answer(a) Stomach

The stomach is a muscular organ located on the left side of the upper abdomen. The stomach receives food from the esophagus. As food reaches the end of the esophagus, it enters the stomach through a muscular valve called the lower esophageal sphincter.

The stomach secretes acid and enzymes that digest food. Ridges of muscle tissue called rugae line the stomach. The stomach muscles contract periodically, churning food to enhance digestion. The pyloric sphincter is a muscular valve that opens to allow food to pass from the stomach to the small intestine.

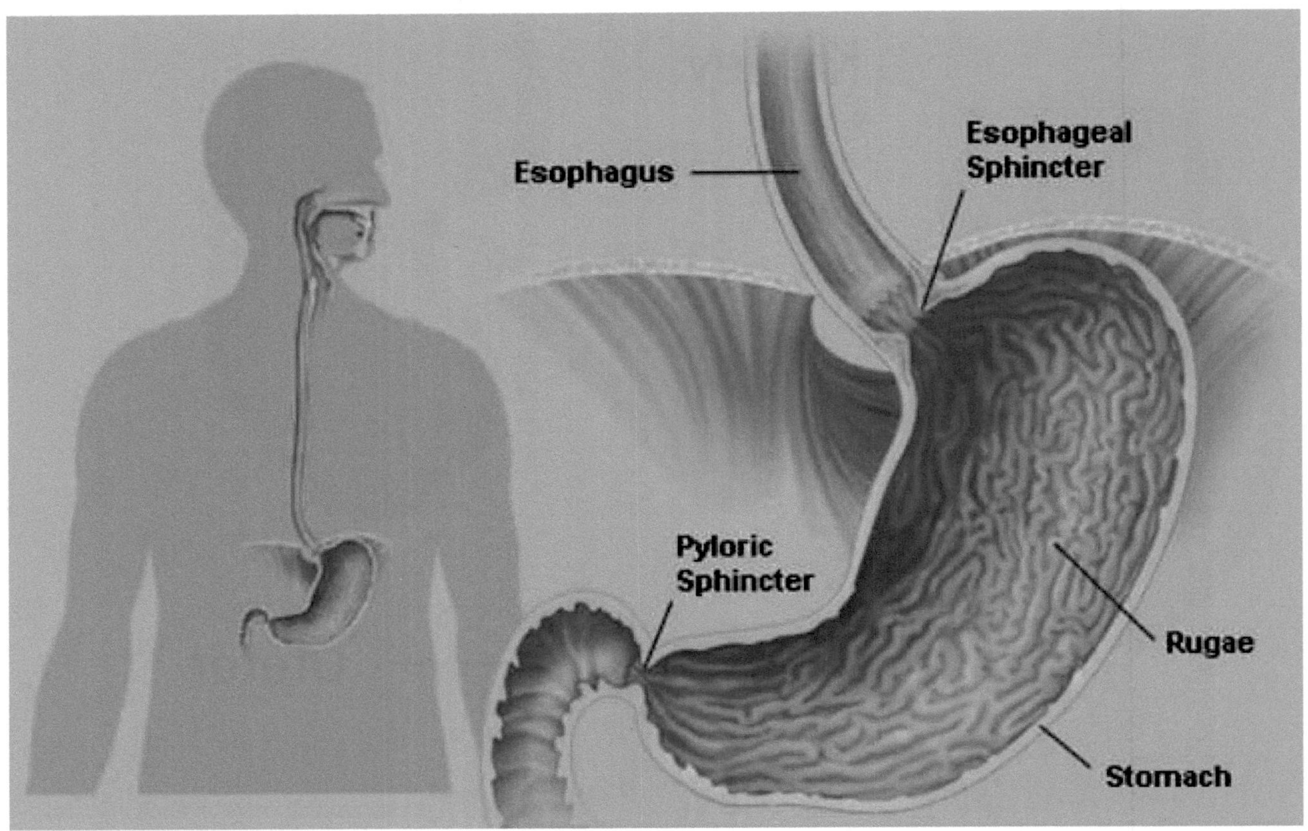

Stomach

Stomach Conditions

- Gastroesophageal reflux: Stomach contents, including acid, can travel backward up the oesophagus. There may be no symptoms, or reflux may cause heartburn or coughing.
- Gastroesophageal reflux disease (GERD): When symptoms of reflux become bothersome or occur frequently, they're called GERD. Infrequently, GERD can cause serious problems of the oesophagus.
- Dyspepsia: Another name for stomach upset or indigestion. Dyspepsia may be caused by almost any benign or serious condition that affects the stomach.
- Gastric ulcer (stomach ulcer): An erosion in the lining of the stomach, often causing pain and/or bleeding. Gastric ulcers are most often caused by NSAIDs or *H. pylori* infection.
- Peptic ulcer disease: Doctors consider ulcers in either the stomach or the duodenum (the first part of the small intestine) peptic ulcer disease.
- Gastritis: Inflammation of the stomach, often causing nausea and/or pain. Gastritis can be caused by alcohol, certain medications, *H. pylori* infection, or other factors.

- Stomach cancer: Gastric cancer is an uncommon form of cancer in the U.S. Adenocarcinoma and lymphoma make up most of the cases of stomach cancer.
- Zollinger-Ellison syndrome (ZES): One or more tumours that secrete hormones that lead to increased acid production. Severe GERD and peptic ulcer disease result from this rare disorder.
- Gastric varices: In people with severe liver disease, veins in the stomach may swell and bulge under increased pressure. Called varices, these veins are at high risk for bleeding, although less so than oesophageal varices are.
- Stomach bleeding: Gastritis, ulcers, or gastric cancers may bleed. Seeing blood or black material in vomit or stool is usually a medical emergency.
- Gastroparesis (delayed gastric emptying): Nerve damage from diabetes or other conditions may impair the stomach's muscle contractions. Nausea and vomiting are the usual symptoms.

Answer (b) Bronchopulmonary segments

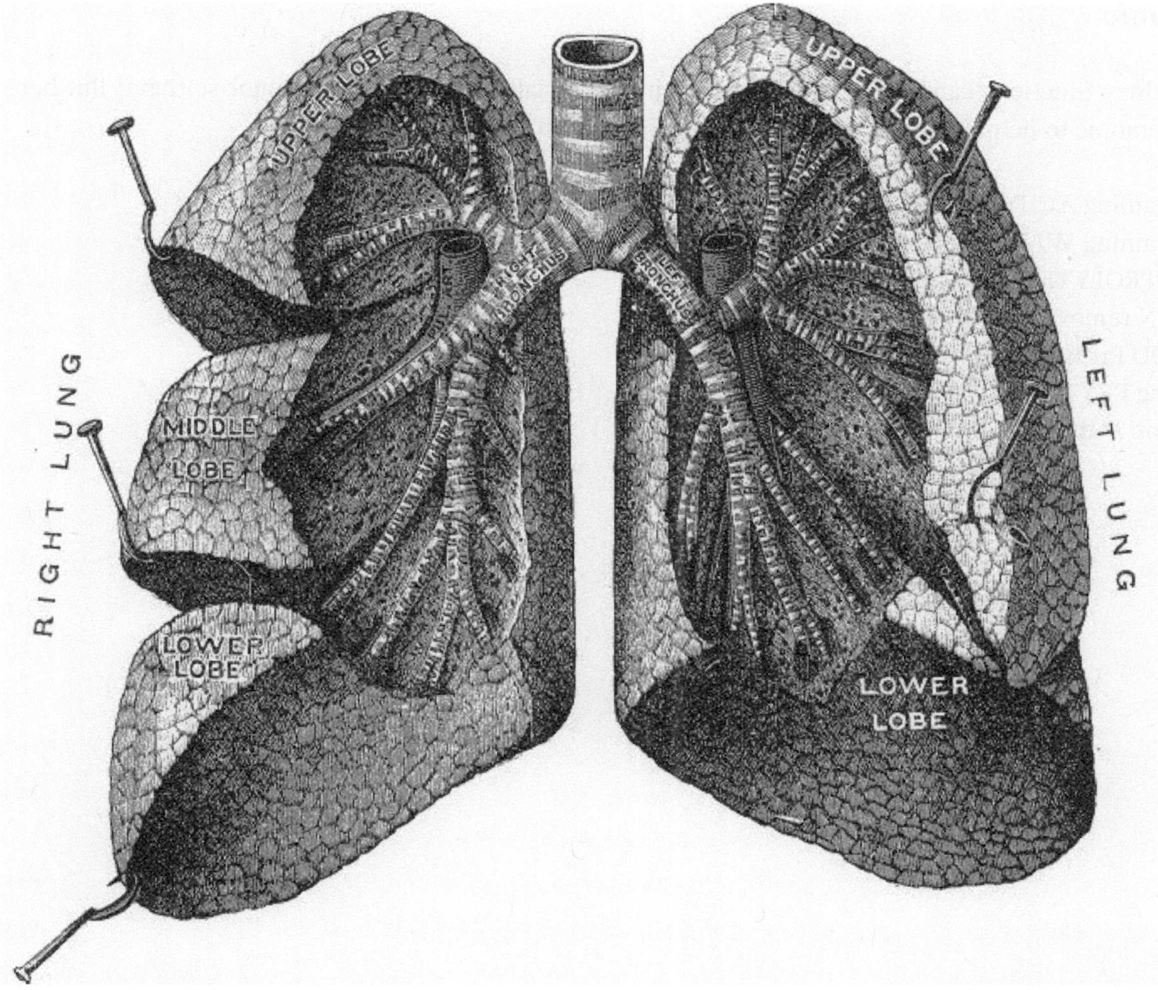

LUNGS

- A bronchopulmonary segment is a portion of lung supplied by a specific segmental bronchus and its vessels. These arteries branch from the pulmonary and bronchial arteries, and run together through the center of the segment. Veins and lymphatic vessels drain along the edges of the segment.
- The segments are separated from each other by layers of connective tissue that forms them into discrete anatomical and functional units.

- This separation means that a bronchopulmonary segment can be surgically removed without affecting the function of the others.
- There are ten bronchopulmonary segments in the right lung: three in the superior lobe, two in the middle lobe, and five in the inferior lobe. Some of the segments may fuse in the left lung to form usually eight to nine segments (four to five in the upper lobe and four to five in the lower lobe.

Answer(c) Kidney

The kidneys are bilateral organs placed retroperitoneally in the upper left and right abdominal quadrants and are part of the urinary system. Their shape resembles a bean, where we can describe the superior and inferior poles, as well as the major convexity pointed laterally, and the minor concavity pointed medially.

The main function of the kidney is to eliminate excess bodily fluid, salts and byproducts of metabolism – this makes kidneys key in the regulation of acid-base balance, blood pressure, and many other homeostatic parameters.

Mnemonic

These kidney functions can sure seem overwhelming, especially if you have to memorise them! But here is a neat little mnemonic to help. Just remember ' **A WET BED**', which stands for:

- Maintaining **A**CID-base balance
- Maintaining **W**ATER balance
- **E**LECTROLYTE balance
- **T**OXIN removal
- **B**LOOD Pressure control
- Making **E**RYTHROPOIETIN
- Vitamin **D** metabolism

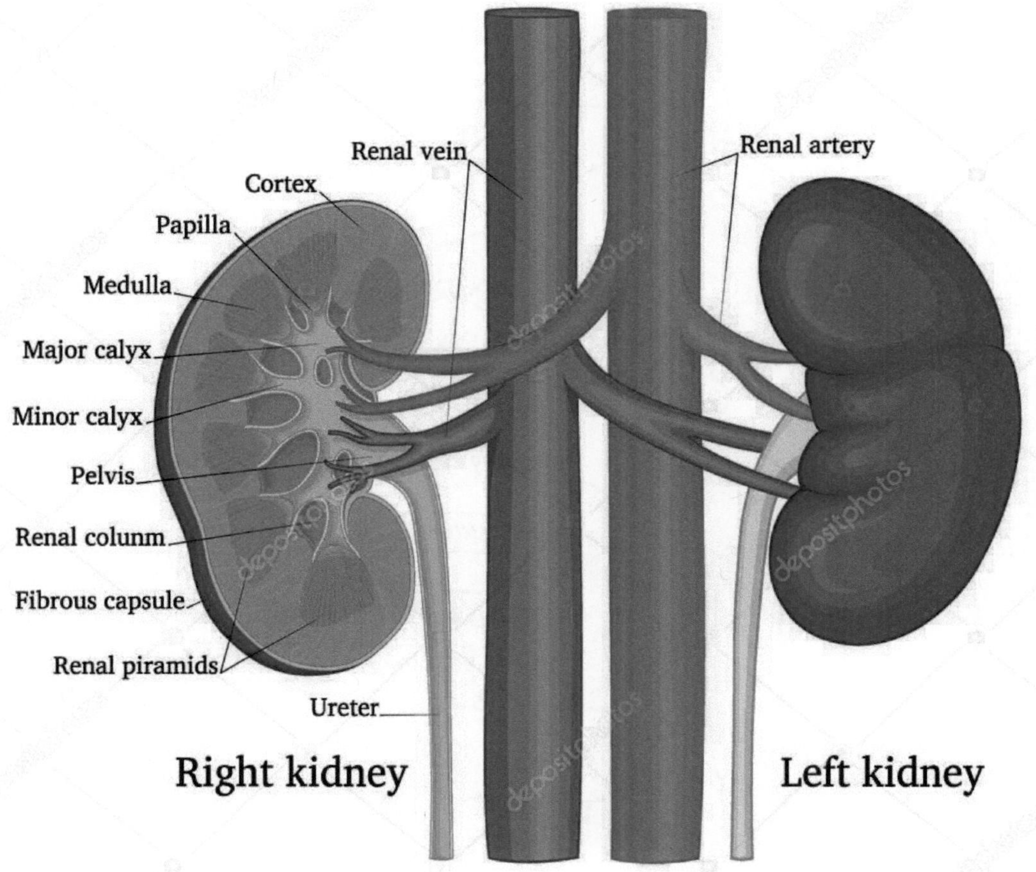

KIDNEYS

Functions

Eliminating toxic metabolites through urine, regulation of blood homeostasis and blood pressure, production of some hormones

Mnemonic: A WET BED

Morpho-functional characteristics

Positioned retroperitoneally, consists of the cortex and medulla, empties urine into the ureter (which carries urine to the urinary bladder)

Artery

Renal artery (branch of the abdominal aorta)

Vein

Renal vein (drains to the inferior vena cava)

Innervation

Renal plexus

Clinical relations

Third kidney, horseshoe kidney, kidney agenesis, kidney stones, acute kidney failure

Part-II (Physiology)

Q4. Write short notes on:

(a) Spermatogenesis

(b) Factors regulating cardiac output

(c) Juxta glomerular apparatus

Answer(a) Spermatogenesis

Spermatogenesis and the factors affecting it

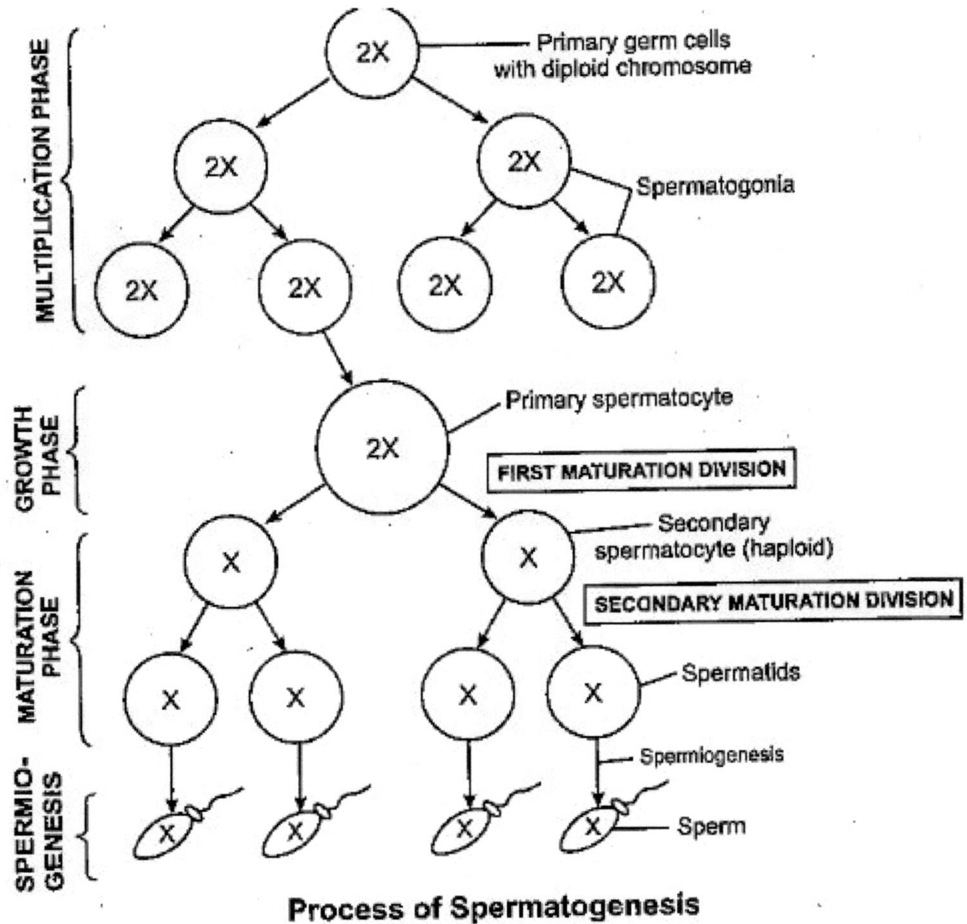

Process of Spermatogenesis

The factors affecting spermatogenesis

- The process of spermatogenesis is highly sensitive to fluctuations in the environment, particularly hormones and temperature.
- Dietary deficiencies (such as vitamins B, E and A), anabolic steroids, metals (cadmium and lead), x-ray exposure, alcohol, and infectious diseases will also adversely affect the rate of spermatogenesis. In addition, the male germ line is susceptible to DNA damage caused by oxidative stress, and this damage likely has a significant impact on fertilization and pregnancy. Exposure to pesticides also affects spermatogenesis.

Answer (b) Factors regulating cardiac output

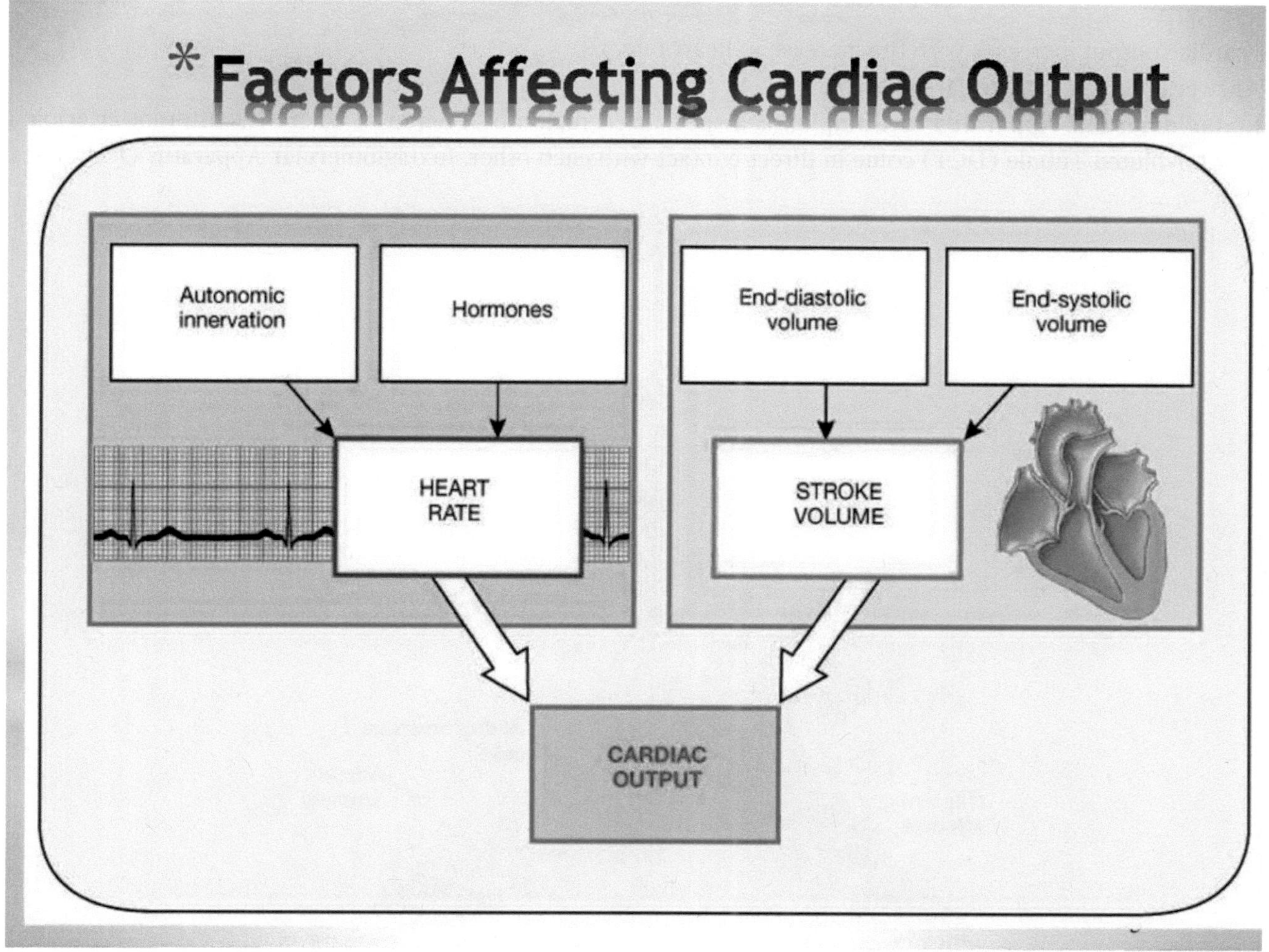

The cardiac output comprises 2 vital components:

- **Heart rate:** It refers to the number of times the heart beats per minute (bpm).
- **Stroke volume:** It refers to the quantity of blood pumped out of each ventricle with every heartbeat.

Factors Determining Cardiac Output

The following factors determine the cardiac output of a human heart:

Venous Return

This is the amount of blood that enters the heart through the veins per minute. After a certain time, interval, the venous return becomes equal to the cardiac output.

Force of Contraction

The stroke volume and the cardiac output increases with the increase in the force of contraction.

Heart Rate

The cardiac output increases with the increase in heart rate.

Answer (c) Juxta glomerular apparatus

Juxtaglomerular Apparatus or Complex is a specialized region of a nephron where the afferent arteriole and Distal Convoluted Tubule (DCT) come in direct contact with each other. Juxtaglomerular Apparatus (JGA) consists of:

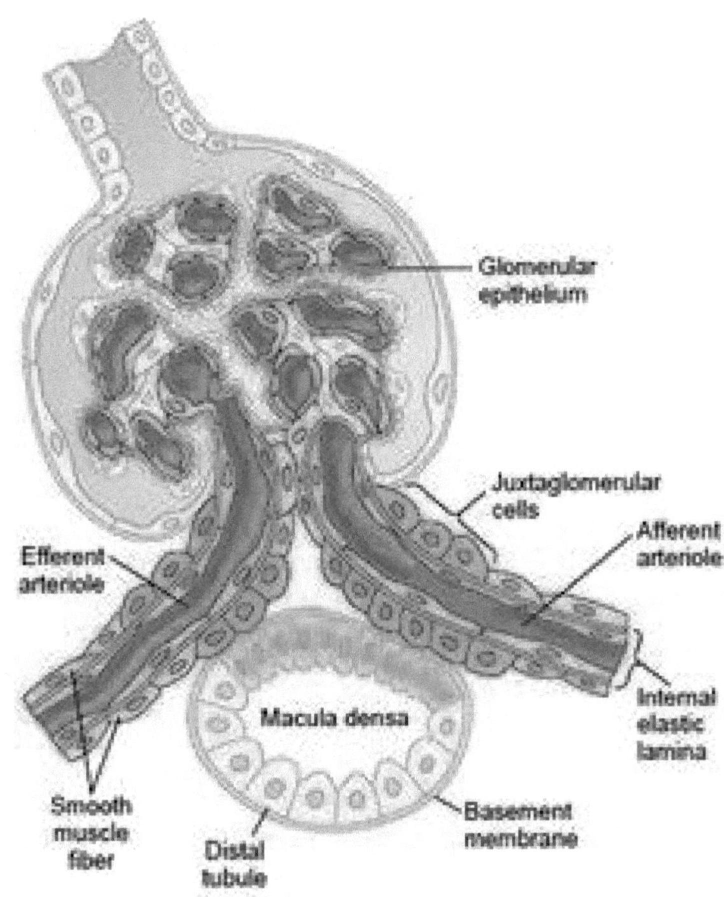

1) **Juxtaglomerular cells** (modified smooth muscle cells) of **afferent arteriole** including **renin** containing (synthesizes and stores renin) and sympathetically innervated granulated cells which function as **mechanoreceptors** to sense blood pressure.

2) **Macula densa cells** (Na+ sensors) of **Distal Convoluted Tubule (DCT)** which function as **chemoreceptors** to sense changes in the solute concentration and flow rate of filtrate.

3) **Juxtaglomerular/Extraglomerular mesangial cells (Lacis cells)** forming connections via actin and microtubules which allow for selective vasoconstriction/vasodilation of the renal afferent and efferent arterioles with mesangial cell contraction.

Functions of Juxtaglomerular Apparatus (JGA):

1. Local transmission of Tubuloglomerular Feedback (TGF) at its own nephron via angiotensin II (AT II)
2. Systemic production of Angiotensin II (AT II) as part of Renin-Angiotensin-Aldosterone System (RAAS)

Tubuloglomerular Feedback (TGF) Mechanism

The tubuloglomerular feedback mechanism has 2 components that act together to control GFR:

1. Afferent arteriolar feedback mechanism
2. Efferent arteriolar feedback mechanism

Increased renal arterial pressure leads to an increased delivery of fluid (increased osmolality or increased flow rate) to the macula densa. The macula densa senses the load and causes constriction of nearby afferent arteriole, increasing the resistance. This will return osmolality and filtrate flow rate to normal.

Decreased renal arterial pressure leads to a decreased delivery of fluid (decreased osmolality or decreased flow rate) to the macula densa. The macula densa senses this and causes:

1. Vasodilation of afferent arteriole
2. Constriction of efferent arteriole as a result of renin release by stimulated JG cells

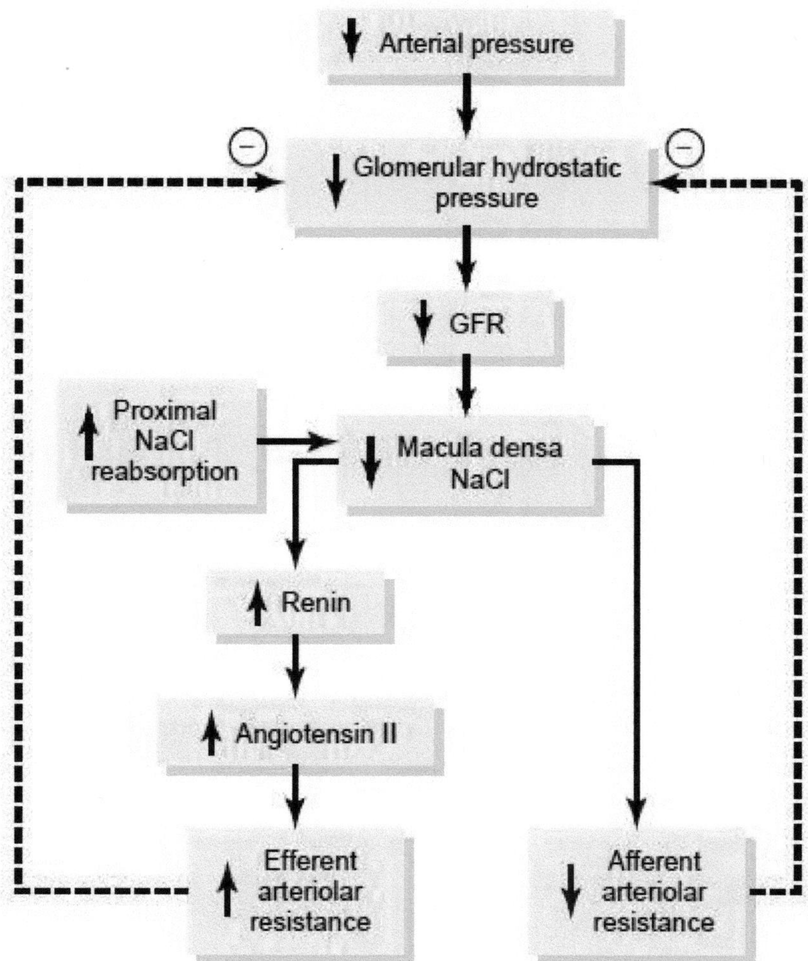

Renin Angiotensin Aldosterone System (RAAS)

When systemic blood pressure decreases, there is decreased stretch of JG cells, which leads to their release of renin. Renin release causes the activation of renin-angiotensin mechanism, which ultimately leads to an increased blood pressure.

<u>**Q5. Write the concept, in short, with the help of a diagram:**</u>

(a) Visual pathway
(b) Regulation of ovarian hormones
(c) Structure of neuron
Answer(a) Visual pathway

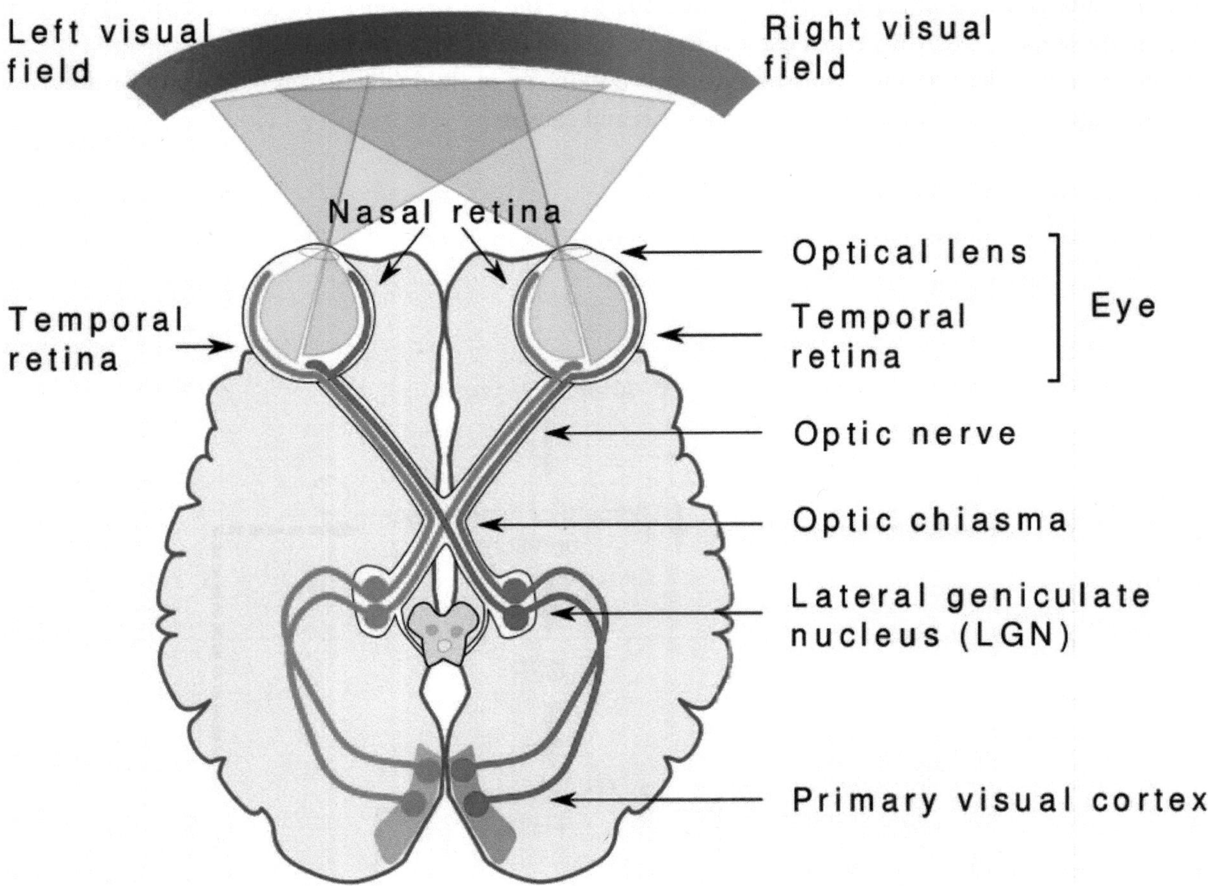

Visual pathway consists of a series of cells & synapses that carry visual information from environment to brain for processing. Components: Retina → Optic nerve →Optic chiasma→ Optic tract L→ ateral geniculate body → Geniculostriate tract→ Optic radiation to visual sensory area occipital lobe 17,18 &19

Answer (b) Regulation of ovarian hormones

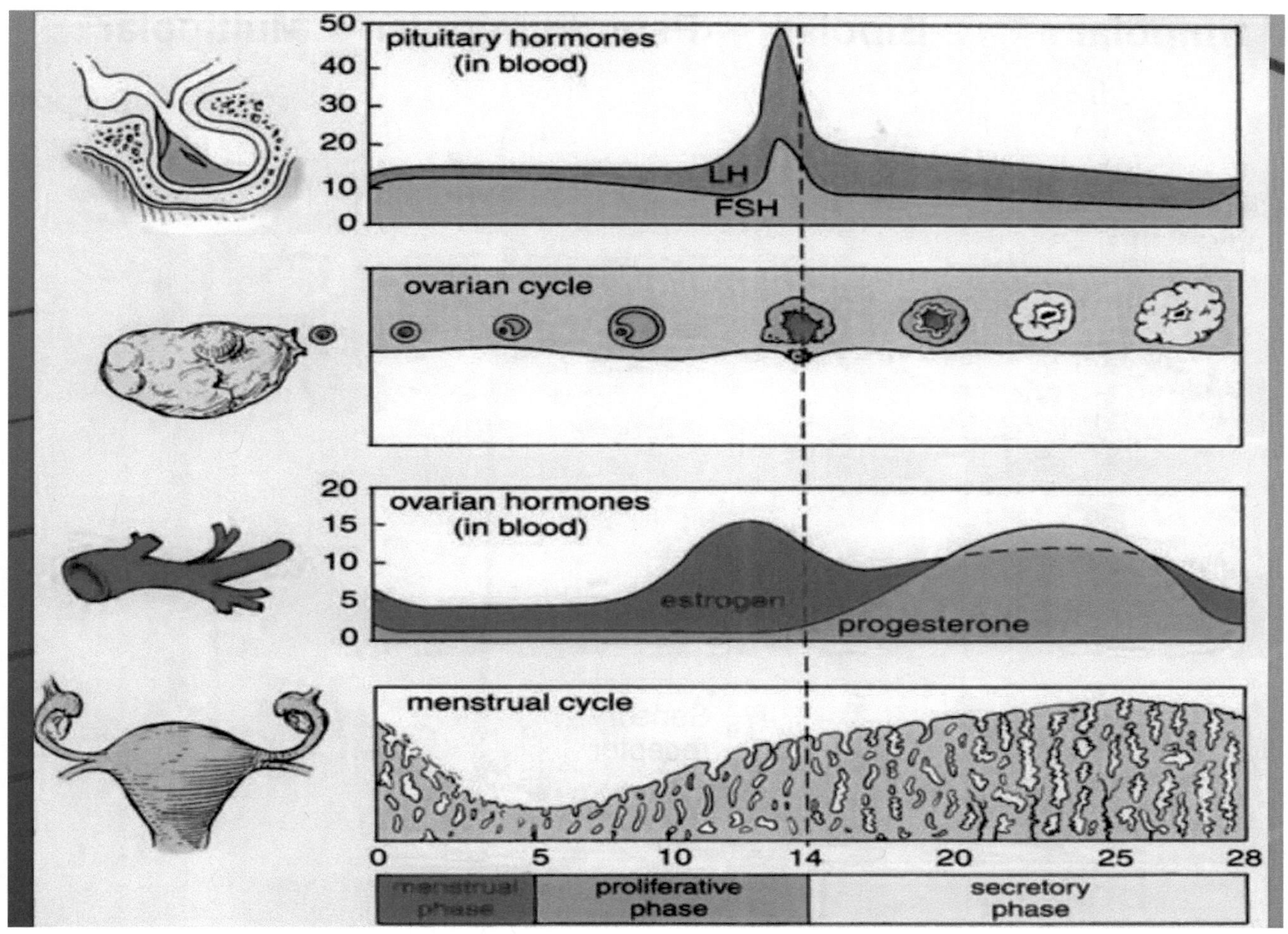

Regulation of ovarian hormones

The ovarian and uterine cycles are controlled by chemical messengers or hormones. Gonadotropin releasing hormone (GnRH) is secreted by the hypothalamus and stimulates the release of follicle-stimulating hormone (FSH) and luteinizing hormone (LH) from the anterior pituitary gland. FSH, in turn, initiates follicular growth and the secretion of estrogens by the growth follicles. LH stimulates the further development of ovarian follicles and their full secretion of estrogens, brings about ovulation, promotes formation of the corpus luteum and stimulates the production of estrogens, progesterone, relaxin and inhibin by the corpus luteum.

Answer(c) Structure of neuron

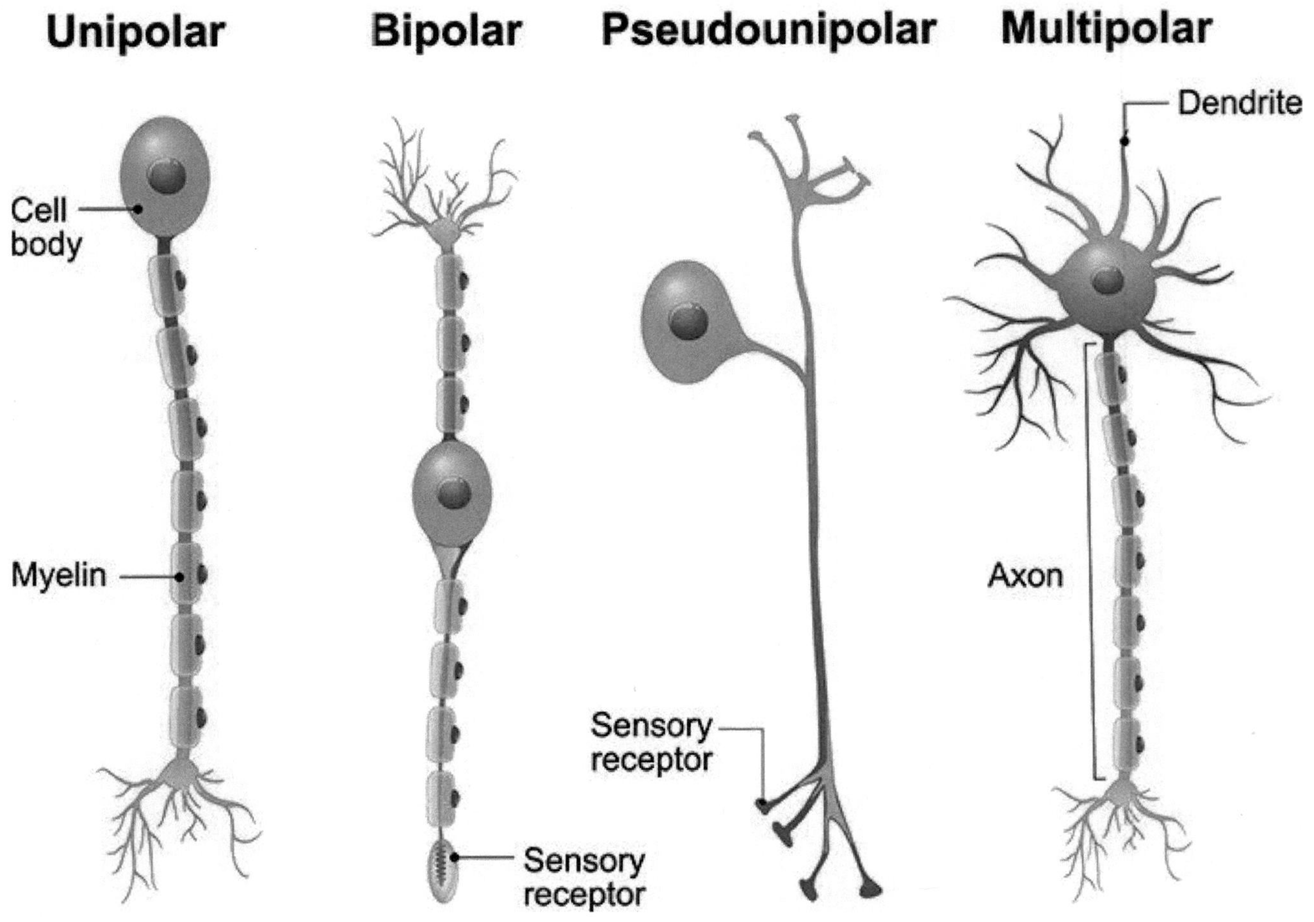

Neurons are the building blocks of the nervous system. They receive and transmit signals to different parts of the body. This is carried out in both physical and electrical forms. There are several different types of neurons that facilitate the transmission of information.

The sensory neurons carry information from the sensory receptor cells present throughout the body to the brain. Whereas, the motor neurons transmit information from the brain to the muscles. The interneurons transmit information between different neurons in the body.

Parts of Neuron

Following are the different parts of a neuron:

Dendrites

These are branch-like structures that receive messages from other neurons and allow the transmission of messages to the cell body.

Cell Body

Each neuron has a cell body with a nucleus, Golgi body, endoplasmic reticulum, mitochondria and other components.

Axon

Axon is a tube-like structure that carries electrical impulse from the cell body to the axon terminals that passes the impulse to another neuron.

Synapse

It is the chemical junction between the terminal of one neuron and dendrites of another neuron.

<u>**Q6. Write Features of:**</u>

(a) Hyperthyroidism

(b) Gigantism

(c) Plasma proteins

Answer(a) Hyperthyroidism

Hyperthyroidism (overactive thyroid) occurs when your thyroid gland produces too much of the hormone thyroxine. Hyperthyroidism can accelerate your body's metabolism, causing unintentional weight loss and a rapid or irregular heartbeat.

Several treatments are available for hyperthyroidism. Doctors use anti-thyroid medications and radioactive iodine to slow the production of thyroid hormones. Sometimes, hyperthyroidism treatment involves surgery to remove all or part of your thyroid gland.

Although hyperthyroidism can be serious if you ignore it, most people respond well once hyperthyroidism is diagnosed and treated.

Symptoms

Hyperthyroidism can mimic other health problems, which can make it difficult for your doctor to diagnose. It can also cause a wide variety of signs and symptoms, including:

- Unintentional weight loss, even when your appetite and food intake stay the same or increase
- Rapid heartbeat (tachycardia) — commonly more than 100 beats a minute
- Irregular heartbeat (arrhythmia)
- Pounding of your heart (palpitations)
- Increased appetite
- Nervousness, anxiety and irritability
- Tremor — usually a fine trembling in your hands and fingers
- Sweating
- Changes in menstrual patterns
- Increased sensitivity to heat
- Changes in bowel patterns, especially more frequent bowel movements
- An enlarged thyroid gland (goitre), which may appear as a swelling at the base of your neck
- Fatigue, muscle weakness
- Difficulty sleeping
- Skin thinning
- Fine, brittle hair

Older adults are more likely to have either no signs or symptoms or subtle ones, such as an increased heart rate, heat intolerance and a tendency to become tired during ordinary activities.

Graves' ophthalmopathy

Sometimes an uncommon problem called Graves' ophthalmopathy may affect your eyes, especially if you smoke. This disorder makes your eyeballs protrude beyond their normal protective orbits when the tissues and muscles behind your eyes swell. Eye problems often improve without treatment.

Signs and symptoms of Graves' ophthalmopathy include:

- Dry eyes
- Red or swollen eyes
- Excessive tearing or discomfort in one or both eyes
- Light sensitivity, blurry or double vision, inflammation, or reduced eye movement

- Protruding eyeballs

Answer(b) Gigantism

Gigantism is a rare condition that causes abnormal growth in children. This change is most notable in terms of height, but girth is affected as well. It occurs when your child's pituitary gland makes too much growth hormone, which is also known as somatotropin.

Early diagnosis is important. Prompt treatment can stop or slow the changes that may cause your child to grow larger than normal. However, the condition can be hard for parents to detect. The symptoms of gigantism might seem like normal childhood growth spurts at first.

causes

A pituitary gland tumor is almost always the cause of gigantism. The pea-sized pituitary gland is located at the base of your brain. It makes hormones that control many functions in your body. Some tasks managed by the gland include:

- temperature control
- sexual development
- growth
- metabolism
- urine production

When a tumor grows on the pituitary gland, the gland makes far more growth hormone than the body needs. There are other less common causes of gigantism:

- McCune-Albright syndrome causes abnormal growth in bone tissue, patches of light-brown skin, and gland abnormalities.
- Carney complex is an inherited condition that causes noncancerous tumors on connective tissue, cancerous or noncancerous endocrine tumors, and spots of darker skin.
- Multiple endocrine neoplasia type 1 (MEN1) is an inherited disorder that causes tumors in the pituitary gland, pancreas, or parathyroid glands.
- Neurofibromatosis is an inherited disorder that causes tumors in the nervous system.

signs of gigantism

If your child has gigantism, you may notice that they're much larger than other children of the same age. Also, some parts of their body may be larger in proportion to other parts. Common symptoms include:

- very large hands and feet
- thick toes and fingers
- a prominent jaw and forehead
- coarse facial features

Children with gigantism may also have flat noses and large heads, lips, or tongues.

The symptoms your child has may depend on the size of the pituitary gland tumor. As the tumor grows, it may press on nerves in the brain. Many people experience headaches, vision problems, or nausea from tumors in this area. Other symptoms of gigantism may include:

- excessive sweating
- severe or recurrent headaches
- weakness
- insomnia and other sleep disorders
- delayed puberty in both boys and girls
- irregular menstrual periods in girls
- deafness

Gigantism diagnosed

If your child's doctor suspects gigantism, they may recommend a blood test to measure levels of growth hormones and insulin-like growth factor 1 (IGF-1), which is a hormone produced by the liver. The doctor also may recommend an oral glucose tolerance test.

During an oral glucose tolerance test, your child will drink a special beverage containing glucose, a type of sugar. Blood samples will be taken before and after your child drinks the beverage.

In a normal body, growth hormone levels will drop after eating or drinking glucose. If your child's levels remain the same, it means their body is producing too much growth hormone.

If the blood tests indicate gigantism, your child will need an MRI scan of the pituitary gland. Doctors use this scan to find the tumor and see its size and position.

Gigantism treatment

Treatments for gigantism aim to stop or slow your child's production of growth hormones.

Surgery

Removing the tumor is the preferred treatment for gigantism if it's the underlying cause.

The surgeon will reach the tumor by making an incision in your child's nose. Microscopes or small cameras may be used to help the surgeon see the tumor in the gland. In most cases, your child should be able to return home from the hospital the day after the surgery.

Medication

In some cases, surgery may not be an option. For example, if there's a high risk of injury to a critical blood vessel or nerve.

Your child's doctor may recommend medication if surgery is not an option. This treatment is meant to either shrink the tumor or stop the production of excess growth hormone.

Your doctor may use the drugs octreotide or lanreotide to prevent the growth hormone's release. These drugs mimic another hormone that stops growth hormone production. They're usually given as an injection about once a month.

Bromocriptine and cabergoline are drugs that can be used to lower growth hormone levels. These are typically given in pill form. They may be used with octreotide. Octreotide is a synthetic hormone that, when injected, can also lower the levels of growth hormones and IGF-1.

In situations where these drugs are not helpful, daily shots of pegvisomant might be used as well. Pegvisomant is a drug that blocks the effects of growth hormones. This lowers the levels of IGF-1 in your child's body.

Gamma knife radiosurgery

Gamma knife radiosurgery is an option if your child's doctor believes that a traditional surgery isn't possible.

The "gamma knife" is a collection of highly focused radiation beams. These beams don't harm the surrounding tissue, but they're able to deliver a powerful dose of radiation at the point where they combine and hit the tumor. This dose is enough to destroy the tumor.

Gamma knife treatment takes months to years to be fully effective and to return the levels of growth hormone to normal. It's performed on an outpatient basis under general anesthetic.

However, since the radiation in this type of surgery has been linked to obesity, learning disabilities, and emotional issues in children, it's usually used only when other treatment options don't work.

(c) Plasma proteins

The proteins present in the plasma of human blood are a mixture of simple proteins, glycoproteins, lipoproteins, and other conjugated proteins are called "**Plasma Protein** ". Salt precipitation, immunological technique, and electrophoresis may separate these.

Types of Plasma Proteins

The three major fractions of plasma proteins are known as **Albumin, globulin,** and **Fibrinogen.** On a finer resolution by electrophoresis, these fractions are separated as follows

- **Albumin** – 55.2%
- **α1-Globulin** – 5.3% (α1-Antitrypsin, TBG, Transcortin, etc)
- **α2-Globulin** – 8.6% (Haptoglobulin, ceruloplasmin, α2- macroglobulin, etc)
- **β-Globulin** – 13.4% (β1-transferrin, β-lipoprotein, etc)
- **¥-Globulin** – 11.0% (Antibodies, etc)
- **Fibrinogen** – 6.5%

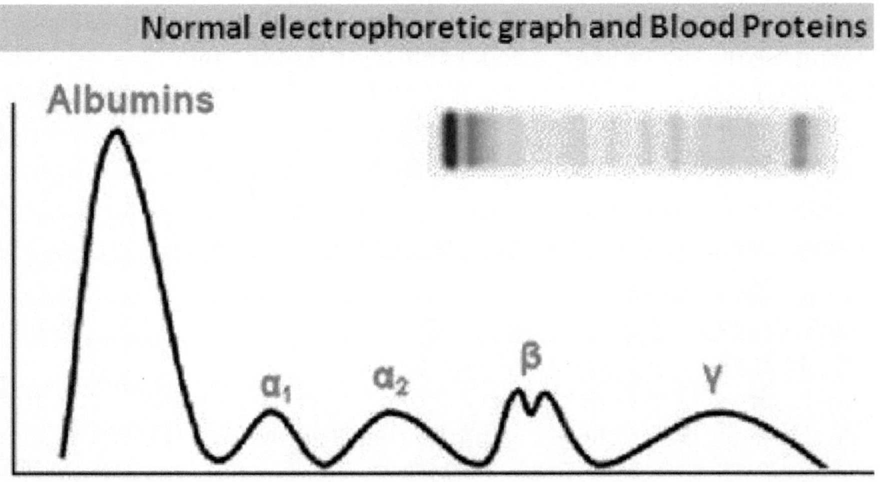

1. Albumin

This is the most abundant class of plasma protein (2.8 to 4.5 gm/100ml) with the highest electrophoretic mobility. It is soluble in water and is precipitated by fully saturated ammonium sulfate. Albumin is synthesized in the liver and consists of a single polypeptide chain of 610 amino acids having a molecular weight of 69,000. It is rich in some essential amino acids such as lysine, leucine, valine, phenylalanine, threonine, arginine and histidine. The acidic amino acids like aspartic acid and glutamic acid are also concentrated in albumin.

The presence of these residues makes the molecule highly charged with a positive and negative charge. Besides having a nutritive role, albumin acts as a transport carrier for various biomolecules such as fatty acids, trace elements, and drugs. Another important role of albumin is in the maintenance of osmotic pressure and fluid distribution between blood and tissues.

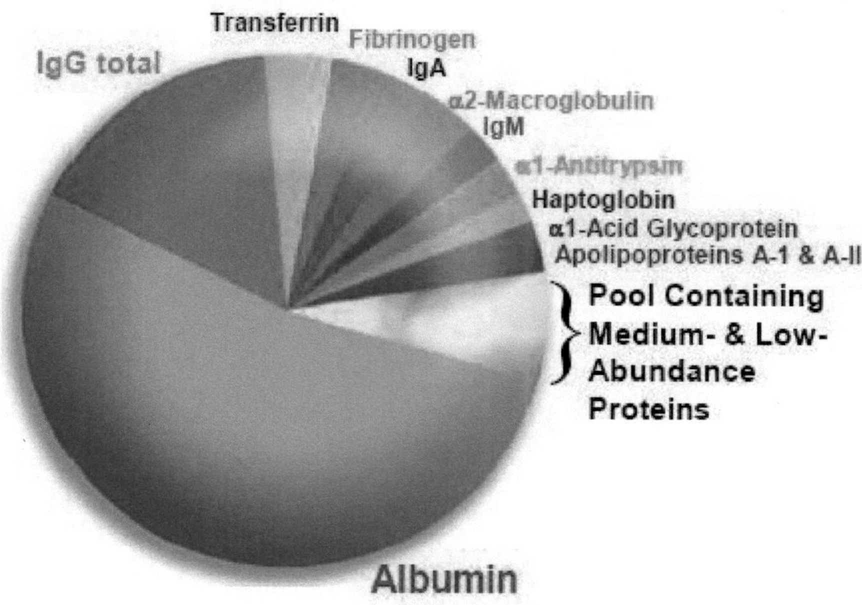

Enter Caption

2. Globulins

By electrophoresis plasma globulins are separated into α1, α2,β and ¥-globulins are synthesized in the liver, whereas ¥-globulins are formed in the cells of the reticuloendothelial system. The average normal serum globulin (total) concentration is 2.5 gm / 100 ml (Howe method) or 3.53 gm/100 ml by electrophoresis.

a. α1-Globulin

This fraction includes several complex proteins containing carbohydrates and lipids. These are *orosomucoid*, *α1-glycoprotein*, and *α-lipoproteins*. The normal serum level of α1-globulin is 0.42 gm/100 ml. Orosomucoid is rich in carbohydrates. It is water-soluble, heat stable and has a molecular weight of 44,000. It serves to transport hexosamine complexes to tissues. Lipoproteins are soluble complexes which contain non-covalently bound lipid. These proteins act mainly as transport carriers to different types of lipids in the body.

b. α2-Globulins

This fraction also contains complex proteins such as α2-glycoproteins, plasminogen, prothrombin, haptoglobin, ceruloplasmin (transports Cu) and α2-macroglobulin. The normal serum value of this fraction is 0.67 gm/100ml. Plasminogen and prothrombin are in the inactive precursors of plasmin and thrombin, respectively. Both of these proteins play an important role in blood clotting.

Haptoglobins are also glycoproteins having a molecular weight of 85,000. These are synthesized in the liver and can bind with any free hemoglobin that may arise in the plasma due to lysis of erythrocytes and thus prevent excretion of Hb and iron associated with it. Ceruloplasmin is a glycoprotein synthesized in the liver and is an important component of copper metabolism in the body. Nearly 95% of plasma copper is bound to this protein.

c. β-Globulins

This fraction of *plasma protein* contains these different β-lipoproteins which are very rich in lipid content. It also contains transferrin (siderophilin) which transports non-heme iron in plasma. The normal serum value of β-globulins is 0.91 gm/100ml. Transferrin is an iron transport protein. In plasma, it can be saturated even up to 33%

with iron. It has a low content of carbohydrates.

d. ¥-Globulins

These are also called Immunoglobulins and have antibody activity. Based on their electrophoretic mobility they are classified as IgG, IgA, and IgM. **Immunoglobulins:** Immunoglobulins are clinically important components of globulins and concerned with "*Immunological reactions*". These are formed by lymphocytes. Two different types of lymphocytes concerned with Immunoglobulin formation of "T-cells of Thymus" and "B-Cells" formed from "Bone marrow".

3. Fibrinogen

It is a fibrous protein with a molecular weight of 340,000. It has 6 polypeptide chains which are held together by disulfide linkages. Fibrinogen plays an important role in the clothing of blood where it is converted to fibrin by thrombin. In addition to the above-mentioned proteins, the plasma contains a number of enzymes such as *acid phosphatase* and *alkaline phosphatase* which have great diagnostic value.

Functions of Plasma Proteins

Plasma protein is very important in our body. Here are the major functions.

1. Protein Nutrition

- It acts as a source of protein for the tissues, whenever the need arises.

2. Osmotic Pressure and water balance

- It exerts an osmotic pressure of about 25 mm of Hg and therefore plays an important role in maintaining a proper water balance between the tissues and blood.
- Plasma albumin is mainly responsible for this function due to its low molecular weight and quantitative dominance over other proteins.
- During the condition of protein loss from the body as occurs in kidney diseases, an excessive amount of water moves to the tissues producing edema.

3. Buffering action

- Plasma protein help in maintaining the pH of the body by acting ampholytes. At normal blood pH, they act as acids and accept captions.

4. Transport of Lipids

- One of the most important functions of plasma proteins us to transport lipids and lipid-soluble substances in the body.

- Fatty acids and bilirubin are transported mainly by albumin, whereas cholesterol and phospholipids are carried by the lipoproteins present in β-globulins also transport fat-soluble vitamins (A, D, K, and E)

5. Transport of other substances

- In addition to lipids, plasma proteins also transport several metals and other substances α2-Globulin's transport copper (Ceruloplasmin), bound hemoglobin (haptoglobin) and thyroxine (glycoprotein) and non-heme iron is transported by transferrin present in β-globulin fraction.
- Calcium, Magnesium, some drugs and dyes, and several cations and anions are transported by plasma albumin.

6. Blood Coagulation

Prothrombin present in α2-globulin fraction and fibrinogen, participate in the blood clotting process as follows.

Prothrombin -> Thrombin (Presence–Thromboplastin)

Fibrinogen -> Fibrin (Clot) (Presence–Thrombin)

Question Paper 2017

B.Sc Nursing 1st year ,annual exam, 2017

Anatomy and physiology

Note Marks 75

1. attempt all questions and draw suitable diagrams, tables, and graphs where required.

2.attempt part-1 and part-2 in separate answer book.

Part –I anatomy

Q1. Describe in detail:5+4+4=18

(a) Describe the formation and growth of bones

(b) Spinal cord

(c) Classify synovial joints. Give one example of each.

Q2. Draw a well labeled diagram to illustrate the following: 4×3=12

(a) Skeletal muscle

(b) Kidney

(c) Uterus

Q3. Write short note on:4×3=12

(a) Thyroid gland

(b) Coronary circulation

(c)Lymph Node

PART-II(Physiology)

Q4. Write short note on the following:5+4+4=18

(a) Fibrinolysis

(b) Neuromuscular junction

(c) pancreatic secretion

Q5. Write on the following with the help of a diagram:5+4+4=18

(a) Feedback regulation of growth hormone (GH)

(b) Hypersecretion of aldosterone

(c) Autoregulation of kidney

Q6. Write features of the following:4×3=12

(a) Peptic ulcer

(b) Stretch reflex

(c) Night blindness

Question Paper 2016

B.Sc Nursing 1st year ,annual exam, 2016

Anatomy and physiology

Note Marks 75

1. attempt all questions and draw suitable diagrams, tables, and graphs where required.

2.attempt part-1 and part-2 in separate answer book.

Part –I anatomy

Q1. Describe in detail:5+4+4=13

(a) Mention the type of muscles and describe the structure of skeletal muscle

(b) Function of blood cells

(c) Liver

Q2. Draw a well labeled diagram to illustrate the following: 4×3=12

(a) Synovial joint

(b) Stomach

(c) Uterus

Q3. **Write short note on:** 4×3=12

(a) Urinary bladder

(b) Lymph Node

(c) Cranial nerves

PART-II(Physiology)

Q4. Write short note on the following:5+4+4=13

(a) Stages of erythropoiesis

(b) Factors regulating heart rate

(c) Cranial nerves

Q5. Write on the following with the help of a diagram:5+4+4=13

(a) Einthoven's triangle

(b) Factors regulating heart rate

(c) GFR

Q6. Write features of the following:4×3=12

(a) Rickets

(b) Cretins

(c) Acromegaly

Question Paper 2015

B.Sc Nursing 1st year ,annual exam, 2015
Anatomy and physiology

Note Marks 75

1. attempt all questions and draw suitable diagrams, tables, and graphs where required.

2.attempt part-1 and part-2 in separate answer book.

Part –I anatomy

Q1. Write note on:5+4+4=13

a. Mention the five types of bones and list its functions
b. Inter vertebral disc
c. Urinary bladder

Q2. Write notes and mention its function: 4×3=12

a. Trachea
b. Cerebellum
c. Lymph Node

Q3. Write short note on: 4×3=12

a. Circle of Willis
b. Mention and organ every region of abdominal cavity
c. List all extra ocular muscles and mention all cranial nerves involved to supply it.

PART-II(Physiology)

Q4. Write short note on the following:5+4+4=13

a. Function of platelets
b. Cardiac cycle
c. Excitation and contraction coupling (write steps only by flow diagram)

Q5. Describe briefly:5+4+4=13

a. Function of hypothalamus
b. Synthesis of thyroid hormones
c. Oxygen Hb dissociation curve

Q6. Write in short:4×3=12

a. Contraception
b. Function of saliva

c. How kidney causes acid bar balance

Question Paper 2014

B.Sc Nursing 1st year ,annual exam, 2014
Anatomy and physiology

Note Marks 75

1. attempt all questions and draw suitable diagrams, tables, and graphs where required.

2.attempt part-1 and part-2 in separate answer book.

Part –I anatomy

Q1. Write short notes on:5+4+4=13

a. Skin
b. Structure and function of bones
c. Autonomic Nervous systems

Q2. Write structure and function of following: **4×3=12**

a. Tongue
b. Lymph Node
c. Trachea

Q3. Describe the structure and function of **4×3=12**

a. Kidney
b. Liver
c. Ovary

PART-II(Physiology)

Q4. Write notes on: **5+4+4=13**

a. Short term regulation of blood pressure
b. Blood groups
c. Neuromuscular junction

Q5. Describe briefly: **5+4+4=13**

a. Function of hypothalamus
b. Anterior pituitary Gland
c. Lung volume and capacities

Q6. Write in short: **4×3=12**

a. Menstrual cycle
b. Digestion and absorption of fat

c. Juxta glomerular apparatus

Question Paper 2013

B.Sc Nursing 1st year ,annual exam, 2013
Anatomy and physiology

Note Marks 75

1. attempt all questions and draw suitable diagrams, tables, and graphs where required.

2.attempt part-1 and part-2 in separate answer book.

Part –I anatomy

Q1. Write short notes on:

a. Blood supply of heart
b. Type of muscles
c. Cranial nerves

Q2. Write short note on:

a. Stomach
b. Pituitary gland
c. Breast

Q3. Write short note on:

a. Kidney
b. Knee joint
c. Muscles of anterior abdominal wall

PART-II(Physiology)

Q4. Write notes on:

a. Erythropoiesis
b. Gigantism
c. Baroreceptors

Q5. Describe briefly:

a. CO_2 transport
b. Immunoglobulins
c. Parkinsonism

Q6. Write notes on:4×3=12

a. Difference between secretin and cholecystokinin
b. Pain Pathways
c. Steps in spermatogenesis

Printed by Libri Plureos GmbH in Hamburg,
Germany